Race, War and Nationalism

The Sailing of the Jamaican Contingent
Source: Courtesy of the National Library of Jamaica

Race, War and Nationalism

A Social History of West Indians in the First World War

Glenford Deroy Howe

 Ian Randle Publishers Kingston James Currey Publishers Oxford

First published in Jamaica, 2002, by
Ian Randle Publishers
11 Cunningham Avenue
Box 686
Kingston 6
www.ianrandlepublishers.com

ISBN 976-637-063-X Paperback

A catalogue record for this book is available from the National Library of Jamaica

Cover painting by Louis Matalon

First published in the United Kingdom, 2002, by
James Currey Publishers
73 Botley Road
Oxford, OX2 0BS

British Library Cataloguing-in-Publication Data

Howe, Glenford D.
  Race, War and Nationalism: A Social History of West Indians in the First World War
  1. Great Britain. Army. British West Indies Regiment 2. World War, 1914-1918 –
  Participation, West Indian 3. World War, 1914-1918, Social Aspects
  I. Title
  940.4' 127292

ISBN 0-85255-482-6 (James Currey Paperback)

Table of Contents

List of Tables

Preface and Acknowledgements

This study, which is based on data presented in my doctoral thesis submitted in the University of London in June 1994, is a contribution to the social history of war and in part an exploration of aspects of the development of working class consciousness in the group of countries formerly known as the British West Indies. It attempts to pull together a number of strands in West Indian history to produce a theoretical and empirical examination of the experiences of blacks who served in the British West Indies Regiment, which was raised to provide service in World War One. The study focuses on the experiences of the regiment during its recruitment, service overseas and demobilisation. The central tasks in this regard were the examination of the processes and politics surrounding black participation in the war, detailing the multiple experiences of the soldiers overseas, analysing how their ordeal affected their perceptions and attitudes towards England and the empire, and exploring the complex manner in which the intensification of working class protest locally between 1914 and 1919 interacted with the agitation of disillusioned ex-servicemen and seamen and the radical political activities of individuals like F.E.M. Hercules and Marcus Garvey. However, as an important sub-theme this study also shows how, through analyses of war and the military, important information and insights can be gained about issues relating to civilian health, disease and medicine during particular historical epochs. A preface should, however, tell us not only about the content of the book or what to expect, but also about the social relations of the book itself; it is to this requirement that I now enthusiastically turn.

The task of producing a study, which ranges across the entire British West Indies, Europe and the Middle East, could have been somewhat daunting but, because of the encouragement of several persons, my interest and enthusiasm never wavered during the period of researching and writing the dissertation. My sincerest thanks to Shula Marks and Richard Rathbone for supervising this study; their impressive knowledge of the historiography of several continents and intellectual rigour profoundly influenced the final outcome of my research and writing and made my task much easier. Thanks also to W.K. Marshall, George Belle and Alan Cobley for the keen interest they showed in my development during my time at the Cave Hill campus of the University of the West Indies. Cobley was my initial supervisor at the University of the West Indies before I transferred to the University of London, and since the completion of my thesis he has continued to provide invaluable guidance. Among the persons in my home country, Montserrat, who deserve mention are Howard Fergus and Dorothy Greenway, and in particular B.B. Osborne, who over the years has been a good friend and a staunch supporter. My appreciation also to the various workers at the libraries of the Institute of Commonwealth Studies, the School of Oriental and African Studies, the Public Records Office and especially those at the British Library newspaper section at Colindale, who took great interest in my work and pleasure in serving their numerous readers. The group of West Indian historians in England and the United States which included, Peter Fraser, Gad Heuman, Barry Gaspar, Tony Martin and Jean Stubbs, Mary Turner, Richard Blackett, Seymour Drescher, Peter Ashdown, Rosemary Mallet, Donald Wood, and others, who also did much to make me feel welcome and a part of the group; they also provided invaluable assistance by way of sources and discussion. In addition, special thanks to the British Council and the Association of Commonwealth Universities for funding this research. Finally, I take great pleasure in thanking my friends, colleagues and especially my parents and other members of my family for their constant interest and support.

Abbreviations

BWIR	British West Indies Regiment
CEF	Canadian Expeditionary Force
CO	Colonial Office
DCM	Distinguished Conduct Medal
GB	Great Britain
GOC	General Officer Commanding
HMSO	His Majesty's Stationery Office
ICS	Institute of Commonwealth Studies
ISER	Institute of Social and Economic Research
NCF	National Cultural Foundation (Barbados)
NCO	Non Commissioned Officer
OAG	Office Administering the Government
PRO	Public Records Office
RAMC	Royal Army Medical Corps
UNIA	Universal Negro Improvement Association
UWI	University of the West Indies
WIR	West India Regiment
WMMS	Wesleyan Methodist Missionary Church
WO	War Office

Foreword

From the perspective of Caribbean scholars, especially historians and social scientists, this is an important and highly necessary book. It is crafted by a historian who has mastered the skill of presenting lucidly multisourced ideas and analyses, cumulatively and purposively based on careful and deep research. The author, while clearly following a definite theoretical, conceptual and methodological scheme, manages to take the reader effortlessly into the temper of the times and does so with realism and honesty. He allowed the words of people of all strata, races and skin-colour shadings to evoke the atmosphere and reasonings of the time without having to impose heavy interpretative analyses upon the various aspects of his arguments. On these bases alone, it was a rare privilege to read this book before its publication.

The author placed his study squarely within the framework which takes directly into account the sociopolitical foundations and implications of all aspects related to the establishment, deployment in the Great War, and consequences thereof, of the British West India Regiment (BWIR). He has demonstrated that the study of the BWIR in many war situations provided a compelling set of contexts within which to examine the larger issues of slavery, race and class, culture, gender, education, politics, demography and social structure, as well as the social psychology of colonialism. He has recovered the history of British West Indians in the Great War which was otherwise dispersed, hidden or discounted. In so doing, he has helped to strengthen the positive side of the dichotomy of non-white West Indian experiences in the Caribbean. It was a history of both shame and triumph but this work has revealed that in spite of incredible obstacles the human spirit of the West Indian shone through with pride and accomplishment.

The range of his presentation - from the daily problems of army life for West Indian recruits, the internal intricacies of army administration, the functioning of West Indians as soldiers, through to connection of these with slavery, race, class, geography and the like – is exhilarating and fully informative of the colonial condition. The particular prism through which these aspects unfold is vital, since war brings out more readily the deepest feelings and fears of humanity. What is especially appreciated is the way in which dynamic forces, undercurrents of thoughts and actions are revealed to demonstrate that subsequent events such as the revolt of labour, the movement for regional integration, the nationalist movement and its search for constitutional decolonisation, fed voraciously on the thoughts of ordinary West Indians. This aspect of his work was path-breaking and substantive. It will cause political scientists to revise their analyses of the foundations of modern Caribbean politics.

Neville C. Duncan
Director
Sir Arthur Lewis Institute of Social and Economic Studies
Mona Campus, University of the West Indies, Jamaica

Introduction

World War One, usually labelled the 'Great War', was an event
unprecedented in the history of European and world warfare. It marked the
major transition from limited to total warfare.[1] Consequently, the extent and
nature of its impact and significance were unparalleled. At the outbreak of
war in 1914, the British Empire was in size and complexity, the largest
occidental empire since Rome.[2] Such was the magnitude of the British
Empire but Britain was not alone as a world power or imperial nation. The
United States had emerged from being a colony of Britain into a powerful
nation, wielding considerable political and economic clout. Russia was also
then rapidly expanding its industrial base as part of its modernisation
process. Both France and Germany had already developed into prosperous,
powerful states with their own colonies. But at 1918, with the cessation of
hostilities, these nations and empires, with the exception of the United
States, had been significantly weakened physically and psychologically.

The war also had major social, economic and often less visible, but
equally important, psychological and political implications for the numerous
colonial peoples of the world. In fact, the first British military operation of
World War One was launched from the Gold Coast against Germany's
colony, Togoland.[3] Throughout the colonial world people were called upon
and many even eagerly volunteered to defend the very nations and institutions which kept them in subjugation and robbed them of their identities.
Ostensibly, this involvement reflected one of the chief ironies of imperialism.[4] However, the irony may not be as great as it appears on the surface,
since colonial domination usually entails more than the disruption of the
lives of a conquered people; it also involves the inculcation of ideas supportive of the new social structures and relations.

It may well be true that nearly 80 per cent of the casualties and 88 per
cent of the expenditure incurred by the British Empire to defeat Germany

came from the United Kingdom and domestic taxpayers.[5] Nevertheless, it is undeniable that the manpower and resources of the dominions and colonies were exploited in an unprecedented manner during the war. Throughout British-colonial Africa the manpower and material resources were brought even closer under the control of Britain to facilitate maximum exploitation.[6] These resources were used in the campaigns in South-West Africa, East Africa and the Western front, particularly in France. It was in the context of this empire-wide effort that the British West Indies, both spontaneously and by request, made their contribution to defeat Germany and her allies.

By focussing on the British West Indies Regiment (BWIR), this book aims to highlight those deeper social, economic, political and psychological implications of the war effort, not only for Britain and the Empire, but more especially, for the West Indians who were involved. Compared to the effort of the other major colonial areas such as India and Africa, the West Indian contribution, both in terms of human and material resources, was small. However, this input was arguably just as significant for the West Indians who were affected by, or participated directly in, the Great War. This book approaches the issue of West Indian involvement in the war from the perspective that the participation of colonial people in the war, as soldiers, transport carriers and in various other roles, as well as policy decisions made in the metropole, provides the basis for understanding the impact of World War One upon these societies. More particularly, it attempts to explore the dialectical and interactive relationship between local processes and British-colonial policy decisions. It shows that the military and wars can provide fascinating contexts for the examination of those larger issues of slavery, race and class, culture, gender, education, politics, demography and social structure, which have come to constitute some of the general areas of historical investigation.

Until now the story of the BWIR has remained largely untold, not simply because of the procrastination and neglect of West Indian historians but also by the intentional design of the early historians of British-colonial history. Unintentionally and intentionally, the war-effort of West Indians has been denied a place in the histories written about World War One. In the *Cambridge History of the British Empire*, for example, the war-effort of the British West Indies is barely mentioned.[7] In the colonies themselves, a similar attitude prevailed among local officials. Arguing in 1938 for a detailed history of the BWIR, C.L.R. James insisted that it was the duty of a federated West Indies legislature to ask for and support the production of 'this necessary piece of West Indies history', since Crown Colony government would not interest itself in such a task.[8]

In arguing thus, James was highlighting the fact that colonial governments and imperial officials, who, having exploited the manpower and material resources of colonial territories, subsequently denied or obscured this contribution. Principally, this was for racial as well as for political reasons, which formed the basis of the relationship between 'mother country' and colony – mirroring the relationship between the local white aristocracy and the black population. White racism exercised a pervasive influence in every sphere of relations between whites and blacks and it was implicit in colonialism to undermine and deny the self-worth and capabilities of colonial peoples. To have done otherwise would not only have contradicted inherent supportive structures in colonial relations but, even more dangerously, inadvertently encourage a mentality of anti-colonial self-confidence and inevitably increase resistance to colonialism.

This book locates the experiences of the BWIR within the processes of change and development affecting West Indian societies at the time. It, for instance, explores the connection between the experiences of the BWIR soldiers overseas and their subsequent role in post-war agitation, in order to realise to what extent these veterans can really be identified as a distinctive group within West Indian societies. These issues have remained unresolved until recently, partly because there has been little historical research on the period between the 1865 Morant Bay uprising in Jamaica and the cataclysmic labour disturbances of the 1930s. This neglect has been symptomatic of a tendency by many historians to ignore social and political movements while they exist as subcultural manifestations and lack sophisticated organisational form. These movements as subcultural manifestations of constant pressure for change in societies, have played critical roles in Caribbean political and social development but have remained largely unheralded, scorned or unrecognised.[9]

Part of the difficulty of assessing the impact of World War One on West Indian societies, as has been perceptively pointed out in the African context, is that 'whereas after World War Two it is surely true "that nothing was ever the same", the lines between cause and effect before and after World War One are far from neatly drawn, and not merely because less is known about the period as a whole.'[10] This book does not seek to prove that World War

One was a 'watershed' in West Indian historical development, but it does suggest that the war was more important than previously thought.

Significantly, the judgements on the blacks who served in the war have not always been well-informed or kind. There has been a tendency by some laymen and historians alike to suggest that these blacks soldiers were misguided patriots who lacked any sense of race and class consciousness and who, therefore, do not deserve to be recognised in West Indian societies as heroes who fought for a great cause.[11] Other individuals have used even more derogatory terms, including 'latrine cleaners', to describe these black West Indians soldiers.[12]

As is often the case in analyses of complicated situations, myth and reality, truth and fiction may become blurred but this book clearly shows that these previous assessments of the West Indian war veterans are not only singularly one-sided but also dangerously misleading. The ahistorical nature of these arguments stem from their failure to locate their analyses properly within the wider context of the socio-cultural, economic and psychological experiences and realities of life in the West Indies during colonial rule. West Indians went to war on behalf of the British Empire for a variety of complex reasons, as this book shows. What has been done in this book, is the pulling together of diverse strands of West Indian history to produce a theoretical and empirical examination of the BWIR during its recruitment, service overseas and demobilisation.

Officers and Men of the West Indian Regiment
Source: Courtesy of the National Library of Jamaica

Reactions to Outbreak of War

With the expiry of the British ultimatum to Germany in August 1914, the West Indian colonies and the rest of the empire became embroiled in war. For the colonies there was no right of neutrality but the unity of empire was more than formal. Even though informal influence was primarily and essentially a result of constitutional and political arrangements born of imperial conquest, it was the informal ties which mainly determined the responses of the cosmopolitan West Indian population at the outbreak of war.

By 1914, the majority of the inhabitants of the British West Indies had been conditioned as faithful patriots, and social progress was, in part, measured locally by the extent to which the subjects of each colony had adopted, internalised and exhibited British ideals and customs. Thus, Barbados, then popularly referred to as 'Little England' was widely regarded along with Jamaica, as among the more developed in the region. Centuries of alienation, indoctrination, creolisation and suppression of the remnants of African cultural practices had by the outbreak of war, created staunchly loyal black Britishers in the colonies. British practices, institutions, language, and religion fashioned the consciousness of West Indians. The physical impress of British ideas was everywhere evident in place names, road patterns, naval and military bases, military bands, architecture, surnames and sporting activities like cricket. Indeed, the various theories and material practices of colonisation were often very specific, ranging from the layout and planning of towns, to the social structure to be established in the newly conquered territories.[1]

Even though black intellectuals in the colonies held strong views on questions of race pride, human dignity and progress, and frequently engaged in fierce denunciation of British colonial policies, they assiduously discouraged extreme expressions of their beliefs or the severing of cultural, social and political ties with England. Indeed, their attachment to, and display of, British social and cultural values formed the basis of their 'respectability' in West Indian society.[2] As such, black intellectuals had out of necessity to articulate their protests within the context of notions of British justice and the equality of all races. Thus, although these educated blacks regularly condemned racism, and the multiple social, economic and political inequalities within the West Indies and the empire, to a large extent their framework of analysis precluded their protestations being translated into more explicit anti-hegemonic action. Ambiguity and vacillation were characteristic features of their politics in relation to Britain and the impoverished populations they claimed to represent.

Robert Love, for example, has been described by Joyce Lumsden as the outstanding black politician and possibly the most prominent politician of any racial origin in Jamaica between 1890 and 1914.[3] To Rupert Lewis, Love represented the 'most radical figure in Jamaican politics at the turn of the century'.[4] Though proud of his colour, Love nonetheless spoke unashamedly of his desire to acquire British values. 'We desire to be English' he declared, 'in spite of some faults which we see and feel, there is much that is good and sound in the great heart of England, and we have confidence in Her good intentions.'[5] To Love, the Negro born under the British flag was an English man regardless of his African heritage.[6] A newspaper editor like Love, T. Albert Marryshow, Grenada's leading intellectual and black nationalist, was equally convinced that 'the education given to British subjects should have a distinct British personality about it so as to impress on the minds of the trained a respect for British consciousness and ideals.'[7] This was the same man whom the governor of Grenada described to the Colonial Office as being well known locally for his antipathy to Europeans.[8]

Likewise whether the West Indian newspapers followed a more liberal or conservative British ideology, they shared for the most part a common objective: the preservation of ties with Great Britain. Despite their frequently disparaging attacks on elites and governors, the liberal papers in Jamaica and the other colonies, which were normally owned and or edited by black and coloured political activists, more often than not merely desired to achieve social and political reform and not the dissolution of the relationship with England. This underlying unity was significant both in terms of the considerable influence the press exercised on public opinion and in determining the attitude and responses of the newspapers to the war.

Following the lead of the British press in response to the outbreak of war was therefore quite natural. The West Indian press systematically reproduced the propaganda of their British counterparts. A barrage of emotive and derogatory descriptions of the Germans including 'Huns', murderers, thieves and barbarians filled their pages. So too did stories of German atrocities to innocent victims, such as Belgian women and children as well as the sick and the elderly.[9] Nevertheless, occasionally the authorities found it necessary to prosecute a newspaper in one of the colonies to ensure loyalty. The *Argos* (the working man's paper) of Trinidad, for example, was fined £50 for publishing an article prejudicial to the good conduct of the police force.[10] In Barbados, the government also adopted measures to suppress the newspapers and other disloyal elements in the society.[11] Legislation was put into action against the *Advocate*, which was charged £100 for publishing a letter allegedly making false statements and comments likely to cause disaffection to the government.[12] It was, then, within the context of these formal and informal ties that the colonies responded to the plight of England in August 1914.

At the outbreak of hostilities, the colonies promptly forwarded expressions of loyalty and pledges of material and financial support to the British government.[13] One of the most touching resolutions received by the Colonial Office was from Marcus Garvey and his followers and read in part:

That we the members of the Universal Negro Improvement and Conservation Association and African Communities League, assembled in general meeting at Kingston, Jamaica, being mindful of the great protecting and civilizing influence of the English nation and people of whom we are subjects, and their Justice to all men, and especially to their Negro Subjects scattered all over the world, hereby beg to express our loyalty and devotion to His Majesty the King, and Empire and our sympathy with those of the people who are in any way grieved and in difficulty.[14]

Because Garvey was already regarded as a potential threat to the stability of the colonies, the resolution was highly praised in the Colonial Office. Perhaps more importantly, this expression of loyalty was reflective of the extent to which Garveyism emerged out of and shared the culture of ambivalence which characterised the late nineteenth-century West Indian black intelligentsia. Calypsonians in some islands also devoted their energies towards composing songs which supported Britain in the war. However, not all of these songs were approved by the officials and the press. The *Port of Spain Gazette*, which usually represented the views of the old proprietor class, observed that in Trinidad, 'Tipperary' and other patriotic songs were superseded by 'senseless refrains in which the Kaiser came in for rough handling'.[15] Other songs confidently predicted the defeat of Germany. Through these songs calypsonians were able to both express popular sentiment as well as assist in generating greater public sympathy for the Allies.

Gifts to the value of several thousand pounds were subsequently contributed by the colonies to the war effort. These included sugar, rum, oil, lime, cotton, arrowroot, rice, items of clothing, logwood and nine aeroplanes to the Royal Flying Corps and the Royal Air Force. A total of 11 ambulances and adequate sums for their maintenance were donated to the British Red Cross Society. The people in the various countries donated thousands of pounds in cash by voluntary subscriptions and contributions to various charities, including the Belgian Red Cross Fund, King George's Fund for Sailors, Prince of Wales' National Relief Fund, the Star and Garter Fund and Queen Alexandra's Field Force Fund. The cash contributions to the British government and the various charities amounted to approximately two million pounds sterling.[16] Part of the funds was raised through the implementation of new taxes in some colonies like Grenada and Trinidad. The most widely adopted were a produce or export tax and a one pence War Stamp Tax. In relation to the donations of the dominion territories and Allied countries, the West Indian contribution may appear relatively minor but given the small size of the region and the poverty of the population, their effort and the spirit in which they gave were second to none.

It is also worth noting that these donations were made in spite of severe hardships caused by major increases in the cost of living throughout the region, which occurred with the proclamation of war. In Trinidad, for instance, the price of milk increased from five pence to eight pence per tin, rice and flour from one and a half pence to three pence per pound (lb.), salted fish from five pence to eight pence per lb. and sugar from one and a half pence to three pence per lb.[17] Similar conditions in British Honduras prompted a group of women to send a deputation to the governor to complain and seek a reduction in the cost of living.[18] There was a reduction in remittances from the United States and Canada and deposits in the saving banks of the colonies also decreased.[19] As a result of popular protest, the various governments quickly instituted price-control schedules but these did little to pacify the public or the press, which regularly accused the merchants and shopkeepers of boldly and unjustifiably violating the price controls. Likewise, a group of unemployed labourers in British Honduras, in a petition to the governor, indicated that they were facing severe privations as a result of the war, while the elites were enjoying prosperity.[19]

The generosity of the colonies was also not uncontested locally. Against the background of the social and economic bludgeoning effect of the war on the population and the perception that the elites were making super profits from the war, some liberal newspapers, though fully sympathetic to the cause of the Allies, had serious reservations about what they regarded as extravagance on the part of the local legislatures. Their commitment to the cause of the lower classes they claimed to represent had to be seen by the public as being no less significant than their loyalty to the British government. This was critical to their credibility locally. Thus, in a series of three fierce articles, Barbados' *Weekly Illustrated*, described by the *West Indian* as a paper 'always violently at war against wrong doing', castigated the Barbados officials for what it regarded as an excessive and unjustifiable war-donation of £20,000:

> Our legislators have absolutely no right to do anything more to make this colony the laughing stock of its neighbours or of the entire empire. The Home government does not expect impossibilities, and since our finances are in such a desperately unsound condition it would be impolitic for those responsible for the government of the country to make promises on behalf of the population which they well know it is beyond the power of the inhabitants to perform. We condemn this method of advertising the loyalty and patriotism of Barbadians for it cannot stand the test of a searching analysis.[21]

In view of the Barbadians' long-standing and indefatigable self-perception as the most 'British' in the region, it is unlikely that the majority of the population would have subscribed to the paper's position. To allow the other colonies to contribute more than Barbados would probably have seemed as a disgrace to many of the inhabitants. However, the paper's alternative opinion was that instead of Barbados playing the 'poor great', the 'Barbadian Rajahs', as the planters were sarcastically described, should donate the money from the profits they were rapidly accumulating.[22]

Objections were equally evident in the Bahamas, which like most West Indian colonies, experienced economic stagnation before the war. The *Tribune* founded in 1903 on the proclaimed principles of impartiality, liberalism and commitment to the upliftment and defence of blacks, was foremost in condemning the legislature's gift of £10,000:

> We cannot see how in view of the economic conditions that obtain at present that our representatives can shut their eyes to the fact that dark days are before us. With our sponge industry, practically the backbone of the country, suspended; our sisal industry, the next in importance, down to unprofitable production; with the certainty of our custom receipts falling far below average owing to decrease importation; with the Government finding it necessary to stop government work; the consequent lack of employment, reduction of money in circulation and diminished spending power of the people, it seems madness to vote away so much which we are more than likely to need for our increasing army of unemployed and dependents.[23]

While it is also likely that the paper's position would not have met with general approval, there probably would have been more public sympathy with its views than in Barbados because unlike the other West Indian colonies, whose industries (sugar, cotton, oil, wood and so on,) stood to benefit from the war, this was not the case in the Bahamas. Because Barbados and the Bahamas functioned under the Old Representative System of government and hence enjoyed greater political autonomy, their liberal newspapers were not encumbered to the same degree, as those in the Crown Colonies, by the need to adopt a sycophantic attitude to the British government or modify their views too frequently to impress the imperial authorities.[24]

This is not to suggest that the liberal papers in the Crown Colonies did not come face to face with the conflict between their self-appointed responsibility to the lower and middle classes and their need to engage in the politics of appeasement with the British officials. The case of the *West Indian* in Grenada, one of the few colonies which had enjoyed pre-war prosperity, illustrates the point. Early in 1915, Grenada and the Windward Islands received a new governor in the person of George Basil Haddon-Smith. In his inaugural speech, the governor warned the people of Grenada that during the war they would be required to make greater sacrifices than ever before.[25] In reply, the *West Indian* assured him that as Grenadians were a loyal people they would endure the sacrifices even to breaking point.[26] In fact, the paper regarded regular contributions by the children to the war effort an ideal method of instilling in them greater patriotism and appreciation for the empire.[27]

Yet, in accord with its promise to protect the interests of the middle and lower classes, the paper also protested vigorously when the one pence War Tax Stamp was imposed in aid of the war effort on the grounds that it was too much for the majority of the people to bear. It argued that while there were some persons in the colonies to whom the additional tax was nothing, since they could pay 'ten times the amount ten times a day', the tax would bring misery to those already suffering from the war.[28] Taxes the paper protested, could be instituted for the war effort but had to be done 'more under the principle of an equalization of sacrifice, according to one's ability'.[29]

The other liberal paper in the colony, the *Federalist*, though sympathetic to the cause of the Red Cross, was very critical of the manner in which the poor were being fleeced by such organisations. The Red Cross fetes, the paper argued, only served to extract more money from the desperate poor while the rich simply organised the functions, did all the talking, and swaggered about but did not really contribute any funds.[30] In fact, as early as September 1914 the paper had launched a fierce attack on the government and elites and bitterly questioned:

> Are the Government going to give the people work? This is the most important question of the day here. It is not to be asked for a moment and then put aside. It is to be dinned in the ears of those in authority until they understand and appreciate its serious significance. It is all nonsense to shout loyalty to Great Britain when British citizens here are being forced into disloyalty through starvation. If those who form the Government of Grenada were not sure of drawing their salaries every month and thus feeding and providing for their families, what would become of their loyalty? It pays them to be loyal, to shout "Rule Britannia", to rail against the Kaiser and all that sort of thing, but stop their allowances from the Public Treasury and where will their loyalty be? [31]

Opposition to the material and financial contributions made to the war-effort was, however, rare throughout the war years. Centuries of indoctrination reinforced by the barrage of war propaganda effectively created an atmosphere of overwhelming patriotism, which tended to cut across and transcend ethnic, class and race affiliations. Equally important, however, in the new social climate created by the war, certain minority ethnic groups, classes, religious sects and cultural forms were subjected to sustained repression.

With the outbreak of war, martial law was declared giving the governors wide-ranging powers to mobilise the local forces, impose strict censorship, control food prices, prohibit the use of lights in the towns at night and adopt other measures for the general defence of the colonies.[32] As a consequence, during the weeks after the declaration of war a state of nervous tension existed in virtually every colony. These anxieties were further intensified by the rumour that two German cruisers were lurking in the waters of the Caribbean.

In some colonies crowds gathered at the telegraph offices daily and the appearance of any ship on the horizon was a signal for unrestrained panic.[33] The arrival in St. Lucia of the British war ship *Bristol* for coal, for example, caused nervous inhabitants to flee into the hills believing it was a German cruiser.[34] Some relief was brought to the residents of the region by the presence of a battalion of the Royal Canadian Garrison Artillery stationed at St Lucia throughout the duration of the war. In addition to the heavy guns which were mounted in a number of colonies, including Barbados, St. Vincent, St. Kitts, Dominica and the Bahamas, a fleet of motor launches based at Trinidad carried out regular patrols around the region.[35]

Inevitably, it was impossible for Germans and Austrians to escape the wrath of nervous authorities and an overwhelmingly patriotic public. Throughout the region they were ruthlessly rounded up, seized aboard ships and placed under arrest or had their movements within each colony severely restricted.[36] Some had their businesses confiscated and summarily auctioned off to support the local war effort.[37] Any association with Germans residing in the colonies was strictly prohibited. In Jamaica, Oscar Lewis, a lower-class boy, was found guilty of delivering letters to his former German employer who had been interned. He was sentenced to five years imprisonment even though the jury recommended he be dealt with leniently.[38] The punishment was widely regarded as unjust, particularly since neither the sender nor the receiver of the letters was prosecuted, apparently because they were members of the propertied class.

The fact that the governor granted Lewis a pardon after he had spent several months in jail did little to appease those who felt the whole matter had been dealt with on a class basis. As the *Daily Chronicle* noted sarcastically of the pardon:

> His Excellency the Governor is being given credit for showing clemency by the release of the prisoner after his incarceration for some months. This we submit, savours of sycophancy and snobbishness. From our point of view, which, we understand is a popular one, he should have ordered his immediate release. It will be said that he was in the hands of judicial advisers, but His Excellency is not an automaton. It is true that the principal characteristic of his regime is procrastination, but it is one thing to dally over the details of government: it is another, to deprive the subject of his liberty.[39]

Incidents like these might have served to revive the bitterly divisive class and race antagonisms, which had been temporarily overshadowed by the perceived need to unite in order to assist the 'mother country'. Yet, if there was a resurgence of such conflict this did not serve to detract from the general paranoia and anti-German feelings in the colonies. On the contrary, as Germans in the United States and England also discovered, the emotional atmosphere of war-politics had the effect of virtually obliterating much of the previously accepted moral and legally sanctioned conduct of behaviour towards ethnic minorities.[40] Behaviour and attitudes towards these groups which were hitherto regarded as repugnant and impermissible quickly became tolerated by the public and only checked by the authorities when extremes were reached or the stability of the country threatened. The cases of individuals of German origin, who had by virtue of their long residence in the colonies become naturalised citizens, often presented great difficulties for the authorities.

On the one hand, the public were categorically of the opinion that all Germans, irrespective of the status of their nationality, constituted a threat and ought to be incarcerated. On the other hand, although the authorities were concerned about the loyalties of naturalised Germans, the tendency was to respect their status as citizens. Thus, the authorities normally allowed these Germans their freedom unless incriminating evidence was obtained or they were suspected of illegal activities. But in the atmosphere of suspicion and with the lack of forbearance or sympathy generated by war propaganda, anyone with the slightest connection with the Germans or their allies was liable to be categorised as a traitor. Legal measures were adopted in some countries to secure the expulsion of anyone of German or Austrian parentage[41] from various organisations like the Chamber of Commerce.

In Belize, members of the public wrote to the newspapers protesting that Germans were allowed their liberties.[42] It was in Trinidad, however, that there was the most serious manifestations of hostility against resident Germans. There, local German businessman Paul Scherer and his family became the focus of a vicious anti-German campaign led by the *Mirror* newspaper.[43] Demonstrations were held in front of the Scherer buildings and his property was stoned. The agitation against Scherer was also supported by the Trinidad Chamber of Commerce, which argued that he was an undesirable alien and probably dangerous.[44] The campaign was so relentless that the government of Trinidad, acting on instruction from the Colonial Office, issued a caution to the paper's editor warning of possible action if the inflammatory and libellous articles continued.[45] Bonar Law was of the opinion that the agitation could not be tolerated since Scherer also had American citizenship and America was a friendly nation.[46] Nevertheless, Scherer was advised by the Colonial Office to leave Trinidad while the question of his citizenship was being settled.[47] On the other hand, the Trinidad government did bring a case against Carl Boos, a German, on a charge of espionage but the lengthy case ended in an acquittal due the lack of incriminating evidence.[48]

In Jamaica, the arrest of Edward Cook, a German by birth but of a British mother, created a sensation.[49] Although feelings of sympathy towards him were expressed quietly on account of his pleasant personality, these were muted because of the intensity of the anti-German atmosphere. In fact, anyone, regardless of nationality, who was suspected of being unpatriotic or having the slightest sympathy for the Germans, was liable to be treated as a spy. One such case was that of T. Colin Campbell, an Englishman who was arrested aboard a ship on its way to Kingston, Jamaica from Liverpool, England; he was hand-cuffed, his feet were bound, he was dragged to his cabin and deprived of drinking water, medicines, electric light and clothing and confined for the duration of the voyage along with his young son.[50] When he protested about his private papers being confiscated he was contemptuously informed by the captain: 'Nothing is private now, you cur.'[51] As if this was not enough, when the ship arrived in Kingston he underwent what was obviously for him, further embarrassment and psychological humiliation by being arrested according to him, by 'three ugly black native' police.

The newspapers even publicised the story that a suspected German spy had been arrested. In the pest-infested cells where he was confined for some weeks, he experienced more psychological torture by being regularly told by the guards to make the most of his time and say his prayers since he was certainly going to be shot as a spy. On one occasion when he requested to go to the toilet, the guard's mockingly indifferent reply was: 'I'll report it to the officer in the morning and let you know.'[52] On hearing that he had been arrested as a spy, the firm he worked for simply ignored him. After a month he was informed that the authorities had arrested him on forged letters of instructions and he was therefore free to go but the governor nevertheless ordered him to leave the island within 24 hours. Because all his funds had run out during his imprisonment, Campbell was unable to comply with the governor's order and was therefore re-arrested and confined until he could be deported to England.

On the afternoon of his departure, he and his boy were put on the police-wagon and escorted by coloured police and detectives through the streets with a loud gong ringing all the way to clear the traffic. The noise naturally enough brought people out to stare at the spectacle of the suspected spy. On his arrival back in England, Campbell attempted to seek redress but neither the police, the shipping company or the War Office showed much interest in his plight and his former employers informed him they could no longer trust him. His attempt to generate public sympathy also failed because the newspapers refused to publish his story since they felt it would violate censorship regulations. Such incidents might not have been widespread in Jamaica and the rest of the region but as the Scherer case also illustrated, when they did occur it was difficult for the victims to receive a fair trial or public sympathy.

Urgent calls were also made in Barbados for the government to adopt strict measures to prevent the 'spy peril.'[53] One American woman living in Barbados who was alleged to have a German grandfather was forced to make a desperate denial in order to avoid arrest. The fact that she was not incarcerated infuriated the *Globe*, which insisted:

> There should be no other room but the barbed wire enclosure for any German seen in Barbados or any other of His Majesty's dominions during the present crisis; there should be no quarter given on the score

of class or sex ... We have no desire to be hard upon any peaceful citizen who may be an alien, but events have proved the necessity for firm action, however unpleasant it might be, and it is the duty of this government to see that such firm action is taken.[54]

Unlike in the United States and England, the relatively small size of the colonies and the fact that the vast majority of the population were non-European made it extremely difficult for persons of German or Austrian parentage to disguise or change their identity as a means of protecting themselves.

Aliens who had the unfortunate experience of being interned in local gaols often suffered severely at the hands of the authorities. Numerous complaints were received by the international committee of the Red Cross from the more than 700 prisoners of war in Jamaica, who claimed among other things, that they were improperly fed, ill-treated, robbed and housed in appalling conditions.[55] These prisoners were mainly German and Austrian seamen taken off ships throughout the region but a small number were Germans living in the West Indies. Similar complaints were made by those prisoners held in Trinidad and St Lucia. Though it is likely that the claims of poor treatment were at times exaggerated or even false, the evidence suggests that some complaints were justified. One German was shot, for example, by a guard who thought the prisoners were deliberately trying to create a distraction to facilitate an escape.[56] Another prisoner who pleaded with the authorities to release him because of his declining health had his application categorically rejected.[57] Another who had been interned in 1914 subsequently died in prison from diabetes and phthisis.[58] Although the odds were heavily weighted against them, interned Germans did not accept their imprisonment passively. Various schemes were devised to escape custody but more often than not these ended in failure. Some held at Glendairy prison in Barbados enjoyed a brief spell of freedom by escaping through a tunnel but were soon caught.[59] At the St James barracks in Trinidad, several Germans were court-martialled after assaulting the commandant of the internment camp, Captain Percy Louis Fraser, who had referred to them as miserable dogs.[60] Most of the prisoners from the region were eventually repatriated to Canada.

The paranoia and politics surrounding the war also gave local authorities the green light to intensify their repression of cultural and religious practices, which they had previously regarded as threats to British hegemony in the colonies. Given significant religious intolerance in the colonies, particularly on the part of the officials and the press, and the officials' deep concern about maintaining social order and temporal authority, the attacks on the Jehovah's Witnesses in the new environment of war excitement was not surprising. By 1895, missionary work of this group was already on the way in South Africa, Switzerland, Colombia and the West Indies, where the religious ideas of Charles Taze Russell, the movement's founder, figurehead and major benefactor, had found a noticeable number of converts by the outbreak of war.[61]

In 1886, Russell had predicted that 1914 would mark the second coming of Christ and the 'end of the time of the Gentiles.' The years immediately before the war witnessed the rapid spread of Russell's messianic ideas among the struggling working classes around the world. Through its organs, the *Watch Tower Bible and Tract Society* and the *International Bible Student's Association* the movement increasingly agitated for relief for the poor and their active participation in society, and intensified its attacks on capitalist businessmen. Russell's doctrines had particular significance in the West Indies where, in the years after emancipation large numbers of disillusioned persons increasingly rejected the established churches and sought refuge from their daily miseries in the smaller but more lively Afro-West Indian revivalist churches.[62] The Jamaican leader of the Russellites, J.L. TaBois, also began prophesying, in accordance with the beliefs of the movement, that debts and mortgages would be repudiated, that the meek would inherit the earth and the kingdom of God established on earth.[63]

Since the outbreak of war seemed to fulfil Russell's prediction, his followers in the West Indies, as elsewhere, intensified their proselytising activities, disseminating leaflets and holding noisy demonstration marches in the streets. Condemnation from the press was swift and caustic. In Barbados, for example, indignant protests were made by the *Globe* which described the leaders as men of 'incomprehensible religious persuasion', whose objective was to prey upon the feelings of the weak and lead them away from their 'inborn patriotism under the guise of religion'.[64] As a warning to the authorities of the possible consequences, the paper declared in characteristically alarmist tone:

It is decidedly dangerous that the weak should be thus deluded, and especially under the pretence of religion, because once convinced in

13

that respect there is no reasonable power on earth to remove the impression, and in steps disloyalty to the crown ... Such individuals are dangerous in a half educated community like this; their mouths should be stopped and their parades abolished. It is true they are only maniacs in the eyes of the enlightened inhabitants, but it is not amongst this class that they seek to labour. They are capable of easily inciting the mind of the weak and seducing them from their allegiance to the Crown. Our masses form an easy prey for invasion by any doctrine of religion; they are ever swift to accept even though their tarry may be short and their progress slow. We counsel the proper authorities to be up and doing and thus sweep from our doors at an early time the menacing evil.[65]

These calls for the suppression of the Russellites did not go unheeded by the officials. Local government authorities throughout the region adopted measures to deal with the group. Laws were enacted in most territories requiring the licensing of foreign preachers and in British Guiana the organisers of the movement were deported.[66]

For somewhat similar reasons the less messianic but equally contentious religious group, the Shakers, were ruthlessly pursued, harassed and even imprisoned in a number of West Indian colonies. The *Sun* in Antigua was just one of the local papers which engaged in angry denunciation of this group, which was accused of being a public nuisance and engaging in noisy practices, including shouting, screaming, falling on the floor, pounding and other 'ridiculous antics' mistakenly believed to be manifestations of the power of the Holy Spirit.[67] Throughout the war the attacks on the movement in Montserrat, St. Vincent and Trinidad were intensified, and legislation prohibited their gatherings.[68] Consequently, in most areas the movement was forced to carry on its meetings in secret but police harassment continued, sometimes resulting in violent confrontation between the two.[69]

Meanwhile, the Church of England and the Catholics, with the tacit approval of the state, launched an attack on those cultural activities which they regarded as incongruent with civilised society and an affront to established Western religious principles. Principal among these were the Carnival celebrations, which were held annually in a variety of forms in a number of territories but which at that point were perhaps largest in Trinidad. The social and political significance of these celebrations, which had their roots in slavery as a means of protest and as expression of an incipient cultural nationalism, has been well documented in several studies.[70] In the light of this history, and more so, because of the social disturbances which occasionally accompanied these events, state and church authorities readily adopted the attitude that carnival represented a threat to public order and moreover that it was unpatriotic to engage in frivolities while others were suffering and dying in the war.

The carnivals in Trinidad and Grenada were condemned as dirty and demoralising spectacles during which all sorts of vulgarities were engaged in by persons wearing masks,[71] and legal measures were adopted prohibiting the wearing of masks in public or processions of persons in disguise or fancy dress.[72] Despite these regulations, the carnivals in both countries continued to be held but on a reduced scale. In these ways, then, under the disguise of patriotism, the war legitimised the repression of a number of minority ethnic and religious groups as well as those cultural movements which allegedly posed a threat to British hegemony. The threat from these groups and practices was unquestionably exaggerated but because of the hysteria generated by the war, distinctions between wrong and right, truth and falsehood, reality and fantasy became even more blurred. However, as we will see, there were other factors which served to confirm the suspicions of the authorities that there was some degree of disloyalty among the population.

Black Aspirations Expressed

Although British hegemony was pervasive throughout the region, there was constantly the realisation that it was prone to be challenged by certain elements within the society. Cultural hegemony is rarely, perhaps never, as we have suggested, so all–embracing that it renders the subordinate groups incapable of contesting prevailing social relations or official descriptions of reality. This subculture of resistance was symbolically highlighted by the fact that when the war began, the question of participation by blacks quickly became the focus of an often antagonistic debate. The controversy in the colonies was to have a profound influence on the discussions and decision–making process among British officials.

In several territories, including Trinidad, Grenada, Jamaica and British Honduras, a number of blacks adopted the position that it was a war among Europeans (a white man's war) and therefore that black people should not get involved. As was to be expected, the West Indian press, regardless of political and ideological persuasion, unanimously condemned such arguments. The *Jamaica Times*, for example, adamantly insisted that persons responsible for spreading such malignant and treasonable lies should receive no mercy under martial law.[1] For its part, the *Federalist* argued that to describe the war as a white man's quarrel was mad and impious.[2] As an institution which prided itself on its ability to debate issues with vigour and intellect, the West Indian press could not, however, confine itself to bluster and indignation. Ideological and pragmatic arguments were carefully crafted, drawing heavily on the corresponding discourse in England to combat and enlighten the dissenters.

Given the fact that West Indian blacks, as indeed colonials throughout the diaspora and Africa, regarded the war as the first real opportunity since slavery to demonstrate their loyalty to and equality with whites, the press naturally utilised this theme. The participation of blacks in the war, it was contended, would provide a significant fillip to their social and political advancement, quite apart from its psychological benefits. Thus, the *Jamaica Times* posited, black people had of necessity, firmly and rationally, to claim the right to shoulder their responsibilities as subjects of the King and members of the empire if they desired to win the confidence of other races.[3] It was only in this way, it argued, that the objectionable tradition of 'the white man's burden' could be broken down. The issues of this line of reasoning, reminiscent of the anti–slavery debate and the articles of faith of the French revolution, were also succinctly summarised in the *Federalist*:

> As Coloured people we will be fighting for something more, something inestimable to ourselves. We will be fighting to prove to Great Britain that we are not so vastly inferior to the whites that we should not be put on a level, at least, of political equality with them. We will be fighting to prove that the distinction between God–made creatures of one empire because of skin, colour or complexion differences, should no longer exist, and that some opportunities should be afforded the Coloured subjects of the empire as fall by right of race to its citizens. We will be fighting to prove that we are no longer merely subjects, but citizens – citizens of a world empire whose watch–word should be Liberty, Equality and Brotherhood.[4]

Integral to these arguments was the conviction among many educated blacks that, in accordance with what they perceived as the 'rhythm and cycles of civilisation', Africa and black people generally, would regain their glorious past.[5] The theme of Africa's great past and the belief that the continent would once again rise to political prominence was systematically developed throughout the nineteenth century by black scholars like J.J. Thomas and Dr Theophilus Scholes.[6]

Although the notion of Africa's glorious past has in recent times been the subject of much scholarship and controversy, the argument provided blacks, particularly the nationalists, with a powerful means of rejecting the inferiority complex inculcated by centuries of denial and humiliation and the claims by English writers and scholars that blacks had never contributed to 'civilisation' and were incapable of self–rule.[7] To educated blacks like Marryshow, then, the war was a confirmation of the process of disintegration and regeneration which all civilisations experienced. In the light of this belief, Marryshow insistently advised that blacks should hold their heads high and feel a deep sense of superiority to the Germans, who before the war had been 'universally acknowledged to be high representatives of white civilisation of Europe'.[8] In addition, a number of arguments cloaked in the language of moral indignation and often verging on hysteria were advanced to justify why blacks should do their utmost to assist in the conflagration. Blacks were urged to forget, at least temporarily, the record of Belgian atrocities among the people of the Congo and to assist in suppressing the Germans who had 'bestialised Belgian women, murdered children and maimed the sick and the aged'.[9] For these reasons it was argued, blacks should eagerly seize the opportunity to use the 'sword of righteousness' against the filthy, criminal and ungodly enterprises of the 'white devil'.[10]

At the same time, the spectre of German rule in the West Indies as a consequence of an Allied defeat was actively raised as a warning, especially to those blacks who wished for a German victory or asserted that it was a white man's war. Those who objected in Trinidad on these grounds were angrily condemned by the *Mirror* which countered:

> We have to thank Providence that we are living in the West Indies, far from the theatres of the war and far from German possessions. Perhaps, however, that is not a blessing for our people. Had not thousands of miles separated us from the German colonies, so that we know little of their ways and customs, we would not have heard as we often hear now, people in their ignorance disclaim that this is a white man's war in which the black people should not take part. It is a pity that there are such people in our midst, and it is more regrettable that they should be allowed to propagate their pernicious ignorance within the limits of the colony of Trinidad and Tobago.[11]

At one meeting of the UNIA in Jamaica, at which a party of black volunteers of the BWIR were present, Marcus Garvey delivered a lecture dealing with German colonial policy in Africa. The volunteers and other members of the audience were told of German atrocities in Togoland and warned that since Germany's aspirations were opposed to the enlightenment of blacks, it was clearly the duty of those interested in the progress of the negro to do all within their power to stop German militarism.[12] At the close of the meeting a vote of thanks was moved by a member of the contingent. At this point, the local authorities were prepared to exploit the Garvey movement and ideology to their benefit but, as we will see, as the war came to a close, the officials became extremely wary of the relationship, regarding it as an unholy alliance.

Proponents of West Indian federation also believed West Indian's support of the war- effort would strengthen their hand and the process of integration. Among those agitating for political reform in the region, federation was accepted as an essential pre-requisite to representative government and greater recognition within the empire. The *West Indian*, as a leading advocate of West Indian federation was quick to argue that the war could enhance the process:

> Even in these days of darkness, ours is not a nightmare but a glorious dream of the future when every portion of His Majesty's dominion capable of responsibility, will play its own great appointed part. The dawn of this auspicious day for the West Indies does not rest with the Authorities of Downing Street, but with West Indians, who should first learn to cultivate the spirit of nationality; to look beyond their cocoa fields and cane fields, their little parishes, and poor "canvas cities" within narrow stripes of seas, into the broader outlook of West Indian interests. The war that is being waged in Europe today affords to the world a great object–lesson in Unity and Self–Sacrifice ... Let us hope then, that when the war–drum throbs no longer ... West Indians, as represented in these scattered islands of the Caribbean, will have long abandoned their mutual suspicions, prejudice and reservations of pride, and be quite prepared to enter into that spirit of oneness of purpose, which ought to receive peculiar advantages in the great days of imperial consolidation and up–building that are ahead.[13]

When the BWIR was eventually formed, the paper happily declared that the first step towards unity had begun.[14]

Black and coloured reformers who were attacking Crown Colony government in the region regarded the war as an important blessing for the movement for representative government. By 1914, the contest of ideas and struggle for power between the planter/merchant elites and the coloured and black middle classes had become acute. The Colonial Office was by no means oblivious to the potential threat to the stability of the colonies posed by these developments. After years of persistent deadlocks and even embarrassing defeats in their clashes with the local legislatures, Colonial Office officials tended to regard the planters as 'ignorant, narrow–minded, shifty, improvident, selfish and provocative'.[15] But some officials also had a long–standing distrust of the black population and of the increasing unity between black and coloured politicians. The first evidence of an organised political union between blacks and coloureds in Jamaica and perhaps the entire region, was the loose coalition in the Jamaica Assembly known as the 'Town' party.[16]

This development had been critical in the decision of the planter\merchant elites to opt for Crown Colony government in order to preserve their influence, even if only informally, after years of vicious defence of their 'rights as Englishmen'. Philip Curtin, has in this regard made the contention that: 'It is difficult to avoid the conclusion that Jamaican fear of the demagogues, combined with the growing British conviction that Jamaicans could no longer be trusted with the control of their own government, would have ended self–government within a few years, even without the rising at Morant Bay.'[17] Significantly, when the British government began reducing its garrisons in the West Indies at the end of the nineteenth century, Montagu Ommanney, Permanent Under Secretary in the Colonial Office, anxiously predicted:

> There are forces at work in the West Indies and rapidly gaining strength, which have to be reckoned with. A disreputable press, [and] an equally disreputable and quite unscrupulous class of half–breed agitators are continually increasing their hold on the ignorant and excitable Negro and they may easily foment disturbances of a kind and on a scale with which the force now available will be unable to cope.[18]

The fundamental political problem of West Indian society at the turn of the century was the fact that blacks and coloureds realised that in most colonies, Crown Colony government had failed miserably to curb the influence of the elite, which more often than not was inimical to the betterment of the majority of the population. It was with this in mind that the *Federalist* concluded in 1914 that Crown Colony government in Grenada had become a fraud and an imposture.[19] The anxieties of the local elites and the Colonial Office were really then only symptomatic of this deeper political and constitutional malaise.

In Grenada, the opposition forces agitating for the abolition of Crown Colony government crystallised in 1917 with the formation of the Representative Government Association and similar organisations were soon established in other colonies.[20] But even before that, in January 1915, the *West Indian* had been established in the capital, St Georges, by local journalist T.A. Marryshow and a lawyer, C.F.P. Renwick, as the official voice of the reform movement in Grenada. Marryshow had previously worked for the older radical paper the *Federalist*. Both papers, but especially the *West Indian*, were at the forefront of the agitation to send a contingent overseas. Their tremendous support for the war-effort was not purely disinterested; it represented calculated practical patriotism. It was not likely, as G.K. Lewis has noted of the Jamaican group, that these 'negro gentlemen' with radical ideas, who looked to the liberal imperialists in British politics for their fulfilment would have had any criticisms of Britain's role in the war.[21]

Like their compatriots in South Africa, West Indian middle–class blacks were aware of the relevance of the war in their struggle for political and constitutional change.[22] Couched beneath their protestations of patriotism was a clear linkage between their support for the war-effort and the grant of the reforms they desired. Not surprisingly, such a connection was strenuously denied by the *West Indian,* which denied seizing England by the throat at a time of crisis.[23] 'We are not asking for representative institutions', the paper objected, 'as the price for our loyalty and sacrifices in this war, but because it is part of the principle for which respectable humanity is fighting with Great Britain in the war.'[24]

Yet, once the United States had entered the war, the reformers were able to state their position more assertively and confidently in the language of Wilsonian idealism. Shortly after Woodrow Wilson had led America into the war, he propounded his now famous Fourteen Points, which had as their core ideology the principle of self-determination. In the light of this declaration, the *West Indian* boldly declared:

The present war has many side issues; a number of different designs and results are dependent on the ultimate decision, but, high and above all these, there is one overmastering issue over which the world is at war, and that is, whether the people of the states of the modern world are to be vested with the responsibility of their own government, or whether the German view is to prevail under which all human needs and aspirations are to be sacrificed to the passions and vanities of a ruling few. This is clearly, the only issue on which the United States entered the war ... The main and greatest issue of the war is to lay a solid world–foundation of "government of the people, for the people, by the people" ... that is the evangel; that is the cause, above, surrounding, and permeating the war. All other hopes and outlooks are of secondary importance. The war is a war for Liberty; a war for public Responsibility of Government, under which, alone, the royal murderers of humanity would be kept in check and, "the world made safe for democracy".[25]

Many years later Henry Hudson Phillips, an associate of Marryshow, recalled that the editor 'conceived the idea that through common sacrifices on the battlefields on the part of the West Indies with the rest of the empire and of the world, a claim to rights of freedom could impressively be made; a united West Indies would be born; a West Indian Dominion having the active sympathy and support of Britain and the other Dominions.'[26] Moreover, it was incomprehensible and unacceptable to the reformers in Grenada that the South Africans could have been granted such extensive liberties as was represented in the 1910 constitution after having engaged in a bloody and embarrassing war with Britain, while the ever loyal West Indians were being denied their meagre demands for reform.[27]

Not everyone in the colonies shared the expectations of the educated blacks for political advance or psychological confidence as a result of local participation in the war. These possibilities were deeply resented by that section of Jamaican society which had, because of ignorance, deceit and prejudice, convinced itself that blacks were inherently incapable of managing their own political affairs. They feared that the locals might become 'swell–headed' from exaggerated notions of the importance of the role they had played in the war. As in Trinidad, scorn was poured on the idea of blacks going to fight for England.[28] To this ultra–conservative, indeed, racist section of the society, the thought of large–scale black participation in the war seemed absurd. The intelligence of the volunteers enlisting for the Jamaica contingent and the entire black population was contemptuously called into question, as was their possible practical use as soldiers. Jamaicans were urged to drop the idea of sending a contingent to the front and be content with material and financial contributions.[29] Such reactionary comments generated many angry reactions in the community, which found expression in a heated debate in the press over the relative intelligence of the West Indian versus the British recruit.[30]

A group of labourers experienced similar rejection when they offered to subscribe voluntarily to the war fund in Jamaica. At the outbreak of the war, a number of estate workers approached the overseer and expressed the desire that he deduct a small amount weekly from their wages for a set period of time as their contribution to the War Relief Fund.[31] They were promptly told that they were not being asked and if they insisted on this sacrifice they were not to see it as charity. The overseer subsequently admitted that pride had compelled him to respond in that way because he did not wish Jamaican labourers to think that English soldiers needed their assistance.

In response to the overseer's insult, the workers defiantly protested that they were giving not only because they desired to give but also because as British subjects they had as much right as he had to contribute. This confrontation illustrated quite clearly the clash of two ideals or currents in Caribbean thought at the time. On the one hand, the blacks, regarding themselves as free members of the empire, desired to act out their perceived rights in all forms. On the other hand, white-prejudice elicited an adverse reaction or confirmation of their determined efforts, as the blacks correctly believed, to keep them in their places socially, politically, economically and psychologically.

While the suggestion of a West Indian contingent elicited contempt in racially prejudiced whites, it also generated a certain measure of anxiety and fear which had historical roots. In 1795, the white population of the West Indian colonies had reacted with violent opposition to the creation of the black slave regiments, even though they faced possible extermination and considerable economic loss from their white French adversaries.[32] Likewise, when the anti–slavery movement was at its peak, whites in the colonies felt that the end of their physical existence was at hand because: 'The idea of a society in which Negroes were released from their subordination and allowed legal equality with whites was so antithetical to the principles on which the slave society rested that it seemed to threaten complete social dissolution and chaos.'[33]

Even though slavery had long since ended and the presence of the West India Regiment (WIR) had become a regular, if not accepted fact of life in Jamaica, the thought of blacks enlisting en–masse in the military to go to the European front created uneasiness among sections of the population. Among whites, oral tradition had kept alive the dreadful stories of slave rebellions and their efficacy as a weapon of black resistance. And if these revolts had been forgotten, many whites would certainly have remembered the series of post-slavery disturbances in virtually every colony, and particularly the 1865 Morant Bay Rebellion in Jamaica, which changed the political landscape of the region.[34] The fear of disturbances was imbedded in West Indian society to a large extent because very little had changed socially, economically and politically for the bulk of the population between 1838 and 1914.

Other changes within West Indian society also contributed to the crisis of consciousness among whites. For example, the whites were steadily becoming a smaller minority, not only in relation to the rest of the population but in absolute numbers. The decline of the white population in Jamaica, for example, meant that increasingly the officials had to depend on blacks to preserve internal security. However, as the controversies in Jamaica and other colonies over the composition of the militia and the constabulary revealed, whites were very uncomfortable about providing blacks with firearms.[35] In addition, the emancipation day celebrations which were celebrated on August 1 throughout the region, were viewed by some as a time when the labouring classes would possibly engage in serious political or social demonstrations.[36] However, this fear of black radicalism was usually tempered by the belief that the labouring classes had always been indifferent to those who claimed that August 1 would be a time of social and political unrest.[37] Nevertheless, during the war years there were again suggestions that labourers would seize the opportunity to engage in industrial action on that day.[38]

Given the persistence of these fears and the constant efforts of black agitators to capitalise on and manipulate them in order to precipitate change, it is not surprising that the thought of more blacks in the military and the possibility of blacks helping to kill whites, even if they were enemies, caused distress, especially among the conservative sections of the society. Commenting on these anxieties with contempt born of relief that their fears had not materialised the *Gleaner* remarked:

We have been amused in the past days to hear the opinions expressed on the loyalty of Jamaica natives; We more than once have heard it said that the people wear a mask, that the police could not be trusted, that West Indian soldiers were dangerous. The people who said all this were not numerous ...Yet they were sometimes vocal. You might have imagined, to hear them talk, that the better classes of these colonies were living on the edge of a volcano and that, an eruption might at any moment occur.[39]

Despite the obvious smugness of this paper, the historical evidence of the region as well as universal comparisons, suggest very strongly that such concerns might have been more widespread than the paper realised or was, because of its own insecurity, willing to admit. Whether or not these fears were actually well–founded is a difficult and complex issue. However, while there may have been good reason for distrusting the labouring classes, as the Morant Bay revolt illustrated, it seems that there was much less of a basis for fearing black soldiers. The history of the WIR shows that it confounded the hysterical objections of the elites by providing reliable and effective service as a colonial police force for well over a hundred years and played a crucial role in suppressing the Morant Bay revolt.

Although it is likely that the overwhelming patriotic response to the war would have relieved those who feared blacks might be radically changed by serving in the military, there is no doubt that these fears remained a permanent feature. By those in favour of creating a West Indian contingent they were mainly regarded as inconsequential and a mere cover for deep–rooted race prejudice. In South Africa where the black population was subjected to even greater inequalities and segregation, a section of the white population reacted to the thought of blacks serving as soldiers in a manner which was reminiscent of the panic which prevailed in the West Indian slave colonies in 1795.[40] This did not go unnoticed in the West Indies. The *Federalist*, for example, prophesied contemptuously:

> The Boers naturally fear that if the Zulus are trained to the use of modern arms it will be a difficult job afterwards to control and dominate them, hence they even refused their services against ... the Germans. But we think the day is dawning when the black man will be more fairly treated in the empire. When that day comes we must thank Kaiser Wilhelm of Germany for it.[41]

The *Times* of St. Vincent, with similar satisfaction, asserted that the necessity which had led to the employment of blacks on the continent of Europe had dealt a shattering blow to racial prejudice.[42] The paper predicted that the destiny of Indians and blacks within the French and British empires was bound to be completely reshaped in the aftermath of the war.

Countering the suggestions that the war would induce a change in the consciousness of blacks to the detriment of the whites, was the belief that military service would have a beneficial effect on blacks, especially those of the lower class who were likely to comprise the bulk of the contingents. It was thought that military service, which emphasised the harshest type of discipline, and the related 'natural' effects of the experience of foreign travel, would be beneficial to blacks. The *Clarion* contended that the majority of the men would return with their minds expanded by foreign travel and habits improved by the strict discipline and fiery ordeal they had passed through.[43] The *Port of Spain Gazette* carried articles emphasising the belief that the war experience would inculcate in the men such Christian virtues as courage, unselfishness, self–sacrifice, cheerfulness, helpfulness and religiosity.[44] The *Gleaner* stressed the prospect for greater social control, arguing that the black man would learn the value of discipline, self–restraint and obedience.[45] Moreover, it was argued, blacks would benefit from an education and their visit to England as well as closer association with British ideals were apt to make them return stronger imperialists and even more proud of their connection with the empire.[46] All of these arguments, and particularly those articulated by the *Gleaner*, reflected the preoccupation of these conservative newspapers and, the elites whose views they represented, with the struggle for cultural dominance in the colonies; they also highlighted the way in which the lower class were regarded by the elites as territory to be subjugated to their conception of morality, social order and progress. As early as 1902, the *Gleaner* had argued that the average black man was not as highly developed in mind and character as most white men because they did not discipline themselves and keep their passions in subjugation and therefore Jamaica's paramount need was 'the training and disciplining of the black race'.[47]

Significantly, however, even among the black liberals there were those who, because of their education and informal association with the elites, partly shared the 'official' view of ex–servicemen as barbarised; they were believed to have a penchant for violence which would constitute a serious threat to society if they were not properly reacculturated and reintegrated. In this respect, the participation of blacks in the war created a minor dilemma for the liberal segment of the press. Although they tacitly shared the 'official' perception of the veterans, they had out of necessity to their cause, nevertheless, to articulate the opposite socialistic conception of ex–soldiers, which saw them as comrades unhindered by class divisions and hence representing a major hope for the resolution of class tensions within capitalist society. Thus, in spite of its agitation for blacks to participate in the war, the *West Indian* found it possible to question sceptically:

> Are we sure that many old established principles of religious experience, moral law, civil law, social order, and such things, will not be undermined by the grown power, the realized power, of the strong arms of men who passionately have fought for others and passionately may fight for themselves? Are we sure that what we praise and acclaim as "splendid stoicism", "Spartan courage", "bull–dog tenacity" in enemy territory overseas will not suddenly work out in internal affairs, just as a crazy clock that is wound up is capable of striking the midnight hour some time, and at any time?[48]

The extent to which the black reformers were willing to dwell on the possible negative consequences of sending large numbers of locals to the war was, however, effectively reduced by their need to secure as many allies locally and in England in their own war against the planters and merchants. As we have seen, they hoped participation in the war would effect this.

The debate on West Indian involvement in the war was no less informed by economic considerations. Given the historical propensity of the planters to cry ruin at the slightest indication that their labour supply was being affected adversely, it was to be expected that they would object to the sending of men overseas. It was asserted in Belize that the country needed more labourers for its development and that the loss of men to the military would not only set the colony back, but also cause the loss of tax revenue.[49] Similar concerns about the probable loss of labour were also voiced in Jamaica.[50] However, the need to appear patriotic in the light of the general euphoria and expressions of loyalty from the public, as well as the attacks from the reformers, meant that these objections were rare and muted.

Nevertheless, economic arguments were put forward to justify sending men overseas. It was argued that as with the migration of men to Panama and Cuba, the colonies could benefit substantially from the remittances of the soldiers.[51] It was also asserted that the departure of men to the front would ease the problem of the large numbers of unemployed in most colonies.[52] In fact, the *Gleaner* argued that in spite of the departure of men to the front, thousands of able–bodied labourers would still be available to meet the country's needs and, moreover, although their place was preferably in the home, women could be used to supplement the labour force if the need arose.[53] Another hope expressed was that the presence of West Indian soldiers overseas would draw attention to the region, so that after the war, British ex–soldiers would be encouraged to migrate and establish agricultural enterprises in the colonies.[54] The clamour and intensity with which the arguments for participation of blacks in the war were articulated by the local population provided the basis for official representations to the Colonial Office.

The Great Dilemma

Under pressure from the various sections of the population in the different colonies, the governors of the West Indies realised that they had to heed the wishes of their people. The possibility of a contingent was initially raised with the Colonial Office by the governor of Jamaica.[1] The offer of black troops from the West Indies placed the cat among the pigeons in that it was made in the midst of a bitterly divisive discourse taking place within official circles and the public in England. Among British officials opinion was unequally and unfavourably divided on the question of using blacks as soldiers, especially on the western front. The possibility of using them in a non–combatant role did, however, receive more favourable consideration.

The case for utilising the services of blacks in both capacities was strenuously argued by those military officials who had formerly commanded black soldiers in various parts of the empire, but especially on the African continent. The fine physique and 'natural fighting qualities' (a notion premised on the European preconception that blacks were a semi–barbaric and war–like people, as well as on previous bloody battles with various African groups) of blacks were extolled to justify their deployment against the Germans.[2] It was partly against this background that, long before the outbreak of war in 1914, there were those like P.H. Silburn, a member of the Defence Committee of Natal, who advocated the greater use of blacks as part of an imperial army drawn from all parts of the empire.[3]

Those opposed to deploying blacks against the Germans, however, denied their fighting abilities on the grounds that as a race, blacks were inferior in every capacity. One senior military official insisted that Africans were so uneducated that if employed in throwing bombs they would be a greater source of danger to their friends than to the enemy.[4] The argument that blacks were uncivilised was thus a two–edged sword cutting on both sides of the discourse. Unfortunately for the West Indians, it was the perception that blacks were useless which was most actively championed within both the Colonial Office, and especially the War Office. However, as the debate escalated, it became clear that the refusal to employ blacks was based on a wider range of seriously problematic social and political issues.

In view of the intransigence of the War Office, a number of other arguments were articulated to bolster the contention that blacks should be utilised. The seemingly inexhaustible number of blacks on the African continent, as well as the ostensibly cheaper cost of employing blacks as soldiers and carriers, since most did not require pensions or separation allowances, were cited as powerful justifications for their use, especially in view of the increasing shortage of white soldiers.[5] As early as November 1914, Sir Robert Paterson Houston, whose shipping company operated in such diverse places as London, New York and Cape Town, offered to raise, equip and transport battalions of Africans at his own expense but his offer was flatly rejected by the War Office.[6] Nevertheless, a small lobby in Parliament, consisting of men like Sir Harry Johnston and Josiah Wedgwood, continued to press for the creation of a large black army to be used against the Germans.[7]

Some officials who had worked with blacks had become deeply conscious of the persistence and consistency of their desire to reclaim their dignity and achieve self–fulfilment. Wedgwood argued in Parliament that many blacks were clamouring to serve in the war because they felt that if they were able to fight side by side with British troops the colour–bar would disappear and they would gain more self–respect.[8] Whatever the accuracy of this perception it did not impress many because it struck at the heart of deeply embedded fears within official circles. Moreover, wider political considerations, such as fear of the reactions of South African whites, further served to harden the opposition among some British officials.[9]

In response to such concerns, arguments based on notions of Britain's responsibility to uplift blacks from their alleged state of barbarism to a state of civilisation were put forward as a warning of the fearful consequences for blacks should Germany win the war.[10] Meanwhile, the fact that the French were actively recruiting blacks to serve in their army provided the Wedgwood group with another argument which seemed to them to expose the hypocrisy of the British attitude.[11] The War Office disagreed that the French black battalions had been a success in Europe.[12] In spite of the barrage of criticisms and the tremendous difficulty of not raising the question of colour too openly, the War Office remained hostile to the calls for blacks to assist in the war–effort while continuing to press for more and more whites to enlist or be conscripted. Indeed, in the midst of one of the greatest crises Britain had ever faced, concern was expressed that the Germans would object to the use of black soldiers.

Inevitably, the British public and press were drawn into the debate and in some quarters the suggestion that blacks should be allowed to fight was fiercely contested and the spectre of a black menace in Europe raised in alarm. Given the negative connotations of blackness and the prevalence of hardened racial attitudes, this reaction was perhaps not surprising. Advocates of black participation were on occasion subjected to the most virulent criticism and verbal abuse. A post card to R.P. Houston, for example, threatened him and his compatriots with violence for suggesting that blacks be brought to Europe where they might slaughter 'decent white people'.[13] While these threats were naturally unpleasant, they probably did even greater harm by further evoking the anxieties of the public and intensifying the intractable attitude of the officials toward black recruitment.

Understandably, then, the offer of black soldiers from the West Indies created a major dilemma for the Colonial Office, for though its officials shared the prejudices and other concerns of those in the War Office, they were acutely aware of the possible consequences of ignoring such widespread agitation in the region. Additionally, in time of war, military bodies usually acquire greater influence and within the British cabinet the Secretary of Defence had unprecedented power and influence. Lord Kitchener, for example, was accused by his adversaries in Parliament of being a virtual dictator on occasions.[14] The Colonial Office was therefore usually apprehensive about any matter which could draw it into conflict with the War Office.

In fact, however, even before the offer was formally made by the West Indian governors the Colonial Office officials had had to deal with the question of blacks and coloureds who had come to England through their own effort to volunteer. Among the men who had paid their passage or stowed away aboard ships to England were a number of these blacks and dark mulattoes. Although the official position was that blacks were not desired, some were able to gain acceptance into British regiments in a variety of mainly non–combatant roles. A number of others were, however, unceremoniously rejected even though they were of middle–class background in the West Indies. W.A. Moore, for example, was a manager of one of the great stores in Trinidad when he paid the considerable but normal sum of £25 for his passage to England to serve his 'mother country'. Much to his surprise the military authorities refused to sign him on because of his colour.[15] He could not understand why he should be rejected while Indians were being accepted. The matter was brought to the attention of the Colonial Office but by this time its officials knew that some blacks had been able to gain admission into regiments in spite of the colour–bar. Cases such as that of W.A. Moore were therefore a source of concern. Nevertheless, George Grindle, then the Principal Clerk, but by 1916 the Assistant Under Secretary at the Colonial Office, minuted that he had heard that some military officials were prepared to accept blacks but that this should be discouraged.[16]

Thus, when the question of black participation was raised by the local governors it immediately occasioned scepticism and resistance within the Colonial Office, which was not keen on taking up the matter with the War Office. Anticipating certain rejection from the War Office, one Colonial Office official suggested that perhaps the governors should simply be told what the War Office's response was likely to be.[17] Another suggested that the governors be told, by secret communication if necessary, to discourage the enlistment of blacks locally, without raising the colour issue. The latter approach was adopted and the governors found themselves having to formulate excuses to pacify their restless population. While urging that some way be found to utilise the services of blacks, the governor of Barbados, Sir Leslie Probyn, stated that he would try to discourage the blacks with, among other objections, the excuse that their colour would make them dangerously conspicuous to the Germans.[18] A more widely used and credible objection offered by the governors was that the colonies could not afford the financial cost of sending contingents to the front.[19]

Reluctant to confront the War Office but realising that the problem would not go away, the Colonial Office eventually communicated the West Indian desire to send a contingent overseas, to the military authorities on August 28, 1914.[20] As expected, the War Office immediately rejected the offer on the grounds that the blacks were required for local defence purposes and to maintain order locally.[21] Thinking that the War Office's rejection was absolute, the Colonial Office informed the local governors of the decision, hoping that the matter would finally be laid to rest. The news was received in the different colonies with mixed feelings. Two German cruisers were rumoured to be in the vicinity of the Caribbean at that time, so there was some acceptance of the War Office's arguments, though many people suspected a racial motive.[22] One letter of protest characterised the reason for the denial as absurd, since there was no way that a few local rifle men could withstand the guns of a German cruiser.[23] In fact, in Antigua there were those who felt it was safer to surrender or negotiate with the enemy rather than open fire and experience the destruction of the capital and the loss of lives.[24] Moreover, there was a certain faith among West Indians that 'England ruled the waves' and this served to allay somewhat their fears of German attacks.

However, once it was realised that the threat no longer existed since the German ships had been captured or destroyed, West Indians renewed their agitation with even greater determination, believing that the War Office no longer had any reason to reject their offers. As a result of mounting local pressure, the governors again raised the matter in December with the Secretary of State for the Colonies, Lewis Harcourt. By this time, the agitation in the West Indies was causing some anxiety among the officials in the Colonial Office. Despite his reservations, on December 8, Harcourt wrote once more to the War Office on the subject of West Indian participation.[25] He conceded that there were several problems, not least of which was the colour question, which made the suggestion of a West Indian contingent serving in Europe impracticable. He warned them, however, that he had begun to feel some anxiety over the possible negative political effects the continual rejection would have and that he feared that West Indian loyalty to the empire might be undermined. Thus, while acknowledging that military considerations were paramount, Harcourt pleaded that some means be found to draw the black population of the West Indies into the war, and suggested that they could be used in Egypt against the Turks.

The War Office was still not too impressed but was prepared to make a minor concession. On December 14 the Colonial Office was informed that the Army Council did not consider West Indian troops to be suitable for Egypt and that their value in East Africa was doubtful.[26] Nevertheless, it was prepared to accept a West Indian contingent to serve as a peace–keeping force in the territories the Allies had captured in West Africa. The Colonial Office promptly objected that the War Office's compromise offer was incongruent with West Indian desire. Harcourt insisted that the West Indians were anxious to fight for the empire and would deeply resent this peace–keeping proposal.[27] Moreover, he asserted, West Indians were no less susceptible than white troops to 'West African diseases', such as malaria, and would be as difficult to move and as expensive to maintain as white soldiers. It was more advisable, Harcourt believed, for West Africans to be recruited for these duties. With neither group willing to alter its position, the protracted discussions soon developed into an impasse, which was not without its impact on the debate in the West Indies.

Procrastination on the part of British officials led to increasingly intense public anger in the colonies. The War Office's explanations were caustically and contemptuously rejected by several of the liberal newspapers. In response to the assertion that the West Indians were of limited military value, the *Federalist* pointed out that the WIR had done outstanding service on behalf of England since its formation in 1795.[28] And to those who questioned the fighting abilities of blacks, it pointed out that the British had on occasion suffered humiliating defeat at the hands of African groups like the Zulu.[29]

These observations, plus the fact that France was recruiting blacks from its West Indian colonies, led the *Federalist* to conclude that the only reason why the British authorities were not using blacks was 'the nasty cowardly skin prejudice characteristic of the empire'.[30] The realisation that Harcourt was in part responsible for stalling the negotiations led the *Clarion* to accuse him of making excuses of a 'ridiculously transparent character' and piling impediment on impediment in the way of local participation in the war.[31] Moreover, the paper insisted angrily:

> Until the war is carried into Germany; until the Allied commanders sit in the imperial palace in Berlin, and dictate terms of peace; until the holocaust of blood, rapine and horror indescribable, offered in Belgium by Germany to her gods of demonical hate, arrogance and barbaric militarism has [been] avenged, the empire cannot dispense, unless she is obsessed with the spirit of self–destruction, with the services of her blackest and humblest citizen. Englishmen take long to learn their lessons. The killing of a German is an imperial duty of obligation, as the churchmen say; and God forbid that the complexion of the man who does the killing shall stand in the way of the victory, without which the England, which we all love, in spite of her many faults, shall stand humbled at the foot of an arrogant and despised conqueror.[32]

While these criticisms and agitations were effective in bringing the aspirations of the black population to the attention of the colonial and war offices, their inaction seemed to demonstrate the limitations of local pressure.

Meanwhile, however, influential individuals in England with interests in the West Indies had joined the debate. One such person was the Earl of Dundonald, to whom W.H. Moore had gone to seek representation after being rejected by the military officials. Like the authorities, Dundonald feared that the introduction of blacks into British regiments would eventually be detrimental to their imperial affiliation as they would become more politically conscious. But to him there were concerns of a more immediate and pertinent nature. Although conceding that the issue of using blacks was 'in some ways a difficult question', he was nevertheless deeply worried that great harm would be done if the officials persistently 'offended the susceptibilities' of the black population.[33]

Dundonald warned the Colonial Office that if the aspirations of the West Indians were not in some way appeased, it was possible that they would seek to replace the Union Jack with the Stars and Stripes of the United States. His contention was obviously based on certain trends which had been developing in some of the colonies. By 1914, British hegemony in colonies like Jamaica was facing a small but growing challenge from the spread of American influence. The 1898 war against Spain for the possession of Cuba and Puerto Rico had established America's power in the Caribbean. More importantly, America's economic influence was increasingly being exercised through trading organisations like the United Fruit Company. Increasing trade with America and Canada was slowly eroding British economic and political hegemony among some sections of the population. In 1884, for example, planters discussed the possibility of annexation to the United States or confederation with Canada in order to protect their economic interests.[34] Some officials like Sydney Olivier also feared that increasing migration of Jamaicans to Central America was undermining British imperial hegemony in favour of American influence.[35] At the same time, the economic progress of Cuba and Puerto Rico led some in the poverty–stricken West Indian colonies to wonder if England was willing to do the same for her territories.[36]

Although Dundonald's warning was made against this background, he was certainly exaggerating. Even in the worse social disturbances, expressions of disloyalty in the colonies were usually directed at local officials and rarely at the imperial connection; and even when attacks were targeted at the imperial union, they were usually confined to a very small section of the population. The separatist faction which suggested union with the United States at emancipation, for example, was in effect merely, 'a movement with no emotional basis beyond a false nationalism that ran counter to the stronger attachment to England. It was separatism out of fear and social necessity alone.'[37] As a result, it was quickly pressured out of existence. The relatively weak economic and military position of the colonies made secession without consent virtually impossible. Moreover, by stimulating patriotism and sympathy for the 'mother country', the war had the effect of reinforcing the imperial relationship. Indeed, the occasion of Queen Victoria's anniversary celebrations on June 20, 1897 had already gone a long way in boosting loyalty and patriotism throughout the West Indies and the rest of the empire.[38] Although the Anglo–Boer war had the effect of shattering the myth of an indissoluble and united empire, it also generated much sympathy for England in the West Indies. For these and other reasons, including press reports of institutional racism and the lynching of blacks in America, Dundonald's argument had little reality. However, in view of the propensity of Colonial Office officials to get jumpy and nervous at the slightest agitation in the colonies, it is possible that Dundonald's views would have assumed a measure of importance and credibility. Moreover, by 1900, American industrial growth and its challenge to British industrial competitiveness worldwide had become a major political and ideological issue among British officials.[39]

A more realistic argument forwarded by Dundonald focussed on the question of the safety of property within the region. Among the property–owning classes in the West Indies as well as the absentee proprietors and the elites in England, the question of the sanctity and inviolability of private property constituted a critical aspect, perhaps the core, of their hegemonic ideology. Knowing how vulnerable their property was during times of social unrest, the elites were constantly anxious not to precipitate conflict. As Dundonald stated frankly and unashamedly to the secretary of state: 'I have property in the West Indies and have considerable knowledge of the feelings of the coloured population, and therefore think you might like to have my views.'[40]

The fundamental difficulty to be resolved, then, was the clash of these two long–standing elements of British society, which the war had brought into conflict namely, race prejudice and the inviolability of private property. As a property–owner, for Dundonald the choice was naturally weighted in favour of property. This meant that some alteration in the colour–bar was necessary. Thus, Dundonald argued for a West Indian battalion to be formed for service in a temperate climate. In this way, the problem of having blacks on the Western front would be resolved and ostensibly the blacks would benefit since they were unlikely to withstand the cold climate of northern Europe. But more importantly, the aspirations of the black population would be appeased and the safety of property ensured.

Yet, these concerns failed to give impetus to the negotiations between the Colonial Office and the War Office, which remained in deadlock. However, in a demonstration of his political astuteness and interest in the empire, King George intervened as arbitrator. On April 17, 1915 the King instructed his emissary Lord Stamfordham to write to the Colonial Office indicating that he could not help 'thinking that it would be very politic to gratify the wish of the West Indies to send a Regiment to the front'.[41] The King suggested that the West Indians might be usefully employed in Egypt. At this point the proposal was clearly tempered by diplomacy but the Colonial Office and, in particular Harcourt, failed miserably to take the hint. In what can only be regarded as a manifestation of his ignorance and lack of political tact, on April 20, Harcourt informed the King of the insuperable difficulties which rendered West Indian participation impossible.[42] Chief among these difficulties was the War Office's intransigence.

The King promptly consulted Lord Kitchener. It is worth noting here that at the time, the senior officer core of the British army was characterised by a great deal of jockeying for position in which the ability to gain Royal patronage was a crucial factor.[43] Kitchener therefore, not surprisingly, denied that the War Office had ever refused to accept the West Indians, and informed the King that he would be glad to accept a contingent from the region. In a determined effort to keep the blacks away from the Western front in large numbers he insisted, however, that the West Indians would only be accepted without any conditions as to where the regiment should serve, since troops ought to go where they are sent. In the light of this conversation, on April 22, the King wrote to the Colonial Office reiterating the political importance of not refusing the patriotic offers of the West Indians.[44] He expressed the hope that this time the Colonial Office would make an acceptable proposal to the War Office. This virtually amounted to a direct order to the Colonial Office to make provision for West Indian participation in the war. More significantly, as a result of Harcourt's poor diplomacy, the Colonial Office had been portrayed as the obstacle to gratifying the aspirations of the black population.

Embarrassed and clearly perturbed by Kitchener's apparent distortion of the truth, Harcourt wrote to Kitchener on the same day pointing out that it had in fact been the War Office which had been responsible for frustrating the wishes of the West Indians.[45] He accused Kitchener of giving the King false information regarding the role the WIR was then playing in the war in West Africa. No longer desirous of going against the wishes of the King but apparently seeking to minimise the Colonial Office's involvement in the whole affair, Harcourt suggested to Kitchener that if he wanted more West Indians he should raise another battalion of the WIR which was 'wholly under War Office control'.[46] In a determined effort to absolve the Colonial Office of blame and shift responsibility to the War Office, a copy of the letter was also despatched to the King. The decision of the King to intervene effectively ensured that West Indian involvement in the war would no longer be frustrated by the bureaucratic and racial attitudes of the War Office and the Colonial Office. It was important, however, that unlike in the case of other Africans, the decision to employ West Indian blacks was primarily motivated by political rather than military or manpower concerns. This meant that once the West Indians arrived overseas their status as soldiers was not altogether clear, particularly for those who arrived at the western front subsequently as a result of manpower shortages.

In late May the decision to accept a contingent from Jamaica in the first instance was communicated to the local governors.[47] It evoked tremendous enthusiasm and a sense of victory among the public, but less so among local officials. The newspapers, particularly the radical sections, welcomed the news with unprecedented accolade. The *West Indian* rejoiced:

This is history. We have before us today a blank page on which to write our glorious record. This is an hour that will not sound again for centuries. Our fathers have been deprived of this day, and our children will be deprived of it also. The gods have reserved it for us. Our fathers would have been proud of this opportunity. Our children when they read the thrilling history of these times will sigh in that they were born after this glorious day and generation. And we are here. The grand spectacle has been left for us – West Indians, most of whom are descendants of slaves, fighting for human liberty together with immediate sons of the Motherland in Europe's classic field of war made famous from ancient Grecian days to the days of Malborough on Wellington. The bones of Clarkson and Wilberforce rattle in their graves today.[48]

Finally, it seemed that blacks would get the chance they had long clamoured for.

Bonar Law, who replaced Harcourt on May 27, 1915 as Secretary of State for the Colonies, was praised by the *Clarion* for not being prejudiced like Harcourt, and being able to resolve the problems of the region.[49] What the papers obviously did not know, or failed to appreciate, was that although Law was unquestionably a more able administrator than Harcourt, he was also determined to keep blacks, particularly from South Africa, from the Western front since he believed this would create difficulties for white supremacy after the war was over.[50] Nevertheless, anticipating the inevitability of West Indian participation, Bonar Law arranged a meeting of former West Indian governors and other officials on August 30. This led to the formation of the West Indian Contingent Committee. The organisation raised approximately £32,000 in England and looked after the welfare of all West Indian soldiers overseas with efficiency.[51]

Between May and the end of September 1915, the public and press of the various territories became increasingly frustrated as the local governments, Colonial Office and military officials engaged in protracted negotiations over the terms and conditions under which the West Indian contingent would be recruited as well as the financial contributions of the individual colonies. During this period, the governors were subjected to the most derogatory criticisms and comments for their apparently lethargic attitude in raising the contingents. One paper concluded in condemnation of the governor of Jamaica, that the state of indifference which existed could not have been possible under previous governors.[52] Reacting to the frequent verbal attacks on the officials, the *Jamaica Times* observed despairingly:

A great deal has been said, sometimes bitterly, and often excitedly, of the alleged coldness of the Governor and the War Office towards the idea of our Contingent. As is our way, we have worked ourselves up to a state of what may be termed impulsive suspicion, and comment has varied from the crude and somewhat stupid efforts of men who are utterly thoughtless, to the much more refined and well thought out criticism ... [53]

In response, Governor Manning wrote to George Grindle at the Colonial Office, complaining of the agitation but admitting that though he was still opposed to the contingent he would be glad to see its departure so as to end the local controversy.[54] Meanwhile, men who had registered for the contingents but had become frustrated with the delay sailed for England on their own.[55]

In Trinidad comments about officials were no less vulgar and contemptuous. One letter to the press noted bluntly: 'There is no higgling over the statement that there is utter disgust and unfortunate lack of confidence in our government in regard to this vexed question of a contingent from Trinidad.'[56] In Barbados registration for the contingents had to be temporarily suspended as negotiations continued.[57] Meanwhile, Governor Haddon–Smith of Grenada was forced to inform the Colonial Office that he could no longer contain local determination to send a contingent to the front.[58] A telegram from William Wilson, chairman of the Jamaica Contingent Committee Fund warned the officials that there was considerable dissatisfaction and that feelings were running high because of the War Office's procrastination.[59] Frustrated by the incessant barrage of telegrams from the West Indies, Grindle minuted: 'If only the W.I. would stop telegraphing for a bit! This dropping fire of telegrams will only delay the [decision] by the War Office of the main questions, but of course, the colonies cannot realize that.'[60]

By the beginning of October, negotiations relating to the financing of the West Indian contingent and its pay were completed and recruiting began in earnest.[61] With a few minor exceptions it was agreed that the West Indians would be recruited on the same terms and conditions as British recruits.[62] This represented a major triumph for West Indian blacks and a significant about turn by the British. Crucially, however, this 'victory' for the West Indians was not intended by the War Office to represent the beginning of large–scale use of blacks in Europe; it would not be until late 1916, as we will see, that manpower shortage would force the British to employ large numbers of black and other colonial troops in Europe.

Recruitment Strategies

By November 1918, approximately 15,204 West Indians had been recruited and sent to do military service in Palestine, Egypt, Mesopotamia, East Africa, India, France, Italy, Belgium and England as members of the BWIR.[1] One of the main features of recruiting for the war was the similarity of the themes used and methods employed throughout the empire to get recruits. With the exception of, for example, some areas in West Africa, where recruiters sometimes resorted to coercive measures such as 'recruit catching', which resembled conscription tactics used in France's African territories, recruiting methods in the British Empire were relatively mild, with emphasis on moral suasion. Local recruiting agencies such as the churches, the press, and government agencies, for the most part, adopted those strategies developed and disseminated by British organisations like *Wellington House* and the *Parliamentary Recruiting Committee*.[2] As we have seen, in a number of the West Indian colonies, however, it was newspapers which initiated recruitment campaigns while governments procrastinated. Whilst attacking government for its inaction, the *Port of Spain Gazette*, for example, began registering volunteers to form a Trinidad contingent.[3] Newspapers were able to develop and maintain enormous influence over the recruiting process. The *West Indian*, for instance, was widely acknowledged by Grenadian officials as the major influence in the colony which could either significantly stimulate or hamper recruitment.[4]

The major religious denominations such as the Baptists, Anglicans, Catholics and Wesleyans also did their part by emphasising the moral obligation of local populations in supporting the 'mother country' in what was variously described as a war for peace, justice, and righteousness and a struggle between Christ and Satan.[5] The latter view was reinforced with newspaper cartoons showing the Kaiser and Satan affectionately embracing each other.[6] Once the terms and conditions of service had been finalised with the

British government, local authorities established various committees to organise recruiting meetings and co–ordinate the enlistment of men.[7] These gatherings were often chaired by the governors.

After decades of violence against the Caribs and attempts to undermine their ethnic identity by means of education, religion and other British cultural institutions, local authorities used notions of the 'martial' or 'fighting' races to try to get the Caribs to volunteer.[8] Those in British Honduras were urged by the governor and other recruiters to remember their glorious tradition as fighters against the British.[9] Similar efforts were made to recruit the Maroons in Jamaica who also had a tradition of successful resistance against British forces; but as with the Caribs, cultural indifference and problems of illiteracy rendered this strategy ineffective. Interestingly, the rumour that the Maroons were coming to enlist brought out large crowds, who obviously still held them in awe, to witness the event but the Maroons never turned up.[10] On the other hand, the general black population were specially reminded of the British government's 'generosity', which led to their emancipation, and they were urged to reciprocate this act of 'kindness' by volunteering.[11]

Posters were plastered throughout the various towns and villages calling on men to do their duty for king and country. Films distributed as part of the official British propaganda were shown in the colonies to stimulate patriotism and encourage men to volunteer.[12] These films portrayed an 'illusion of reality', since most people were quite oblivious to the fact that the scenes were often carefully staged. Pamphlets received from *Wellington House* were also freely distributed. Officials in Trinidad, St. Lucia, St. Vincent and Grenada all testified to their effectiveness.[13] The Administrator of St. Vincent claimed that the pamphlets were most desirable because they provided the local population with their only means of acquiring 'accurate' information about the war.[14] The Colonial Office was therefore given the incentive to obtain a liberal supply of the shorter, illustrated pamphlets for distribution throughout the West Indies. Specially written and illustrated propaganda material was obtained for the large East Indian immigrant communities in Trinidad, British Guiana and Jamaica because most could not understand the pamphlets printed in English.[15] Propaganda material was also obtained for the tourists coming to Jamaica from South American countries, where the authorities believed German influence was significant.[16] Under secret instructions from the government, the *Jamaica Institute* distributed this literature to the various hotels and other places visited by tourists.

A number of 'carrot and stick' measures were also adopted to induce men to come forward. They were repeatedly told by recruiters of the 'very distinct advantages' of enlisting. Among these were the prospects of gaining medals, glory, discipline, exercise and free land at the cessation of hostilities.[17] They were also informed that military service would make them better men and citizens. The example of a former 'yard–boy' who was subsequently promoted to the rank of corporal in the BWIR was proclaimed by recruiters in Trinidad as evidence of how the character of blacks could be significantly improved and social mobility achieved when they came into contact with 'superior civilisations' overseas.[18] These arguments were rooted in a belief common among officials in England and the colonies that the army rather than society was capable of giving meaning and direction to life by systematically simplifying the myriad and contradictory choices that faced individuals in civilian life.[19] Recruiters therefore regarded their advice as particularly pertinent to those they saw as loafers, vagabonds and the unemployed.

This belief prompted one magistrate at Falmouth, Jamaica to give a group of 16 delinquents who had been charged with disorderly conduct the option of enlisting in return for dropping the charges against them.[20] After listening to his recruiting speech, half the men accepted the offer. Men with previous criminal convictions were also allowed to enlist, but unfortunately some never made it to the front. For example, before he could depart the colony, a city rogue named Nathaniel Quimby, who volunteered in British Guiana, was sent to jail for assault.[21] Likewise, Randolph Griffith who had been caught trying to stow away, was given the chance to avoid jail by enlisting but failed to show up for registration; a warrant was promptly issued for his arrest.[22] In another case, a notorious recruit, 'Bobo' Reece, who had been granted a year off a seven–year jail term for manslaughter, enlisted in one of the Barbados contingents, but because of unruly conduct was recalled by the civil authorities to finish the unexpired portion of his sentence.[23] Precedence for the use of these discretionary measures by the civil courts had been established in England under the Mutiny Act in 1703 when the Sovereign was empowered to order the release of capital offenders who had been pardoned on the condition that they enlist in the army.[24]

The economic advantages of enlisting also constituted a central theme of recruiters in virtually every territory. Some employers like L. Nunes, a merchant of Kingston, Jamaica, guaranteed their clerks part or the whole of their salaries for the duration of the war if they enlisted.[25] To encourage small land–owners and peasants to volunteer, the Jamaica legislature enacted a law in 1916 which exempted from tax any property of or under the value of £150 belonging to any person who enlisted. The exemption was for the duration of the period of service and 12 months thereafter.[26] In the prevailing conditions of high unemployment, spiralling cost of living, and depressed wages, the groups most susceptible to the economic incentives included plantation labourers, artisans and the many unemployed of the working class in the towns.

Among these groups, issues of loyalty, duty and patriotism were of less immediate importance, and migration was generally regarded as a more viable alternative to economic deprivation and starvation. Recruiters usually pointed out to the labourers that military pay and increments were not only more lucrative than local wages but also, provided a greater degree of economic security for their families.[27] These efforts often proved successful because the plight of labour in West Indies made the army, despite the dangers of war, an attractive option to many poorer people. This is reflected in the table below. For those not enthusiastic about military service, the possibility of employment in the munitions factories in England seemed a better prospect, so that attempts to stow–away to England to achieve this aim were not uncommon.[28]

Although the evidence is too fragmented to establish a clear correlation between economic deprivation and enlistment, it seems that recruiters had greater problems in areas where wages were higher due to prosperity in industries which supplied goods for the war. In his review of recruiting in Jamaica for the period prior to August 1916, J.H.W. Park, the chairman of the Central Recruiting Committee, complained that the high prices of sugar and logwood were discouraging men in areas like Westmoreland, Hanover and Trelawny from volunteering.[29] It is worth noting that these three parishes, along with St James and Clarendon, had experienced the lowest rate of abandonment of estates in Jamaica.[30] Recruiters in Jamaica were also bluntly told by men holding good jobs that the pay offered to recruits was not enough.[31] Similarly, a number of Hondurans expressed amazement that men had relinquished lucrative positions to expose themselves to the dangers and horrors of war.[32] Those who expressed such views were savagely condemned by the West Indian press as selfish and unpatriotic. The *Clarion* concluded that those who spoke of fighting for a shilling a day

Table A.1 Occupations of the First 4000 Men (Jamaica) Enlisted

Bakers	245
Boot and Shoemakers	176
Butchers	33
Barbers	10
Cultivators	657
Clerks	249
Coachbuilders and Wheelrights	24
Chemists and Hospital Assistants	17
Chauffeurs	43
Coachmen, grooms, drivers, etc	159
Carpenters and Cabinet Makers	356
Coopers and Sawyers	20
Cigar makers	20
Constables	42
Engine, motor drivers and trackmen	52
Engineers, smithers and mechanics	196
Fishermen	56
Foremen and Overseers	17
Goldsmiths and Jewellers	9
Hat and Basket makers	8
Labourers	1,033
Musicians	3
Masons and Builders	102
Occupation not stated	40
Plumbers and Tinsmiths	20
Printers	69
Printers and Binders	17
Potters	1
Sugar boilers	1
Shop keepers	39
Servants	37
Seamen	11
Saddlers	21
Shipwrights	7
Tanners	5
Tailors	165
Teachers	40
Total	**4,000**

Source: Hill, *Who's Who in Jamaica*, p. 246.

were so low in the intellectual scale that it was 'difficult to decide on their exact position in the animal kingdom'.[33] Among groups like public servants who had regular employment, the question of job security was an additional obstacle. Members of the Trinidad constabulary and the fire brigade, for example, feared that there would be no jobs for them when they returned from overseas.[34]

Inflated promises of royal treatment on their return home were also used to persuade men to volunteer and to boost the morale of those who had enlisted.[35] Heavily censored letters which idealised and romanticised conditions overseas and portrayed the 'happy go lucky' soldier were often read at recruiting meetings and reprinted in the newspapers to allay the concerns and fears of potential volunteers.[36] Soldiers returning from the front on furlough were asked to give encouraging talks to potential volunteers. As in England and throughout the empire, some men were encouraged to volunteer by the excitement created by the playing of recruitment bands.[37] Others were fascinated by the King's uniform and the feeling of increased status and power it afforded them.[38] Generally, however, most men were prompted to volunteer by a combination of factors including patriotism, curiosity and a desire for adventure, a sense of duty as in the case of police men and boys scouts, or the desire to escape some unhappy economic or social situation.

Meanwhile, many West Indian blacks who had emigrated to the United States were actively agitating to be allowed to serve with the British forces. A petition was sent from the West Indian Protective Society of America to various British and American officials asking for permission to form a group to be known as the West Indian–American Battalion.[39] The society was based in New York and among its objectives was the task of uniting blacks and promoting their interests generally; it also supported the movement for representative government in the West Indies. The British authorities in New York regarded the organisation as harmless but the executive secretary, Augustus Duncan, a naturalised American of West Indian origin, was considered as 'something of an agitator'.[40]

After America entered the war in 1917, Brigadier–General W.A. White was sent by the Army Council to New York to organise the recruiting of British subjects residing in the United States.[41] By the beginning of 1918, over 2,000 blacks had registered but British army officials could not decide what to do with them. The root of the problem was that while the blacks desired to enlist as combat troops, the Army Council was adamantly opposed to putting them in white regiments, and the War Office wanted to employ them as non–combatants. This procrastination again generated much indignation among the West Indians because the inaction on the part of the British officials meant that they were liable to be conscripted into the forces of the United States.[42] A difficult, if not embarrassing, problem was thereby created for British officials.

The situation also generated some degree of political anxiety for British officials who feared that the continued exclusion of blacks was being used by some people to foster anti–Allied propaganda. They tried to explain the delay in terms of transport to bring the blacks to England. However, it was subsequently arranged that blacks who had registered for military service would be exempted from military duty in the American forces until it was found possible to enlist them in the British army. By that time large numbers of West Indians from islands like the Bahamas had returned home hurriedly lest they were conscripted into the American army.[43] British officials were aware of how quickly information flowed from the metropole into the West Indies. Thus, a circular was sent to the various governors instructing them that if they became aware of any references to the ill–feelings of blacks in America because of the recruitment issue, they were to immediately publish a statement of the decision to exclude these blacks from conscription.[44] Severe manpower shortages forced the Army Council to rethink its attitude, however, and in June 1918 it was decided that blacks could be enlisted into combatant or other units provided that their eating habits (diet) and language met the conditions stipulated by army regulations.

Blacks in Canada, including many West Indians, also experienced great difficulty in their attempts to join the army. Although official policy allowed blacks to be enlisted in the Canadian Expeditionary Force (CEF), a number of commanding officers fiercely opposed the enlistment of blacks in their battalions.[45] They found support from the chief of the general staff at Ottawa, Major-General W.G. Gwatkin, who bluntly objected: 'The civilized negro is vain and imitative; in Canada he is not impelled to enlist by a high sense of duty; in the trenches he is not likely to make a good fighter; and the average white man will not associate with him on terms of equality.'[46] Moreover, he argued, 'in France, in the firing line, there is no place for a black battalion, C.E.F. It would be eyed askance; it would crowd out a white battalion; and it would be difficult to reinforce.'[47] He therefore proposed the formation of one or more labour battalions of blacks and suggested that the British government be asked if it would be able to employ them on special duty, perhaps in Egypt; he agreed that in the interim blacks could be enlisted in white battalions at the discretion of the commanding officer. As in the United States, however, as manpower shortages became acute, white officers began to enlist blacks in greater numbers. Nevertheless, most of the blacks in Canada were eventually enlisted in the No. 2 (Negro) Construction Battalion which received authorisation on July 5, 1916. They were subsequently sent to France, where they were attached to the Canadian Forestry Corps, a labour unit whose duty involved logging, milling and shipping. The experiences of blacks in Canada, the United States and the West Indies illustrate quite clearly the extent to which racist notions were prevalent in these societies and adversely influenced recruiting decisions and policies.

Race and Recruitment

As can be seen from the controversies over recruiting, class, caste and especially colour, were the principal variables defining the character of social relations in the West Indies. These intersected with ethnicity, gender, occupation, religion and nationality. Although there were various forms and levels of intercourse among the inhabitants, each was usually, as Bridget Brereton writes of Trinidad, 'conscious of belonging to definite and separate groups'.[48]

Once the War Office had reluctantly decided to allow black West Indians to participate in the war, the contradictions inherent in the plan to have contingents composed of the multiplicity of classes and ethnic groups in the region surfaced. The social divisions between whites, coloureds and blacks immediately became a major issue. Conflict was most acute in Trinidad and Barbados but was also evident in the other colonies. Given the option of enlisting in the BWIR or the public contingent, as it was called, in most colonies the whites and mulattoes, usually referred to by the press as the 'better' or 'intelligent' classes, refused to volunteer, despite the lamentations, urgings and condemnations of the recruiters.[49] Whenever these young men of the 'better' classes did agree to enlist in the public contingents they insisted as a precondition that they be made officers. C.L.R. James remembered that when the white boys from his school joined the public contingents as officers they would come back to the college to see them, 'with chests out and smart uniforms and shining buttons'.[50] Generally though, these 'better' class men continued to refuse to enlist.

Their refusal to enlist conveniently allowed the merchants and planters to demonstrate their loyalty in view of allegations of disloyalty and greed from the public and the radical sections of the press. Before blacks were accepted for service, the merchants had contributed to sending individuals to the front, but by this time they also wished to match the public effort by raising a contingent of their own. They were, thus, very much in sympathy with the view that blacks, whites and mulattoes should not be in the same contingents. Those in Trinidad and Barbados decided to raise their own contingents of whites and 'lightly coloured' men. However, because of the sensitivity of race and class issues in the colonies, and the belief that 'intelligent' men were needed to lead the public contingents, local officials tried quietly to discourage the movement to create the white contingent in Trinidad. The group was deprived of police protection and officials refused to grant them the services of the band.[51]

In response, the Trinidad group sent a delegation to England headed by George F. Huggins, president of the local chamber of commerce to complain to the Colonial Office about the 'cold shoulder' they had received from the local authorities and to ensure that civil servants who enlisted in their contingents would not have their employment jeopardised.[52] The delegation was received by the principal clerk, George Grindle, who was unenthusiastic about their intentions and refused to encourage Huggins's subtle attempt to secure a message praising the merchants for their patriotism. Nevertheless, he felt that the merchants had a 'good excuse' for their actions and had put a considerable sum of money into the project. He therefore acceded to the group's plea that the whites should have their own contingents, whose members would join various British regiments on arrival overseas, and the Colonial Office instructed the governor of Trinidad to assist the merchants in their endeavour.[53]

The selection process for these contingents was crude and irrational and, as C.L.R. James discovered, the merchants carefully ensured that all members were of the right class and shade of colour:

The rumour was, and the facts seemed to show, that the merchants selected only white or brown people. But though I was dark, I was widely known as a coming cricketer and I kept goal for the college team in the first–class football league. I was tall and very fit. So on the morning when I should have been at school I went down to the office where one of the big merchants, perhaps the biggest of all, examined the would–be warriors. Young man after young man went in, and I was not obviously inferior to any of them in anything. The merchant talked to each, asked for references and arranged for further examination as the case might be. When my turn came I walked to his desk. He took one look at me, saw my dark face and, shaking his head vigorously, motioned me violently away.[54]

This incident highlighted the extent to which colour often took precedence in defining West Indian social relations. Although James claims that he was not 'unduly disturbed' and that 'it didn't hurt for long', the mere fact that he remembered and wrote so vividly about the incident many years later, is perhaps some indication of the scar left on his consciousness even if he did not realise it at the time. In any case, this rebuff would have at least suggested to him the limitations of blacks striving for status in societies demarcated by acute class and colour divisions. James probably also realised that the congenial atmosphere at the Queen's Royal College which had, as he admitted, protected him from the 'crude intrusions from the world', also, had inhibited the development of a more realistic image of colonial race relations in the wider society.

H.H. Vernon was even more humiliated by the Honduran authorities. Vernon was a prominent middle-class creole, a member of the town board, and treasurer to the Contingent Committee, but he was denied access to the governor's entourage on the court-house verandah during ceremonies to send the contingent overseas. He was informed by the police that access to the verandah required a special pass, but since he noticed that none of the whites, even those not invited, had to produce a pass he concluded, with justification, that the special invitation meant 'a white face'.[55] Vernon expressed his chagrin in a letter to the press in which he stated that had he not been a law–abiding citizen, he would have forced his way up the stairs and reacted violently if the police had intervened a second time. As in the James case, Vernon's experience emphasised the importance of colour, even over class, in the region. More than that, the incident also symbolised the persistent conflict between the entrenched white elites and the upwardly mobile, but still relatively weak, coloured and black middle classes.

The formation of the white contingents in Trinidad and Barbados did not go unnoticed in the other colonies. The *West Indian* angrily denounced both white contingents as the result of prejudice, deceit and snobbery, and the blacks of a 'yellower hue' in the contingents were accused of trying to 'play white'.[56] With regard to the name of the Barbados group, the paper queried with contempt and disbelief:

> Citizen's Contingent! What a name! What splitting of hairs. If there is a Citizen's Contingent, what condition does the Barbados Public Contingent represent? Those who are not citizens?[57]

The quality and fitness of the men being recruited into these contingents simply on the basis of class and colour was also seriously questioned by the Grenada paper. Even the usually conservative *Port of Spain Gazette* was forced to report on the allegedly high rate of rejection among these whites on arrival in England or soon after having started training.[58] Despite the hostility and allegations of snobbery the merchants and planters proceeded with their recruiting.[59] Approximately 260 men were enlisted in Trinidad and 79 in Barbados.

Although these contingents accommodated whites and coloureds of very light complexion, many other coloureds, however, were left stranded. Too dark for acceptance in the merchants' contingent or English regiments, they considered it unacceptable to be associated with the black artisan and labouring classes of the public contingents.[60] Efforts were made by the Barbados officials to create a special contingent to accommodate this category of men from throughout the region but these proved unsuccessful. Officials regarded the reluctance of these and other men from the 'better classes' to enlist as a major problem because it created a severe shortage of officers. Thus, the officer commanding the local forces in St. Lucia described the shortage there as an 'unsurmountable difficulty',[61] while officials confronted with similar problems in Jamaica and British Honduras attempted, with some success, to lure more men of the 'better classes' to enlist by virtually guaranteeing them positions as non–commissioned officers (NCOs).[62]

Meanwhile, the controversies over racism were intensified by the cases of coloured doctors who volunteered to serve in the Royal Army Medical Corps (RAMC) but who were categorically rejected or refused commissions because of their colour. West Indian doctors residing in England were perhaps the first to experience this situation. In 1914, for example, Dr James

Jackson Brown, a Jamaican graduate of the London Hospital, offered his services to the RAMC but was only offered the rank of warrant officer. Brown declined on the basis that white doctors received commissions.[63] However, it was the rejection of doctors actually residing in the West Indies that generated the most controversy. Among the most publicised and hotly debated was that of Dr W.S. Mitchell, the acting resident surgeon of Grenada. He was only 'slightly coloured' but had 'the African wooly hair'.[64] Having read in the papers that medical men were required by the army, Dr Mitchell applied to work with the RAMC in 1915 but did not specifically seek a commission as he merely wanted to serve with the medical corps.

The War Office bluntly informed him that as commissions in the RAMC could only be granted to persons of 'pure European blood' he was not eligible for such an appointment.[65] The reply created quite a stir in Grenada but much to the relief of the governor the press did not indulge in the inflammatory agitation which he had expected.[66] The governor nevertheless immediately warned the Colonial Office to suggest to the army to use greater tact when dealing with the 'colour question' in future.[67] The Colonial Office agreed that the affair had been rather poorly handled and that an effort should have been made to conceal the real reason for the rejection.[68] This was in tune with the Colonial Office's position with regard to public debates of race issues in the colonies, it was a position which had been expressed by a senior clerk, R.A. Wiseman, who minuted, in reference to black participation in the war: 'On the whole I think it is our policy if possible to prevent any public discussion of the colour question in the West Indies ....'[69] The local elites would probably have fully endorsed Wiseman's statement because they too had a policy of avoiding or suppressing debates on issues of colour and race.[70] Mitchell subsequently enlisted in the BWIR and was given the rank of surgeon-lieutenant.[71] For a relieved George Grindle this was 'a happy solution to a difficult problem'.[72]

Although the Mitchell case was thus resolved, the denial of commissions because of colour prejudice continued to be provocative locally. In July 1917, the governor of Grenada was severely criticised by the press for discrimination for not assisting more readily in obtaining a commission for Sergeant E. Gresham who had been temporarily invalided from Egypt.[73] By September 1917, the issue of commissions, especially with regard to coloured doctors, was also being debated by the press in Jamaica, and recalling the case of Dr Mitchell, the *Gleaner* denounced the army officials for their 'pure snobbishness', which it saw as one of the greatest failings of the English character.[74] The renewal and intensification of the debate on race prejudice may have increased the apathy and resistance to recruitment, which had been slowly developing.

Women and Recruitment

Significantly, although women were not recruited for combat service in the war, they played an important but ambiguous role in recruitment.[75] From the beginning there were many men who felt no inclination to enlist. These men, whose actions and motives we will examine in more detail later, were bitterly denounced by the press and recruiters. A whole range of derogatory epithets including slackers, shirkers, contemptibles and loafers was unsparingly applied to describe these resisters. More important to the authorities was the problem of getting these men to change their minds. One tactic was to try to make them feel ashamed and guilty. The Grenada papers, for example, carried a poster culled from the British press in which a child asked: 'Daddy, what have you done for the war?'[76] This form of moral suasion effectively exploited male pride in societies which attached a great premium on masculinity. Recruiters also brought indirect pressure to bear on the draft resisters by appealing to family members, and especially women to urge their men to enlist. Mothers, sisters, wives and partners were frequently criticised by the press in most of the colonies and other recruiters who complained that men were being prevented from volunteering by family pressure.

Local women were naturally urged by recruiters to follow their counterparts in England and play an active role in recruiting. They were encouraged to make speeches at recruiting rallies. 'Inspire the men with a zeal that would make them wish to give their life's blood for their country', one woman urged her audience at a rally in Antigua.[77] In a determined effort to embarrass the 'slackers' at Montego Bay, Jamaica, a female recruiter brought along a skirt to taunt them with at the recruiting meeting.[78] It was not unusual for women in Jamaica to organise their own recruiting meetings.[79] Every effort was likewise made to convince the women of Grenada not to encourage men to shirk their duty,[80] while the *Clarion* too pleaded with Honduran mothers: 'Don't let them hide behind your petticoats. Don't you pull out your petticoats to give them a chance to hide behind.'[81]

Collectively, these recruiting tactics which sought to capitalise on culturally constructed notions of femininity and masculinity were effective because of the importance attached to patriarchal ideas in West Indian societies. Men were socialised into specific gender roles which required them to present themselves as tough, strong, controlling, emotionally inexpressive, aggressive and dominant. Moreover, instead of war being regarded as a tragic necessity, it was conceived and projected as a rite of passage and an opportunity for men to prove their masculinity and triumph over physical fear.

Recruiters were able to capitalise on these stereotypes by formulating their language in a way that reflected the discourses of patriarchy, and more specifically, linked notions of masculinity and war. The *Clarion*, for example, warned: 'No parent has the right to advise his son to become a poltroon and a coward; to be branded as that most contemptible of all men, a Slacker, is the limit of national and individual disgrace.'[82] Men with exaggerated or distorted notions of their masculinity were a prime target for these recruiting tactics because as Virginia Woolf perceptively argued, the excessive stress on courage and pugnacity as prime attributes of manliness, made men particularly vulnerable to what she calls the 'manhood emotion', or fear of the taunt of cowardice.[83] It was a recognition of this weakness that prompted recruiters to read letters from the soldiers overseas which sought to get slackers to enlist by denouncing them as cowards.[84]

Recruiters also mobilised stereotypical notions of motherhood to make women view their role in recruitment as a sacred duty. The *Clarion* expressed profound praise for mothers who did their 'duty' by encouraging their sons to enlist, but conversely insisted: 'A mother who advises her son to shirk his duty as a man and a British subject, is a reproach to the sacred name of mother.'[85] The paper's comment was intended as a serious attack on women guilty of inhibiting recruitment because 'Motherhood' is usually regarded in patriarchal societies as being endowed with notions of a natural maternal instinct, compelling women to self–sacrifice for the good of their children and, if needs be, for that of the species in general.[86] Critically, however, these dual images of the patriotic and nurturant mother at times, such as during war, do not always co–exist well. The interests of the nation were not always perceived by these women as being paramount to themselves or their children.

For many West Indian mothers, the issues were quite complex and elicited different and ambiguous responses. For some, the thought that their brothers, sons and husbands were going off to war and possibly never returning was painful. The mother of private James Bramwell found some solace in pleading with her son to pray regularly and to read the ninety-first psalm.[87] At the departure of the first Grenada contingent, family members freely wept and wailed.[88] On the other hand, because of their internalisation of patriarchal values and the pre–eminence of the image of the patriotic mother engendered in the euphoria, especially in the early stages of the war, some probably felt it was their duty to encourage their sons to enlist. Nevertheless, in some cases maternal considerations were stronger. The *Clarion* was partially prepared to recognise the 'excuse of maternal affection', but contended that it was a pity that such mothers had not applied maternal affection to keep their sons on the paths of rectitude.[89] The paper strongly suggested to such parents that service overseas would rescue their sons from a life of idleness and ignorance and convert them into desirable citizens. It predicted that on their return they would be a credit to, instead of a dead-weight on, their country.[90]

Whatever its merits, the advice of the newspapers was perhaps not of immediate significance to many working–class women whose husbands, brothers and sons were being recruited. As a marginalised, chronically underpaid and generally underprivileged group, their main concern was to secure food, shelter and the other basic necessities of life for themselves and their families. As the vast literature on the West Indian family has shown, these women were, in varying degrees subjected to the simultaneous triple oppression of class, race and gender, which meant that their social and economic deprivations were generally worse than perhaps any other group in society.[91] This was (and still is) highlighted by two related significant features of West Indian families and societies, which to a large extent determined the attitudes and responses of many women to recruitment.

Firstly, for a variety of reasons the region was characterised by very high levels of 'illegitimate' births or children born out of wedlock.[92] Secondly, a high percentage of the households in the region were female–headed and as several empirical studies have established, these were usually the poorest households.[93] These two features, along with a number of other structural inequalities in West Indian societies, placed most working–class women and families in a vulnerable economic position. The social and economic crises created by the war further disrupted the unstable balancing act which most of these families were engaged in on a daily basis for their survival. Thus, gaining access to an army wage was likely to be part of the survival strategy of households in which the man was unemployed. Many mothers therefore had strong economic reasons to persuade their sons or partners to enlist. On the other hand, in households where the male labour input was crucial, women were probably more likely to try and discourage the man from enlisting. The serious conflict which quickly developed between many women and recruiting officials seems to have been largely rooted in these difficult economic choices.

A major point of bitter conflict between women and local officials arose over the question of separation allowances. This was an allowance instituted by the army for issue during war in cases where the soldiers formerly supported their relatives. On enlisting, each recruit was required to declare who these dependents were and he also had to be willing to contribute a portion of his pay so as to enable an amount not exceeding his previous level of support to be continued.[94] Under the regulations dealing with the allowances, there was no specific clause directly addressing the question of 'illegitimate' children although allowances were made to dependents other than wives and legitimate children, provided the soldier agreed to contribute some share.

The possibility that unmarried women and their children might not be provided for immediately became a source of concern to these mothers. Anticipating that these anxieties would develop into infectious and active discontent, the *Gleaner* promptly protested that if this were to be the case, the male partners of these women should not be enlisted.[95] However, as a special concession to the West Indian situation, the military authorities allowed the unmarried mothers and their children to rank as dependents.[96] Significantly, while Bonar Law approved the separation allowances for West Indians, he was very opposed to doing the same for the West Africans because, in his view, they were 'polygamous as a rule' and, unlike the West Indians, likely to be 'naked savages' who could not speak English.[97] Yet, given the complex and misunderstood nature of West Indian family structure, confusion and conflict between the women and local officials was perhaps inevitable. Moreover, the authorities were intent on keeping expenses to a minimum and for this reason among others, including army tradition, preferred to enlist single rather than married men.

On occasion, when the volunteers desired or were pressured by their partners to claim the allowance, the officials refused to grant the amounts requested.[98] While acknowledging that these unmarried women had to be provided for, the governor of Grenada, for instance, was equally adamant that the government had to guard itself against fraud.[99] He warned that if allowances were made without careful discrimination, the government was likely to be imposed upon by men, perhaps on behalf of women they had not previously regarded as their 'wives'; each claim had therefore to be verified. The governor was probably quite right in thinking this would be the case, not simply because of the economic crisis which confronted these women, but more fundamentally because, many lower–class West Indian women tended to conceptualise the male's role in narrowly economic terms.[100] The attitude of the authorities in Jamaica was similar to that of their Grenadian colleagues and as a result, 75 per cent of the claims made for the allowance were rejected as fraudulent.[101]

Nevertheless, the women were determined that, regardless of their previous experiences in obtaining child support, they should receive as much of the allowance as possible. The recruiting process naturally became the focus of their anger. Alarmed at the negative impact which their actions would have on recruiting in Grenada, the *Federalist* pleaded with the women to lodge their complaints before the governor, instead of 'bruiting it about town'.[102] The press in Jamaica received several letters from members of the public which made 'savage attacks on the authorities'.[103] The *Jamaica Times*, however, objected that while some of the complaints were perhaps justified, there was nevertheless 'a lot of exaggeration, a lot of carelessness in making accusations and far too much bitterness'.[104] The *Port of Spain Gazette* likewise tried desperately to convince disgruntled relatives in Trinidad that the allowance was only intended to provide partial, and not full, material assistance for the families of volunteers.[105] In colonies like Jamaica and Trinidad, where the problems and protests were more chronic, it took more than mere talk to pacify discontented family members: the authorities were forced to make certain compromises.

During April 1917, the Legislative Council of Jamaica adopted a resolution which granted increased pensions and separation allowances.[106] Special committees, including a Central Supplementary Allowances Committee, were also established to consider and deal with cases of hardship among dependents and invalided soldiers.[107] A home for the destitute children of volunteers was opened on June 11, 1917 at the Rio Cobre Hotel in Spanish Town under the direction of F.N. Isaacs. For the 20 children who had moved in by September, the home provided a much needed reprieve from certain starvation and possible death, although one child died soon after arrival.[108] By March 1919 there were 69 children in the home, while three had been discharged on application of their relatives who could by this time afford to support them.[109] In Trinidad, a fund was launched by A.A. Cipriani to provide additional care for the children of volunteers.[110]

Regardless of the high percentage of claims for separation allowances that were rejected, it is arguable that the mere fact that they challenged official policies and that concessions were made, were significant achievements for working–class women in Jamaica, Trinidad and the other colonies where protests took place. Conditions created by war–time hysteria were, as we have seen, very inimical to accurate social observation, sympathy or agitation on behalf of poorer sections of the community. Moreover, the strategies and tactics possible for these women were limited not merely by the political climate, but also by their cultural, gender and class location and the resources available to them. Within the context of the experiences of West Indian women since slavery, their responses to the policies of the recruiting officials, might be regarded as symptomatic of a nascent gender consciousness which was developing simultaneously with, and emerging out of, a wider working–class consciousness during that period. This, it seems, gave them the confidence to develop spontaneously, strategies to capitalise on the army's intervention in society as a highly competitive employer providing good fringe benefits to families of volunteers. In any case, the women's apprehensions and responses to recruitment were clearly another aspect of the more long–running gender struggle over support, responsibility and power, which as numerous studies on the family have shown, have been an historical feature of West Indian societies. While the agitation by the women created difficulties for the recruiters, even greater challenges were experienced during the process of selecting and medically examining the volunteers.

Military Selection and Civilian Health

From the beginning of recruiting, the medical and military examiners were pressured by the press and local officials to be as strict as possible in their selection of volunteers. Against the background of the intense popular agitation to be allowed to participate in the war, it was generally felt by the press and local officials that volunteers selected to represent the respective West Indian colonies had to be of the highest possible moral and intellectual calibre. The political considerations attached to the war by the local reform movements in countries like Grenada, and petty jealousies between the colonies, made the need to subject each volunteer to a searching analysis even more imperative. The Grenadian volunteers were instructed by the *West Indian* that they were to be 'missionaries' of the island's manhood.[1] Examiners in Jamaica were likewise strictly warned not to enlist persons who were unlikely to be a credit to the island or whose educational qualifications would make them inferior in comparison with British soldiers.[2] Thus, to be enlisted, the volunteer had at least to be able to read and write well in English.[3]

Some doctors tried to adhere ruthlessly to the War Office's selection criteria and as a result frequently rejected men for the slightest defect. In Trinidad, for example, healthy men were sent away because their chest measurements were a fraction of an inch less than that stipulated by the regulations.[4] High rejection rates were quite common throughout the West Indies, as they were in England. Of the 2,500,000 men examined in England between 1917 and 1918, over 1,000,000 or 40 per cent were classified as unfit for combat duty.[5] Of the 2,046 men examined in British Guiana by 1917, approximately 1,453 or 71 per cent were rejected and far fewer actually went overseas.[6] The rates of rejection for the Jamaica drafts were also significantly high. The first and second contingents had a rejection rate of 53 per cent, the third 58 per cent and the fourth's was 66 per cent.[7] The increasing rejection rate in spite of the fact that the selection criteria were being gradually relaxed as the demand for men intensified, provides some indication that the men volunteering at this point were of increasingly poor physical stock.

As early as February 1915, the selection criteria used in England had been relaxed so that men with defective teeth were being passed as fit, subject to dental treatment when the recruit joined his depot.[8] However, it was not until about May 1916 that a similar relaxation occurred in the West Indies. In Jamaica, parish officials undertook to treat men with temporary disabilities so that they could be enlisted.[9] By November, the War Office had also agreed, because of the heavy losses on the Western front, to accept men who were unable to read and write, if they were of 'good physique'.[10] This also meant that non–English speakers from colonies like St Lucia and British Honduras could be enlisted.[11] The officials in Jamaica had hoped that with the abandonment of the literacy test rejections would be reduced but instead rejections for medical reasons increased. This was despite the fact that men infected with venereal diseases were, as in England, being accepted and treated.[12] By the time recruiting in Jamaica had been terminated on August 21, 1918, some 26,667 men had been examined at camp, although the number who actually volunteered at recruiting meetings was much higher.[13] The table below shows that 13,940 or 52.2 per cent of the 26,667 were rejected for the reasons listed. Approximately 10,645 or 40 per cent were accepted and 2,082 or 7.8 per cent were discharged (or had died) mainly because of disease after enlistment.[14] No specific information was given about the diseases affecting those discharged; the general description was 'Medically Unfit'. The table below shows that of the 13,054 men rejected on medical grounds, the percentages were distributed as follows: underdeveloped and underweight 28.80, venereal diseases 11.55, skin diseases and so on, 9.95, poor physique 9.80, anaemia and so on, 8.82, teeth 5.40, undersize 3.92, flat feet and so on, 3.76, varicocele and so on, 3.38, deformity 3.06, hernia 2.67, other causes 8.89.

Even the most cursory glance at the causes of rejection, and the high rejection rates, naturally raises questions about health conditions in Jamaica, and West Indian society more generally, during the period under discussion. From the rejection statistics, it seems that Jamaican society was characterised by a high degree of diseases and other health problems related to poor dietary and environmental conditions. The picture is made even more

Table A.2 Causes of Rejections

* Cause of rejection not known	379
* Illiterate	255
* Under age	143
* Over age	96
* Refused to sign on	13
# Defective speech	63
# Flat chest	68
# Enlarged glands	84
# Periostitis, stiff joints	147
# Sundry causes	208
# Sight	230
# Rejected by M.O. as not likely	347
# Hernia, Rupture	348
# Deformity, (includes phimosis)	399
# Varicocele, varicose veins	442
# Flat feet, knock knees	493
# Undersize	514
# Teeth	706
# Anemia, heart, lungs, pulse	1,151
# Poor physique	1,280
# Skin diseases (sores etc.)	1,297
# Venereal diseases	1,512
# Undeveloped, underweight	3,765
Total	**13,940**

* Non–medical causes – (886); # Medical causes – (13,054)

Source: Hill, *Who's Who in Jamaica*, p. 247.

complete when one reflects on the fact that the army tended to prefer men who were under the age of 30. In any society this segment of the population would normally represent the most fit and healthy. It is instructive to note that 74 per cent of the British soldiers who died during the war were below the age of 30.[15] The pattern in the West Indies was similar.[16] Approximately 96 per cent of the first 4,000 recruits from Jamaica were between the ages of 17 and 30. Since the male population of Jamaica between the ages of 20 and 35 at November 1916 numbered between 93,178 and 96,472, the 26,667 men actually examined at camp was a significant sample of that segment, even if its selection was not based on any of the scientifically accepted methods of modern statistics. The figures suggest quite strongly that ailments and diseases related to persistent undernutrition or malnutrition were chronic among the working class in Jamaica from which most of the recruits were drawn.

The rejection statistics become even more significant when it is realised that most of the men examined at camp, including the 13,054 rejected for medical reasons, already had been given a preliminary examination by the district or country physicians, who turned away many others as unfit.[17] It should be noted, however, that as the war progressed and more doctors left for the front, it became increasingly difficult to get physicians to accompany the recruiting parties to the country districts, and those doctors who remained at home were so busy that they could not provide any assistance. As a result, officers in charge of the recruiting parties had to depend on physical tests and use their own judgement to decide if a volunteer was fit enough to be sent for final examination at Up Park Camp.[18]

It is now commonly recognised by medical researchers that the incidence of disease and mortality are strongly influenced by a variety of social and economic factors, including education levels, environmental conditions, poverty, the quality and efficacy of health services, income levels and distribution and especially diet. In the light of this, one immediate observation which can be made about recruitment is that the rejection statistics seem to support those doctors and social observers in Jamaica, who argued at the time that the diet of the working class was highly deficient in protein and that this deficiency was an important underlying cause of the numerous ailments and diseases prevalent in the society. In 1900, W.P. Livingstone, who had been editor of the *Gleaner*, claimed in his book *Black Jamaica* that in general, the black population was physiologically half–starved and were frequently dyspeptics because their diet was deficient in quantity and quality.[19] A study conducted in 1911 by the director of agriculture, H.H. Cousins, also pointed out that the diet of the working class was very deficient, particularly in protein.[20]

Cousins analysed the nutritional content of the locally grown foodstuffs which constituted the bulk of their diet and concluded that with the exception of peas and beans, all the local produce were strikingly deficient in protein substances and that the 'bread–kind' in Jamaica were almost entirely carbohydrate foods. He also argued that this deficiency led to a 'starving and stinting of young growing persons or the consumption of a wasteful and distensive amount of food by the mature worker'.[21] Cousins therefore insisted that imported sources of food which he demonstrated to have a higher protein value, was absolutely necessary in Jamaica unless local production of meat was greatly increased. Many of the studies conducted from the 1930's onwards, from which time there was a growing awareness of malnutrition throughout the empire, would all point to prevalence and serious implications of protein–calorie deficiency in Jamaican society. One such study done by H.D. Chambers, a medical doctor in Jamaica, argued not only that the diet of the poorer classes was deficient, but also that as a result their powers of resistance to disease was not high.[22] In Chambers' opinion malnutrition easily ranked as the first cause of morbidity in Jamaica, even though its seriousness was not recognised.[23]

Although these studies may be criticised for lack of scientific rigour, and the failure to recognise variations in diet among the black population in terms of class, location and seasonality, they nevertheless accurately pointed out one of the major causes of sickness and death in Jamaica at the time. A child who is malnourished may lag behind successively as each developmental milestone is passed and may become physically, socially and mentally retarded.[24] In fact, malnourished children may not even survive infancy. Poor nutrition was identified by doctors in Jamaica as a significant cause of infant mortality and 20 per cent of the infant deaths in Kingston between 1912 and 1916 were attributed to Marasmus, an extreme form of malnutrition, caused mainly by inadequate calorie intake and insufficient supplement; it is also possible that deaths among older children were partly the result of Kwashiorkor or extreme malnutrition, caused mainly by inadequate protein intake. The relationship between protein and calorie deficiency and their relative importance in causing the different types of malnutrition is, however, a complex one and still the subject of recent medical research.

Perhaps more importantly, it is now well recognised by epidemiologists that the incidence of malnutrition and infections are interrelated and can aggravate each other. Thus, if one looks at the rejection statistics it would be difficult to differentiate the root causes of the numerous skin diseases, sores and ulcers from, for example, the cases of deformity and poor physique. Similarly, while pulmonary tuberculosis, pneumonia and diseases of the digestive system were, in addition to outbreaks of epidemics of typhoid and influenza, for example, among the main causes of sickness and death in Jamaica, these conditions are usually terminal events which may obscure the underlying incidence of malnutrition which facilitate deadly attacks on poor people and they also make the detection of malnutrition difficult. Despite this, it does seem strange that there are no specific references to tuberculosis and other pulmonary afflictions in the rejection statistics. However, this may be because such cases were eliminated by the district medical examiners or perhaps they were included under the heading 'Anemia, heart, lungs and pulse', or any of the other vague categories like 'Sundry causes' or those rejected as 'not likely'.

Rejections because of venereal diseases were also significant because they suggested that there was a high incidence of infection in all the parishes. The percentage rejections for venereal diseases from the different parishes were as follows: Kingston 8.6, St Andrew 8.1, St Thomas 12.7, Portland 12.9, St. Mary 14.0, St. Ann 13.5, Trelawny 19.7, St James 10.4, Hanover 15.9, Westmoreland 8.6, St. Elizabeth 10.2, Manchester 11.4, Clarendon 11.9 and St. Catherine 12.1.[25] The comparatively lower figures for Kingston and St. Andrew, the two urban parishes which were most regularly attacked by the newspapers as being infested with venereal diseases because of the high level of prostitution, are somewhat surprising. However, the chairman of recruiting in Jamaica, J.H.W. Park, may have been correct in asserting that the lower rates for venereal diseases there was not due to freedom from the diseases, but to the greater knowledge of them in the town areas as opposed to the country; they may have avoided recruitment or had easier access to treatment.[26] In any case the rejection figures did not accurately reflect the extent of infection in Jamaica partly because of the later practice of accepting and treating infected men. Also, medical examiners normally checked the physical features of a recruit such as height, weight and chest size before eventually checking for venereal diseases, which meant that some of the men rejected for other causes would probably also have been turned away in the initial phase of recruitment because of venereal infections.

At the same time, however, the rejections for venereal diseases may have been to some extent understated, although the opposite could have occurred, because of the confusion between syphilis and yaws, which are caused by related micro–organisms and which caused some doctors in the West Indies as in Africa, to misdiagnose one disease for the other.[27] More generally, the overall statistics on the causes of rejection also need to be accepted with some degree of caution and not only because of the unscientific method of their collection. Individual complaints were often symptomatic of the confusion which characterised the selection process in a number of colonies. There was often a conspicuous absence of consensus among doctors in their interpretation of the selection criteria laid down by army officials. In Trinidad, for example, volunteers unfamiliar to the medical officers would simply change their names when rejected and get accepted by another doctor.[28] In other cases men approved by district medical doctors as 'doubtful' were passed without the slightest hesitation by the final board of examiners. Conversely, in other instances, men accepted initially without any objection were categorically rejected by the final examination board.[29]

This confusion partly resulted from the ignorance of the civil doctors of the physical requirements for the army, or of what it meant to be fit for service overseas. The selection problems also reflected the subjective nature of the examinations, the vagueness of the guidelines for selection and the wide margin of discretion doctors were allowed. The desired rigidity but usual arbitrariness may have confused the statistics to some extent, although it should be pointed out that, as in England, many more unfit men were passed as fit than the other way around. In spite of these problems it is still possible to suggest that the figures highlighted many of the health problems in Jamaica and reflected the general pattern of diseases affecting the working class.

Reactions to Rejection Statistics

What is perhaps even more important than the actual figures was their impact on public consciousness and reactions in the various colonies to the high rates of rejection. The figures precipitated national debates on a variety of issues but especially on public health and the prevalence of venereal and other contagious diseases in the region. The views expressed were similar and indeed, drew upon a parallel discussion which recruitment had stimulated in England.[30] The debate in England really started during the Boer War (1899–1902) when a high proportion of the volunteers were rejected as physically unfit for service, but World War One broadened and intensified the discussions. In the West Indies, as in England, expressions of alarm, fear and embarrassment emanating from the age–old perceptions of disease as both a corrupting corporeal invasion of the self and a threat to labour availability, were the typical reactions to the rejection statistics.

The high incidence of venereal diseases was described by F.R. Harford, a member of the Grenada Legislature, as frightful.[31] Though alarmed, the *Federalist* was nevertheless thankful that recruitment had revealed the presence of the 'loathsome syphilis' and other diseases which were 'sapping the manhood of the country and ruining its womanhood'.[32] The paper observed that syphilitic men reeking of death and emanating the foulest odours were walking the streets of the town disturbing the nasal organs of the clean passer–by.[33] L.O. Crosswell, the medical officer for Kingston, Jamaica, concluded that the high rejection rates made it evident that stringent measures were required to meet the peril and that the vagrancy law needed to be amended so as to give the police extended powers to apprehend vagrants of both sexes and subject them to examination and when found necessary, to segregate them for treatment.[34] The *Gleaner* admitted that it felt humiliated and ashamed as well as concerned for the loss to Jamaica's and empire's fighting forces.[35]

Inevitably the debate was carried on in more explicitly moralistic terms and the prevalence of venereal diseases was viewed by some church men and self–righteous members of the public as indicative of a deeper moral corruption within society, manifested also in the prevalence of prostitution and drinking.[36] In a letter to the *Gleaner,* one R.E. Clarke argued that the dreadful state of affairs as regard venereal diseases was inseparable from the utterly corrupt condition of morals, which had for some time characterised Jamaican society.[37] Clarke argued that sin against God was the root of all evil, and it was for this reason that venereal diseases were ravaging the community. He therefore warned that 'all the legislation in the world' could not solve the problem; the only solution was a transformation in the sexual habits of the population.

Although it is difficult to assess from the evidence the extent to which these feelings existed in Jamaica and the region more generally, it is not unreasonable to suspect that such views were more common among the middle and upper classes and not merely, or indeed, even because of their religiosity. Clarke's letter was indicative of the manner in which family and sexual relations among the mainly black populations and especially the lower classes, in Africa and the diaspora, had been stereotyped, pathologised and condemned as immoral by social values and medical ideas emanating out of Europe.[38] Many of these attitudes were adopted by the middle and upper strata of West Indian society in particular. It is true that because of the changing nature of these pathological stereotypes and the new environment in which they interacted after emancipation, the elites were more careful not to express their views too openly or frankly, but this did not mean such beliefs were still not common among these classes. For example, the socialist and former governor of Jamaica, Sydney Olivier, recalled that he was frequently told that the black people of Jamaica were 'devoid of any morality in sexual relations'.[39]

The debates in the region were also expressed in environmental terms, which is not surprising since many church men, health workers and others, tended to associate poor social conditions, like overcrowding, with high levels of immorality.[40] Against this background one writer in a letter to the *Gleaner* argued that while religion could be helpful in controlling the problem of immorality and venereal diseases, the real solution was to undertake a major improvement in the public environment.[41] To this end he instructed the authorities: 'Make the conditions of life sweeter and cleaner, have a brighter and better education system, make the people happy; give them something to live for and you have solved the problem, not only of the dread disease, but also of the worst forms of immorality.'[42] He was convinced that these objectives could be achieved if greater emphasis was placed on cricket, football and other sports as well as on education and productive employment.

In retrospect, the most significant aspect of his contribution was, perhaps, the adoption of the 'enlightened' view that, to make venereal disease notifiable, as advocated by some persons, would frighten victims of the disease from seeking medical advice, cause a great deal of domestic unhappiness, if not actual tragedy and place jobs in jeopardy.[43] In adopting this position, the writer was clearly demonstrating a deeper insight into the more complex and fundamental issues relating to the stereotyping and representation of disease, and especially, the complexities of notification. His comments pointed to the consequences of the tendency of many societies to stigmatise the diseased as the 'Other', who was not only different but also symbolised society's worst fears of social degeneration.[44]

The controversy in Jamaica became even more alarmist and urgent when it was discovered that many of the volunteers had contracted venereal diseases after they had been enlisted and put into training. One spontaneous check on June 30, 1916 revealed an infection rate of 58 per thousand and another on August 30, showed that the figure had increased to 136 per thousand.[45] It is worth pointing out that the average infection rate of British and Dominion soldiers in Britain between 1916 and 1918 was 39.2 and in Egypt, 48.1, but it should also be noted that if the countries were analysed separately, it would be found that the rate of infection among the Dominion forces was at times strikingly high.[46] Further embarrassment was experienced by local officials when the War Office started to complain about the large numbers of men infected with venereal and other diseases being received overseas. They were regarded by the War Office as a serious threat to the health of the troops in France.

When the eighth BWIR comprising 22 officers and about 1,000 other ranks arrived in France, it was immediately segregated in camp because of an outbreak of measles and the prevalence of other diseases.[47] Approximately 20 per cent of the battalion were infected with various forms of ringworm and many were infected with hookworm. Of the 406 men from Trinidad in this battalion, 60 per cent were found to be infected with hookworm. It also seemed that many of the men in the battalion had not been revaccinated against smallpox since childhood and anti–typhoid inoculation had only been partially done. Consequently, anti–typhoid vaccine was obtained from the United States so that all recruits could be inoculated before leaving the West Indies. The authorities in France also estimated that 20 per cent of the recruits of the ninth BWIR, which had been recruited in Jamaica, were suffering from venereal diseases at the time of their arrival overseas.[48] Similarly, when a group of 985 BWIR men arrived in Egypt on November 2, 1916, it was discovered that no less than 139 or over 14 per cent were suffering from venereal diseases.[49] Although the local medical examiners might have been negligent in their scrutiny of recruits there were other factors which contributed to the arrival of infected recruits overseas.

Firstly, even though the understanding of the pathology and aetiology of venereal diseases had improved significantly during the nineteenth century, there remained a strong likelihood of misdiagnosis. The intermittent nature of syphilis, for instance, may have led some medical examiners to believe that the disease was cured when it had only gone into remission. Secondly, many recruits contracted venereal diseases on the eve of their departure from the West Indies. Army regulations stipulated that the recruits were to be examined the week prior to and the day before embarkation, as well as upon arrival.[50] Recruits at training camp in Jamaica were strictly warned and a scale of punishments introduced for those who contracted sexually transmitted diseases.[51] Local medical officers were also warned by the War Office to increase the effectiveness of their inspection and intensify the process of vaccination and inoculation among the volunteers.[52] Thirdly, some of the infected men of the 9th battalion had been sent overseas accidentally because of a lack of communication between the staff and the medical examiners in Jamaica. Some 127 men who had been examined and put aside 'from embarkation' were sent overseas without the doctors' knowledge because the staff had mistakenly taken the instructions to mean 'for embarkation'. [53]

While the decision to accept and treat men with curable diseases might thus have been good for the local societies, it had negative implications for the health and efficiency of the troops overseas, and involved a considerable loss of time. Importantly, however, throughout the West Indies the campaigns to eradicate various diseases such as yaws and hookworm infestation or ankylostomiasis were given additional impetus by the revelations of the military examinations. It was, however, the venereal diseases or the 'Black Evil' which gained the most serious attention. A number of colonies including Grenada and Jamaica hastily enacted legislation to deal with the problem. The Grenada ordinance was passed by the Legislature on August 24, 1917. Among other things, it provided for the compulsory notification of those suffering from venereal disease and made it a criminal offence for an infected person to deliberately infect another.[54] Additionally, persons who failed to attend for treatment were liable to be prosecuted and forcibly subjected to treatment. The penal clauses of the ordinance were brought into force, since women especially were generally reluctant to come forward to be examined because of the shame and intrusiveness involved.[55] A variety of drugs were used to treat venereal diseases but the main ones were mercury and salvarsan, which were sold under various trade names such as arseno-benzol, arsenobillion, kharsivan and diarsenol.[56] There were a number of ways to administer salvarsan, which incidentally was also used to treat yaws, but most doctors apparently preferred to inject an aqueous solution of the drug intramuscularly.

Public lectures were undertaken to sensitise people to the seriousness of the disease problem and notices were posted throughout the colony offering rewards to any one who informed on infected persons who had failed to report for treatment.[57] Penalties were instituted to prevent malicious accusations against innocent persons but this sometimes proved ineffective. Much to the anger of the press, false information was at times maliciously given to doctors as acts of revenge intended to humiliate certain 'respectable' persons.[58] Given the great importance attached to notions of respectability, especially among educated blacks and the middle strata of West Indian society, to be stigmatised in this way was unquestionably a distressing experience. Because of the small size of most colonies, the doctors would obviously have been aware that their actions could be seriously embarrassing, especially to 'respectable' citizens, and would no doubt have exercised their power only after careful consideration. Nevertheless, these 'respectable' persons were on occasions summoned by the doctors.

An extensive programme of treatment was also speedily implemented in Jamaica and legislation based on the Grenada ordinance was enforced.[59] Special evening clinics were held twice weekly at the Kingston Public Hospital in order to cope with the large numbers of infected persons. Between February 1917 and January 1918, approximately 6,722 were treated at these clinics and thousands more were treated at the country hospitals.[60] As in Grenada, however, the effectiveness of the eradication scheme was affected by the 'tendency to secrecy and concealment', which medical officers found difficult to overcome.[61] Fines were imposed to prevent anyone other than doctors from treating the diseases. These fines were targeted mainly at the bush doctors, obeahmen and 'experienced friends', whom many people consulted before going to the medical doctors. The fines were intended to have the double effect of encouraging infected persons to come forward and, more crucially, of asserting the hegemony of Western biomedicine over indigenous healing practices, which were regarded by the authorities as largely ineffective and obstructive.

The clergy were also requested to impress upon the lower classes of Kingston and lower St Andrew the need to come forward for treatment.[62] Members of friendly societies who became infected with venereal disease promptly lost all their benefits and in most cases were barred from attending meetings.[63] Moreover, in 1917, the *Jamaica Social Purity Association*, whose committee was dominated by prominent clergy men, was formed to achieve 'the furtherance of social purity in the colony by combating immorality and venereal diseases'.[64] Recruitment for the war thus helped to highlight the problem of contagious diseases and stimulate corrective measures in several West Indian societies, although this should not be exaggerated. The problems associated with treating the population were by no means minor or easy to overcome. Real progress in the fight against venereal diseases was not made until after the war but especially during and after World War Two, when penicillin revolutionised its medical treatment.[65]

The effect of the rejections on the recruiting process was often negative. In Trinidad, rejected men expressed anger or started malicious rumours with the intent of creating disillusionment and apathy among potential volunteers.[66] The selection committee in Grenada was accused of discriminating against volunteers from the rural parishes.[67] What made matters even worse was the fact that many of these men had given up their jobs and could not get them back because others had filled their positions. Employers in Trinidad were also unwilling to hire men who could be called away at a moment's notice. Consequently, once they had offered their services to go to war many men were left stranded for weeks, being neither soldiers nor workers.[68] Frustration was also exhibited by men in Jamaica who had travelled 20 miles to the capital only to be sent away with a shilling as compensation for their time and effort.[69]

However, the intensity of the newspaper propaganda and the general excitement and debate about the war made it virtually unnecessary throughout 1915 to organise any systematic recruitment campaigns involving mass rallies in most colonies. In Grenada, for instance, men flocked to register in the capital, many coming from the distant rural parishes at their own expense.[70] Enthusiasm to enlist was further enhanced by the belief that the war was going to be a short and successful affair. The newspapers did much to encourage this belief by carrying cartoons showing the Germans being crushed, and predicting imminent victory for the Allies.[71] The early contingents were therefore recruited with great rapidity, particularly in the larger colonies of Jamaica, Barbados and Trinidad. The departure of the first contingents of men from each colony was usually, as we have seen, an occasion of some sadness, but more of tremendous euphoria, excitement and pride. On the day of the departure of the first Grenada contingent, the town was richly decorated with flags, palms and flowers, and singing and rejoicing were every-where evident.[72] When news of the arrival of the troops in England reached the colony, there were more celebrations and expressions of patriotism.[73] But this euphoria soon dissipated and the tasks of the recruiters became increasingly difficult and problematic as more people for a variety of reasons, began to frustrate and oppose the recruiting process.

Resistance to Recruitment

By mid–1916, indifference and resistance to recruitment were apparent in most of the colonies. Initially, a major reason for avoiding the army was self–preservation. Many young men in Antigua, for instance, desired to enlist but feared getting shot.[1] The suggestion from recruiters, that it was better to get shot and die knowing that they had done their duty than lying in a bed dying from rheumatism or some other disease, failed to impress the draft resisters.[2] The anxieties of those Bahamians who held such fears were no doubt intensified by the conspicuous presence of discouraging 'calamity howlers'.[3]

In Trinidad, too, there were those who refused to take any interest in the war. A 'patriot' complained:

> They are too inclined to regard the matter in no serious light and take very little or no interest whatever in trying to understand the perilous times which the British empire is at present experiencing. You speak to them of the retreat from Warsaw and they alter the conversation to football! You ask whether they have read the telegrams and their reply is that 'we don't bother to read the telegrams!'[4]

The fearful in Honduras had their anxieties rationalised by hardened dissenters who questioned them: 'Why should you throw your life away, you are young; and why should you go and offer your life in this great conflict?'[5] Others were only confronted with the deadly implications of volunteering when they actually went to register, where much 'enlightening' debate on the issues of the war apparently took place. Thus, a number of men from the parish of Grenville in Grenada who rushed eagerly to volunteer, thought after further reflection that it was 'stupidness to enlist'.[6] Predictably, the press was generally unsympathetic to those who hung back because they feared being shot. The *Gleaner*, for instance, disdainfully dismissed those expressing fearful and discouraging sentiments as contemptible cowards.[7]

Because of these difficulties, the Jamaica legislature adopted measures enabling recruiters to compel men to show up for examination once they had offered their services at recruiting meetings or elsewhere. Under law number 19 of 1916, it became possible for men to be enlisted by any recruiter appointed by the G.O.C. and attested for service with the Jamaica contingent by a justice. This not only increased the number of official recruiters but also, more importantly, made it difficult for men to change their decision once they had registered. Under the new regulations, recruits who failed to comply with the summons to report for training at camp were liable to be punished under the Volunteer Force Law of 1914.[8] The new regulations marked an important shift in the attitude of local officials towards the principle of voluntarism. During the debates in the legislature, according to the attorney-general, it was quite evident that many members felt that the measure was not severe enough.[9]

Pacifists, such as the Jehovah's Witnesses, also criticised recruitment and suffered the wrath of both the liberal and conservative newspapers as a result. The *Federalist*, for instance, expressed great contempt for those who viewed the war as a disgrace and a break–down of Christianity.[10] In Belize, a pacifist condemned the Reverend William Hornsby of the Cathedral of the Most Holy Redeemer for encouraging parents to send their sons to war. He was accused of transgressing the laws of his sacred oath by aiding the 'heretical butchers' in their 'uncivilised carnage'.[11] The *Clarion* defended the priest and angrily denounced the pacifist for suggesting that Honduran recruits were fighting for avarice and greed.[12] The dissemination of pacifist literature appears to have had little impact on recruitment but the evidence is too limited to allow us to be sure. We do know that on at least one occasion a potential recruit in Trinidad changed his mind after reading pacifist material which was being widely circulated, especially on Sundays.[13] This infuriated the *Port of Spain Gazette*, which urged that the preachers of the 'no war' doctrine should only be allowed to propagate their faith behind prison bars.[14] The *Jamaica Times* also condemned pacifist assertions that the war was unjustified and argued, on the contrary, that it was a 'call to do service for God by defending Liberty and smiting Tyranny'.[15] The local press may have been influenced by the condemnations of pacifists in England, but it was also a reflection of the hostility of the local press, established churches, and officials, towards minority religions which, as we have seen, were viewed as a threat to stability in the colonies.

Women were also accused by recruiters of disrupting recruitment by encouraging the resisters with the argument that there was no need to volunteer and go overseas to endure the hardships of war since there was no war in Trinidad and the possibility of the enemy coming there was quite remote.[16] Moreover, many women appropriated the 1915 American song composed by Alfred Bryan in which mothers called for peace, and popularised it in protest against recruitment. The chorus went as follows:

> I didn't raise my boy to be a soldier.
> I brought him up to be my pride and joy
> Who dares to place a musket on his shoulder,
> To shoot some other mother's darling boy?
> Let nations arbitrate their future troubles
> It's time to lay the sword and gun away
> There'd be no war today, if mothers all would say,
> 'I didn't raise my boy to be a soldier, soldier!'[17]

The adoption of this song by the women and more specifically, their projection of themselves as guardians of life and as peace–makers, were significant. The local societies were historically open to influences from the metropole, and the war further facilitated cultural transmission and the transfer of aspects of European and American culture into West Indian society. It is not clear from the sources how the song got to the West Indies but it may have been communicated by returning migrants. Unfortunately, the sources do not provide sufficient detail for us to be able to establish the size and nature of the group of women who adopted this song or whether they used it to articulate wider social and economic grievances.

Resistance had become so widespread in Grenada by the start of 1917 that the *Federalist* was reduced to pleading: 'Don't let it be said that Grenadians are not loyal to the empire. Don't let it be said that Grenadians are shirking their duty to King and Country.'[18] Such exhortations were in vain, and the resisters in that island remained unmoved.[19] H.A. Berkeley a prominent Grenada planter, claimed that in spite of generous inducements not one of his labourers could be convinced to volunteer.[20] Against the background of the refusal to volunteer, particularly of unemployed men, the press in a number of colonies began agitating for the governments to take drastic action. They urged for stricter vagrancy laws for the hundreds of 'loafers' and 'able–bodied human parasites' loitering about the streets doing 'absolutely nothing'.[21] The *Port of Spain Gazette* was convinced that such measures would reduce the number of 'shirkers' in Trinidad. In the light of West Indian labour relations after slavery, however, it is clear that both the press and the officials were merely using the war to further justify and intensify the harassment of the poor, particularly in urban areas, who were often loosely classified as vagrants and associated with crime, moral degeneration and the alleged labour difficulties of the planters.[22] The attitude of the *Port of Spain Gazette* towards the urban poor during the war years, for instance, was consistent with the views it had been expressing since in the late nineteenth century.[23] In Trinidad, the agitation against those without regular employment, including former indentured labourers, resulted in the passage of the Habitual Idlers Ordinance in 1918, which gave the government power to force so–called idlers to work.

Since issues of race and class oppression were being hotly discussed in the region, some resisters naturally articulated their resistance in those terms. The argument that the war was a white man's conflict was repeated by small but vocal groups in Trinidad, British Honduras and other colonies, as it had been in the context of the earlier debates on black participation in the war.[24] During a conversation between two citizens in Belize, one racially conscious resister was reported as saying in reference to the members of the local territorial force:

> Man, black man never get justice.
> What we got to do with this thing?
> If they go, they please themselves, they are men;
> but if they ask me, "I shall tell them not to go".
> They say it is to save the flag.
> "What we got to do with the flag?"[25]

The argument was also expressed in class terms. When asked why he had not enlisted, one Barbadian bluntly replied: 'England only wants men with money.'[26] Some resisters like those in British Honduras went even further, applying disrespectful epithets to the governors.[27] Not surprisingly, the press was also targeted by draft resisters in revenge for the constant attacks on them. On one occasion, the editor of the *Clarion* had the 'King's appeal' for men unceremoniously torn down from the door of his office and replaced with the remark: 'What the hell have we got to do with the war?'[28]

Racially charged talk was equally common in Trinidad but unlike in most of the other colonies, the government carried out an active campaign to eradicate disloyalty. Official action was aimed particularly at a vocal minority of whom the *Port of Spain Gazette* contemptuously noted:

> Since the commencement of the war there has been noticeable in Port–of–Spain, a minute but noisy element which has opposed itself to the cause of the Allies ... Their country being at war, they seem to think they have the inborn right to criticise the conduct of the war by the Allies and to praise the conduct of the enemy; and when a recruiting march is on, or a recruiting meeting takes place or a war memorial service is held in the churches, or when the public telegrams announce an important event in any of the theatres of war, they regard it as their special privilege to air their adverse opinion for the edification of whoever is ready to listen.[29]

What was even more annoying to the authorities was the frequent harassment of volunteers. Squads of recruits on route march were often subjected to laughs, jeers, taunts and shouts of: 'Look at the German targets, etc.'[30] On one occasion, according the *Port of Spain Gazette*, a group of Trinidad recruits was attacked by a 'gang of loose men and women', and subjected to every form of insult for having enlisted.[31]

This group of resisters was specially targeted by the officials in an effort to suppress the expressions and acts of disloyalty. Maximum fines were usually imposed so that poor offenders were forced into prison. At the city magistrate's court, a number of young men were given 'stiff sentences' for insulting volunteers and using derogatory language against them.[32] Similarly, Alexander Morris and Anthony Gayalee were prosecuted for throwing stones at a group of recruits.[33] A disenchanted mechanic at San Fernando who muttered words to the effect that he wanted Germany to win the war as then poor people would get fair play, was likewise immediately arraigned under the provisions of the Defence of the Realm Act and sentenced to one month imprisonment with hard labour.[34] There were also several other convictions for similar offences.[35]

The contempt which resisters had for volunteers in British Guiana was reflected in an incident during which a number of recruits were taunted as 'German baits' by some excursionists on a government steamer on the Demerara river.[36] One man was charged for throwing an empty bottle during the affair and injuring a volunteer.[37] The government's efforts to increase the size of the depleted territorial force in British Honduras were shunned by the resisters who contemptuously jeered and mocked those who chose to volunteer.[38] Some resisters, as in Belize, were influenced by important people with long–standing grudges and grievances against the government. They believed that by dissuading men from volunteering they could put the government in a difficult position and cause the officials great embarrassment.[39]

As a warning to the potentially disloyal in Barbados, the *Globe* published the case of a Norwegian seaman, who was a naturalised British subject who had been heavily fined for saying 'to hell with England.'[40] Such warnings were deemed necessary because in Barbados men had been discouraged from volunteering by the argument that the West Indians would be used to provide domestic service for other regiments.[41] The *Gleaner* also chose to warn dissenters of the consequences of disloyalty by publishing the case of a Jamaican working in Canada who was jailed for six months for asserting that it was only alright for fellows to enlist if they had no brighter future.[42]

By the middle of 1916, men rejected in England as unfit or as invalids had begun to return to the West Indies. The exaggerations in the promises which recruiters had and were still making would have become apparent to these men and the public because, without exception, the local governments had made little preparation for the invalids. Moreover, those men discharged as unfit or undesirable were not entitled to any benefits or pensions, while those who were entitled to benefits experienced excessively long delays before they received assistance.[43] In Jamaica the men were usually given a few shillings, a cheap suit of clothes and free railway transport to their home, but because of transportation problems, some had to remain in Kingston for several days. This exhausted their money even before they actually left for home.[44] The situation created major dissatisfaction because many had no other form of support.

Having relinquished their jobs to fight for King and Country, these men were left to experience destitution and poverty. The *Mirror* reported Trinidadians in 'dire straits'.[45] The case of Reginald Stamford was one of the more serious examples of the neglect of invalids in Trinidad. Having returned to the island with fractured knees, he waited for months without receiving his pension and the government was unable to provide him with any employment.[46] Those in Jamaica were described as being 'in a bad way'.[47] Many of the injured experienced a substantial reduction in their quality of life. For example, a stevedore who lost one foot, and four toes on the other had his 30 shilling a week wage, that he obtained from the officials, reduced to a mere seven shillings a week for nine months.[48] With such a meagre pension and little prospect for good employment he was virtually doomed to poverty given the high cost of living. The rising tide of anger in Jamaica prompted the *Gleaner* to warn the authorities: 'There is a murmur, growing louder and louder every day against the pension system which is applied to the men of the Jamaica contingent.'[49] In Trinidad, where a similar situation existed, the *Port of Spain Gazette* tried desperately to defuse the anxiety and anger over the treatment of the men by dismissing the allegations as the work of 'evil rumourists' and 'busy bodies'.[50]

The group which perhaps harboured the greatest amount of animosity towards the officials were the artisans and tradesmen who had, in many instances, given up lucrative employment to volunteer. Many had sold their workshops and tools and had lost their customers, only to return a few months later as invalids. One disgruntled Grenadian tradesman protested angrily that all the government did for such men was to discharge them without giving them assistance for a fresh start, after having pauperised and made fools of them.[51] The dissatisfaction which resulted was infectious, and those not directly affected must have thought even more seriously about job security when considering the question of enlistment. By December 1916, the enthusiasm and excitement surrounding recruitment had virtually disappeared in Grenada and people viewed the departure of recruits with apathy.[52]

As the war progressed, many people began to realise that the war was not going to be the very short affair they had been led to believe. The authenticity and accuracy of the newspapers coverage of the war was questioned time and again and held in contempt. It was rumoured in Belize, for instance, that the press was not trustworthy and was concealing the fact that every time the British encountered the Germans, the Englishmen were beaten.[53] Similarly, in Jamaica it was alleged that coverage was distorted and biased.[54] In spite of the tight censorship it is not unlikely that people in the various colonies had received news or rumours of the catastrophic losses the Allies had suffered on the Western front. The *Gleaner* asserted that there were hundreds and probably thousands in Jamaica who were depressed and spoke anxiously about the Allied's progress in the war, while there were others who were convinced that the Allies would be defeated.[55]

Although some Jamaicans were simply sceptical of the 'wild sensationalism' of the press, there were others whose conviction that Germany would be victorious was rooted in antipathy for the British. The uselessness of adopting a conciliatory approach towards the latter was well recognised by the *Jamaica Times* which observed in desperation:

> They see disaster and try to make their neighbours see it, because that is what they really long to behold falling on England and the empire. It is a waste of time trying to reassure them, for reassurance is the last thing they really desire. It is no good trying to convince them; they are preconvinced by their prejudices against British rule.[56]

Similar attitudes were evident in Trinidad but the authorities in characteristic fashion rigorously prosecuted the dissenters. One Joseph Hypolite, for instance, was arrested for stating in obscene language that the Germans were smashing up the British, and they had to 'mash them up to a finish' because the British were a damn set of filthy people.[57] He was given the option of a fine of 50 shillings or one month in prison with hard labour.

The spectacle of returning invalids had a sobering effect on potential recruits. The sight of men hobbling on sticks and crutches was evident in Grenada, and there were in Trinidad 'many pathetic scenes to be witnessed'.[58] At the same time several Vincentian recruits returned maimed for life or suffering from bullet wounds, trench feet and bronchial problems.[59] In Jamaica, however, it was the catastrophic journey of their third contingent that dramatically brought home the possible dangers which awaited potential recruits. On March 6, 1916 the third Jamaica contingent comprising 25 officers and 1,115 other ranks departed for England on board the *Verdala*. Due to enemy submarine activity in the region, the Admiralty ordered the ship to make a diversion to Halifax but before it could reach its destination it encountered a blizzard. Since the *Verdala* was not adequately heated and the black soldiers had not been properly equipped with warm clothing, substantial casualties resulted.

Approximately 600 men suffered from exposure and frostbite and there were five immediate deaths. The first to succumb to the cold were the NCOs who had been selected largely on the basis of race and class. On the other hand, the men from the country districts withstood the blizzard much better.[60] As a result of the disaster, 106 of the victims had to remain at Halifax to have amputations, ranging from toes to both legs.[61] Another 200 whose feet were not as badly swollen were sent to Bermuda where the climate was warmer. The disaster was hushed up in the British press but reported in Canadian papers which were received in the West Indies, and exaggerated and alarmist reports of what had happened spread rapidly in Jamaica. The fact that at first the press was forbidden by the censors to deal with these reports did very little to contain speculation and rumour and probably made matters worse.[62] The intensity of these rumours brought home to the authorities the need to act quickly or face severe disruption of the recruitment process. Consequently, the press was allowed to print the official version of the incident. Every effort was made to shift the blame away from local authorities to the Admiralty, which was accused of making a stupid blunder.

A Sufferers' Fund was established by the *Gleaner* to assist victims of the disaster and the Canadian government provided artificial limbs and established training programs in the crafts to enable the affected men to earn a living when they returned to Jamaica. This generosity at a time when there was much debate on the question of union between Canada and the West Indies was highly commended by a number of newspapers, which expressed the hope that as a result, relations would be even better.[63] To allay local anxieties, the War Office granted the victims of the disaster full status as soldiers, which entitled them to pensions.[64] There is no evidence to suggest that the Halifax incident had the effect of the Mendi disaster in South Africa, which was also reported in the Jamaican press, but it apparently did have severe medical consequences for Kingston, Jamaica.[65] It was subsequently believed by medical officers to have been partly responsible for an outbreak of pneumonia which reached epidemic proportions in Kingston and which claimed the lives of several recruits at training camp. Returning convalescents of the Halifax incident were suspected to have introduced a virulent strain of the disease into the island.[66]

The Halifax incident also seriously damaged the recruitment campaign which had to be temporarily suspended.[67] On June 29, 1916 a large group of the victims returned to Jamaica and were greeted by a curious and sympathetic crowd.[68] The gruesome spectacle aroused further fears and resentment. After the disaster, large numbers of women and children attended recruiting meetings but relatively few men did.[69] Women were again pressed to assist by encouraging men to volunteer. At the same time, the recruiters adopted a more vigorous strategy of house–to–house visits.[70] The problems in the way of recruitment were, however, deep–seated, as its temporary suspension had dampened the spirit of the recruiters who were less than enthusiastic about resuming their task.[71] As a result of these difficulties, greater efforts were made, particularly after America's entry into the war in 1917, to obtain more volunteers from Panama, and it was to a large extent these mainly Jamaican and other migrants in Panama that allowed further Jamaican contingents to be formed.[72]

By this time, recruiters in Grenada were also finding it extremely difficult to procure more volunteers and the men in training at the Quarantine Station camp had developed an increasingly rebellious attitude because of the long periods of training and unnecessary delays before being sent overseas. The boredom and irritation of the recruits were intensified by the monotonous nature of the training, which consisted merely of drills, marches and lectures. The transport to take the volunteers overseas was expected in June 1916 but between that time and March 1917 when the ship did arrive, its arrival had already been cancelled at least four times. This had a demoralising effect on the men.[73] To make matters worse, a number of the local training camps experienced outbreaks of fever which caused severe casualties. During the months August to November 1916, 65 per cent of the men at camp in Grenada suffered from fever.[74] There was also an outbreak of measles among recruits in Jamaica.[75]

Frustrated volunteers began overstaying their leave and had to be forcibly brought back, while others tried secretly to emigrate from the island.[76] Eventually a large number of the men had to be dismissed from training camp because of misconduct.[77] In Jamaica where there were similar difficulties, one recruit was given six months imprisonment for deserting twice but subsequently had his sentence reduced to three months.[78] Likewise, a considerable number of recruits who had been passed for the fourth Trinidad contingent failed to turn up at camp for training.[79] The difficulties with transportation and the problems at training camp were brought to the attention of George Grindle at the Colonial Office by Governor Haddon–Smith.

Grindle agreed with him that everything had to be done to avoid the delays since they were likely not only to inhibit recruiting but also to undermine the morale of the black soldiers, who, he believed, were easily affected by monotony and restraint.[80]

Meanwhile, the recruiting campaign in British Honduras, particularly in its northern districts, had also run into serious difficulties. In the district of San Estevan the calls for men to enlist in the second contingent resulted in an exodus of young men unparalleled in the history of the area.[81] It was rumoured that the governor was going to compel them to enlist. Although the recruiters attempted to convince them that the British would never force anyone to fight, it was, the *Clarion* concluded, 'easier to try to wet the back of a duck by pouring water on the feathers than to convince them of the fact'.[82] Many fled across the border into Mexico, leaving their crops to rot. Another group who heard that the governor was coming to recruit in their area quickly deserted into the bush on the pretence that they had business of great importance to attend.[83] The men returned several days later in single file to the cheers of groups of schoolboys who were expecting them. As late as March 1916, not one man from the large villages of San Roman, San Antonio or San Estevan had enlisted for active service.[84]

This response was in part due to the fact that the northern districts of Honduras were largely populated by descendants of people who had migrated from Mexico over several generations. Thus, as the *Clarion* rightly observed, those pro–imperial ideals which had triggered the enthusiastic response in the English–speaking parts of the colony were lacking.[85] Moreover, the history of the colony as a logwood settlement, its isolation and the plurality of the population (blacks, caribs, maya–indians, asiatics, creoles and so on,) meant there were competing cultural identities in different parts of the country. While the capital, Belize, and its environs had a West Indian atmosphere, the more rural areas were characterised by a markedly Central American environment.[86] In the early stages of recruitment, many people in the northern areas were able to take refuge in the excuse that they could not speak English.[87] Because the people of these districts were predominantly Catholic, saboteurs wishing to disrupt recruitment deliberately circulated the rumour that the war was a conflict between Catholicism and Protestantism, the Germans being Catholics and the British the Protestants.[88] Some people in these areas therefore refused to volunteer since they believed that by fighting for England they would be fighting against people of their own religion.

Attempts by the recruiters to counter–act these arguments by pointing out that Belgium, which had suffered German attack, was predominantly Catholic, proved useless.

Throughout 1916 and 1917, the attraction of the King's uniform and the prestige which recruits held in the various colonies was drastically undermined by the poor character and behaviour of some of the volunteers. People increasingly viewed the recruits as nuisances and rogues who were frequently in conflict with the police and members of the public. There were regular clashes between the police and recruits who believed that they were superior in authority to the police and that soldiers were immune from civil law. Thus, when the police in British Guiana attempted to arrest contingent member Ernest DaCosta for misconduct, he became even more unruly and insisted that he could not be arrested as he was wearing his uniform.[89] The contempt which recruits had for the police was also displayed in several altercations in Barbados.[90]

It was, however, in Trinidad and Jamaica that the largest and most destructive clashes occurred. The first major row in Trinidad took place during December 1916 between members of the Demerara contingent sojourning there and men of the Trinidad constabulary. The trouble began one Saturday afternoon after a group of the Demerara men were attacked by a Chinese shopkeeper whom they had verbally abused. From that moment onwards, reported the *Port of Spain Gazette*, it was 'a hot time in Queen Street'.[91] On passing and seeing their comrades in the affray, another group of Demerara men promptly joined in and together they quickly demolished the shop. The conflict escalated when the city police arrived on the scene and immediately proceeded to engage the soldiers in combat but suffered defeat. A much larger police force arrived soon after and having learnt that their colleagues had been abused went on a rampage, beating and arresting every recruit they could find, even those who had not been involved. The action of the police infuriated soldiers in camp who demanded that their comrades be restored to them or they would 'break' barracks and do it themselves, irrespective of the consequences. A number of them broke into the guardroom in an effort to secure rifles. Fearing the worst, the authorities immediately acceded to the wishes of the soldiers and the arrested men were peacefully retrieved from police cells and placed in military custody.

Press coverage of the incident was decidedly in favour of the recruits, in spite of reservations expressed about their conduct. The *Port of Spain Gazette* argued in their defence: 'As soldiers who have volunteered their lives for the empire, although we have absolutely no sympathy with any undue disrespect for order by them, we think it might be less hurtful to their dignity that they should be controlled by a military picket of their own comrades than that they should for every little trifle be liable to be run in by a police man like any ordinary criminal.'[92] The *Mirror* likewise condemned the police for allowing the recruits to be, 'insulted and ridiculed by all and sundry' and protested: 'A man who is desirous of joining the army and of serving his King and the empire should not be treated like a criminal and marched along the public thoroughfares as if he were a murderer or a thief.'[93] While the press was relatively tolerant towards the indiscretions of the recruits, the frequency of similar disturbances gradually changed its attitude. By June 1917, recruits were again severely criticised by the *Port of Spain Gazette* which described one incident as 'a dastardly attack'.[94] On this particular occasion, Adolphus Stewart of the Volunteer Fire Brigade was forced to flee under a hail of stones from recruits of the fourth Trinidad contingent who mistook him for a constable.

The disturbances in Jamaica were the most intensive and costly. As early as December 1915, the riotous conduct of soldiers in the vicinity of the Cross Road police station necessitated the calling out of the WIR to maintain order.[95] Supported by a group of onlookers the soldiers pelted the police station with stones.[96] The real problems began with the fourth contingent. Extensive delays at camp, poor conditions and the practice of accepting men of bad character seriously undermined the morale of the contingent. There were numerous cases of 'shirking, insubordination and unfitness'. [97] A number of men were prosecuted in civil courts for disorderly conduct. In June 1916, the contingent had to be confined to barracks as a result of misconduct at the racecourse. At camp some of the men again made trouble requiring the authorities to requisition an armed party of the WIR to preserve order.[98]

The morale of the fifth contingent was marginally better than that of the fourth but by this time there was not much public sympathy in Kingston for the recruits. Tension between volunteers and the public, particularly those civilians described by the papers as the lower strata or 'riff–raffs', reached crisis proportions in 1917. The conflict was in part a consequence of the contempt which the men in the town had for the recruits, who were mainly from the country districts. The contingent men were regularly subjected to jeers and derogatory remarks. Some men were mocked for allegedly wearing shoes for the first time, while others were heckled with comments such as, 'contingent man can't walk in boots' or 'him get a clean suit of clothes.'[99] While it was true that some of the men were not accustomed to wearing shoes, there was also a problem with the quality and type of shoes given to the volunteers.

The boots were found to be of poor quality and the narrow structure was not suitable for the broad feet of the West Indians, so that many experienced discomfort.[100] Nevertheless, such comments deeply embarrassed and annoyed the country recruits because of the notions of difference, inferiority and backwardness imbedded in them. Women also contributed to the conflict between soldiers and police by urging contingent men to beat the police. Newspapers accounts of the conflict suggest that some of these women belonged to the vibrant class of over 300 prostitutes who inhabited the Kingston area and who were 'aggressive in the retailing of their wares, contemptuous of the police, and irrepressible'.[101] Further, because the contingent men had more money to spend on women this generated much animosity from the men in Kingston. All these factors contributed to a major confrontation involving police, soldiers and civilians on the night of January 20, 1917.

During this incident civilians assaulted the contingent men, who at one point numbered over one thousand, with stones and bricks, and the police were initially forced to beat a hasty retreat as the soldiers turned on both civilians and police.[102] The men of the contingent, but particularly those described as the 'bad men' and 'scallywags' who were responsible for starting the riot, were castigated by the *Gleaner*, which warned:

> Now we wish to say very plainly and emphatically that this will never do. No one has contended more strenuously for their rights than this paper. But neither we nor any citizen of Jamaica could possibly be prepared to tolerate an exhibition of ignorant behaviour on the part of any of these men; and it has now to be candidly confessed that the frequent riots which are associated with the Jamaica contingent are creating in the entire community a feeling of annoyance and disgust which can only do the contingent much harm.[103]

The paper's condemnation of the recruits was not made merely out of exasperation. It was also made in the context of the paper's long-running discourse on issues of race and black soldiers in relation to social order in Jamaica and the security of the white elite. However, given the demoralised state of the recruits by this time and their animosity towards the police, it seems unlikely that many would have been overly concerned with these changes in the attitude of the press and the public.

Following an inquiry into the disturbance, several of the ringleaders were given long prison sentences.[104] These convictions had little effect as a deterrent, perhaps because of the secrecy with which the trials were conducted. By May 1917, the contingent men were again out of control, looting and wilfully smashing up shops. Again the WIR was sent to restore order since the European troops who had been sent initially to quell the riot only served to further infuriate the rioters.[105] It should be noted, however, that the riots in Trinidad and Jamaica did not represent a new phenomenon in either colony: to a large extent these disturbances reflected the high levels of crime, fighting, gang warfare and other forms of social disorder which characterised the rapidly growing urban areas of several West Indian societies from the late nineteenth century.[106] Nevertheless, the frequently unruly conduct of the contingent men probably assisted in inhibiting recruitment by making the military even less attractive to potential volunteers. More importantly, since the later battalions of the BWIR, particularly numbers seven to 11, were formed from the ill-disciplined drafts, it was to be expected that some trouble would be experienced once they arrived overseas.

Conscription

As voluntary recruiting became more difficult, the idea of conscription became increasingly popular and was viewed by many officials as the only practical solution. Crucially, however, the implementation of conscription in England in January 1916 was not a signal for its automatic transfer to the colonies. Conscription as a policy for the colonies was, for several reasons related to the situation in Africa, regarded as undesirable by the Colonial Office.[107] Nevertheless, there were those in the colonies who felt strongly that the colonies should follow the example of the 'mother country'. The first serious attempt to adopt conscription in the West Indies took place in Jamaica in October 1916, when the matter was raised in the legislature by E.F.H. Cox, the member for St Andrew. The motion was successfully blocked by the governor and his supporters who argued that a conscription measure at that time was not only premature but also likely to provoke serious opposition.[108] The major employers of labour also objected as they did when the question of black participation in the war was being debated, on the grounds that conscription would undermine and dislocate their labour supply. Their fears on this occasion were perhaps more justified. Conscription had the potential to remove most of the able–bodied men, except those in 'reserved occupations', thereby reducing the surplus labour employers had hitherto used to keep wages low and preserve the quality of their labour force.

Six months later, however, as a result of the King's appeal for more men, the issue of conscription was again raised and on March 6, 1917, Cox and H.A.L. Simpson, a noted solicitor and prominent elected member in the House, gave notice to the legislature of their intention to reintroduce the Compulsory Service Bill.[109] Although the Colonial Office had serious reservations about conscription, developments in Jamaica were viewed with cautious enthusiasm because of the manpower shortages the War Office was experiencing. The governor was instructed that no official should propose conscription but he was to support the measure gladly if it were raised by one of the elected members.[110] He was also warned not to resort to actual compulsion unless the voluntary system had been fully exhausted.

Despite the strong support for conscription in the House, the issue was vigorously debated in the Jamaica legislature and press. Significantly, however, the divisions between the conscriptionists and the anti–conscriptionists were never really polarised. Among the arguments in favour was the view expressed by the attorney-general that conscription would make the path of duty clear to men who were 'beset by conflicting influences and disturbed by antinomous considerations' whenever they contemplated volunteering. Legal compulsion he argued would be much more effective than speeches in helping such men to settle the various conflicts in their minds.[111] A popular argument was that conscription was the best way of achieving equality of sacrifice by race, class, occupation and section. It was justifiably regarded by some conscriptionists as the most effective method of getting middle–class draft resisters to enlist.[112] The view that the middle–class men ought to be forced to enlist was, however, fiercely contested by others who argued that since this section of the population had more to lose materially, financially and otherwise, better provisions in terms of pensions and security for their families had to be made before they could be enlisted.[113]

Objections to the conscription of middle–class men were also expressed in context of the British eugenicists' contention that recruitment for the war would have a dysgenic effect by stripping the country of its most intelligent and creative members.[114] A letter to the *Gleaner* from one James Sawers of Port Maria protested that since the middle class was the backbone of Jamaican society, it was not sensible to force too many to enlist.[115] Sawers' contention may also have had an economic basis. Other objections to conscription reflected the anxiety and hostility which Asian immigration had generated among many sections of Jamaican society. Sawers, for instance, contended that if too many Jamaicans of military age were conscripted, the country would run the risk of being over–run by Chinese, East Indians and others.[116] Expectedly, the conscription question was debated in terms of race. Arthur Benjamin Lowe, a planter and member of the Marley and Rose Hall district of St. James, argued that since people of every shade of colour had achieved academic and professional success in Jamaica, it was unjust for commissions to be granted to people of only one complexion or to the wealthy and influential. He suggested that if conscription was inevitable, then an impartial board should be appointed to determine a man's intellectual and moral fitness to hold a commission, among other things.[117]

Some of the letters received by the press from the public were edited to suppress statements which the editors regarded as 'rank folly or bordering on the seditious'.[118] Others, written by a minority of persons described by the *Gleaner* as being of a 'very inferior human type', had to be excluded to avoid prosecution. The acrimonious nature of these letters provoked the editor into replying:

> That there are a handful of disloyal persons here, persons who in their heart of hearts would wish to see the British defeated in this war, we have always known, and if they can find an opportunity to cast a stone at the British empire they will always do it, so long as they think they are safe; but they speak for their traitorous selves alone, not for the people of this country. Curs are to be found everywhere, but they will always hang their tails between their legs and slink away when properly kicked.[119]

The *Jamaica Times* also reported that there was 'mischievous talk' and 'malicious falsehood' with regard to the conscription issue, being circulated around the island by persons intent on inflaming the public mind against law and order.[120] Public opposition to the conscription bill was also reflected in a well–attended rally held on April 2, 1917 opposite Victoria Park in Kingston. The meeting was organised by Alexander Dixon, a former member of the Legislative Council and influential in the political affairs of Kingston.[121] He was out–spoken and often represented the poor in the society. The meeting was held to protest against the Bill and to support the members of the legislature opposed to it.[122] Dixon spoke for 45 minutes after which a protest resolution outlining various reasons why the bill should not be passed, was unanimously adopted to send to the Colonial Office.

The resolution pointed out that the number of men recruited under the voluntary system had, by the government's acknowledgment, equalled their original expectations and protested that more men could have been obtained but for the large number of rejections for minor defects and illiteracy. It asserted that it was the public, initially unsupported by the government, which had agitated to be allowed to serve in the war and, which, had contributed substantially to the various war charities. The resolution argued for increased separation allowances for middle–class men and a pension system which would allocate support in accordance with the invalided soldier's station in life prior to enlistment. It also objected that conscription would reflect negatively on the loyalty of Jamaicans and that a plebiscite would reveal that the majority of the people were against the bill. Finally, it was maintained that such a law would give the governor despotic powers and ignored the rights of conscientious objectors. One such objector asked that he be sent to do Red Cross work at the front.[123] Although the resolution was condemned by the chairman of the recruiting committee, J.H.W. Park, and the commander of the local forces, Brigadier-General L.S. Blackden, the meeting failed to deter the legislature from passing the conscription measure.

The Bill which had been introduced on March 22, passed its third reading on April 4, 1917, with 21 members in favour and four opposed. The four dissenters wanted the measure delayed for six months, after which time they asserted they would readily support it if the voluntary system had proved hopeless.[124] With the adoption of the Bill, a system of registration and exemption tribunals modelled on that in England was established.[125]

Approximately 122,238 men were registered and restrictions were placed on emigration to ensure that physically fit men of military age would not leave the island. The clerical work for this process was almost entirely done by women, many of whom had husbands, sons or brothers in the BWIR. Predictably, events in Jamaica either precipitated or stimulated similar conscription debates in most of the other colonies but not every colony found it desirable to follow the Jamaican example. Conscription legislation was also adopted in Grenada and British Honduras but was regarded by the majority of the Barbados legislature as unnecessary because of the loyalty of Barbadians. The men who arrived overseas from the region to serve in the BWIR were therefore all volunteers even though, as elsewhere in the empire, some joined because of economic, legal and private pressures.

Service and Working Conditions Overseas

After their arrival in England in late October 1915, the first group of West Indian black recruits were sent by train to North Camp, Seaford, in Sussex, for training under Colonel A.E. Barchard of Jamaica. More contingents arrived from Barbados, St Lucia and the Leewards along with Jamaica's first draft which included a few recruits from the Bahamas and Panama. These were happily accepted by the Army Council, which had asked Bonar Law about the possibility of another 2,000 men in order to form and maintain another battalion.[1] This led to the formation of the second battalion of the BWIR which, like the first, was composed of men from all the colonies. This chapter details the organisation, duties and conditions under which these and subsequent battalions served.

Crucially, the War Office instructed that 41 Indians from Trinidad who had been included in the contingents be repatriated on the grounds that they were unsuitable and unlikely to become efficient soldiers because of their ignorance of the English language and difficulties with food.[2] The War Office had previously discouraged the recruitment of East Indians in the region on the basis that there were already numerous in the imperial forces.[3] The department was, however, willing to accept the inclusion of 'creoles of Indian descent', who had been born in the colonies and were therefore British subjects, could speak English and eat the normal rations given to the other West Indian soldiers. These constraints imposed by the War Office effectively put an end to recruiting among the large Indian population in Trinidad and British Guiana.

In January 1916, a third battalion was created which consisted mainly of Jamaicans, but with a few Bahamians and Jamaican migrants living in Panama; it was put under the command of Lieutenant-Colonel C. Woodhill, who was subsequently transferred to the first battalion. The third battalion was sent to Withnoe Camp, Plymouth, on account of the bad conditions at

Seaford where the black soldiers were housed in hastily erected huts which provided very little protection from the cold and rain. These 'death–traps', as Woodhill described them, resulted in sickness 'so terrible that hospitals in the locality were filled to overflowing and the entire life and training of these two battalions paralysed thereby'.[4] Obviously, the military authorities had not considered the consequences of deploying men from the tropics in England in the middle of winter without adequate accommodation. The situation of the group at Withnoe Camp was not much better, and these men suffered as badly from the effects of the cold.[5] Early in June, 129 men were discharged as unfit and on the twenty-second of that month a Travelling Medical Board, which visited Withnoe Camp and examined the fourth BWIR, dismissed 298 men as being permanently incapacitated by frost–bite caused by the unusually harsh winter climate.[6] Of a total of 2,991 men who left Jamaica between May 30 and September 8, 1919 approximately 573 were returned as unfit and about 391 of them belonged to the third contingent which had been involved in the Halifax incident.[7] Several disgruntled men wrote to the officials protesting against the 'miserable conditions' in which they lived.[8] The manpower deficiencies created by these losses were partly alleviated by the enlistment of West Indian seamen and others, including a South African and several Americans, living in England, who joined up under the Lord Derby recruiting scheme.[9]

Strike at Seaford

The plight of the soldiers at Seaford was exacerbated by delays in their remuneration. This resulted in a strike during October 1915 involving a group of the soldiers led by Henry Somerset, an ex–policeman and engineer from British Guiana, and several other 'ringleaders' from Trinidad. The men refused to turn out for parade and the notice 'no money, no work' was boldly written up in chalk.[10] The actual number involved is not known, but the strikers probably constituted a significant minority or Colonel Barchard would not have responded in the way he did: on the grounds that the men were 'ignorant of discipline', he decided not to take disciplinary action against most of them. Instead he attempted to regain their confidence by explaining that the delay was unavoidable and by promising to resolve the problem quickly.[11]

Although Barchard believed he could have brought a charge against the leaders for conspiring to cause a mutiny, he decided instead to repatriate them. On October 19 they were, along with several other 'undesirables', including six Barbadians, marched before Barchard and informed that as a result of their insubordination they were to be returned to the West Indies. Somerset was denied permission to speak and within 15 minutes was escorted away with the others to Tilbury Docks, London, where they were put on board the *Magdalena* for the voyage home.[12] To emphasise the punishment, Barchard had their uniforms confiscated and sent them back in civilian clothes. The expulsion was done so hurriedly that Somerset, for example, had no opportunity to collect his clothes except for one set of underwear. It was only when he arrived in Trinidad that he was able to borrow a singlet and a shirt from a friend.

Some of the rogues and convicts who had enlisted also suffered the same fate. One of these was Randolph Pond, a recruit from St Kitts, who was described by Barchard as having a most undesirable character and as being totally unfit to be a soldier.[13] Pond had lived in several West Indian colonies and had a criminal record in each. In Antigua and Dominica he had been convicted for disorderly conduct and larceny and was allegedly well known in St Kitts as an 'inveterate beggar' and a 'suspected' thief. At the time of his expulsion from Seaford, he was serving a 21 days sentence as an undesirable.[14] He was sent back on the same ship as Somerset. The authorities were, however, unsuccessful in repatriating all the undesirables. On the way to Tilbury Docks, one obtained his freedom by bolting through the crowd at St Pancras Station.[15] Although it is possible that he was subsequently recaptured by the military police, he may have been able to hide among the growing number of blacks coming to England to work.

News spread rapidly in the region and hence, not surprisingly, Somerset's arrival in British Guiana on November 5, 1915 was preceded by rumours of his return and this aroused considerable interest in Georgetown.[16] Thus, as soon as the steamer's rocket was heard, people flocked to the docks from all directions forming a crowd of 'respectable proportions'. Somerset was marched off the ship by military guards and taken to the barracks where he was ignominiously discharged.[17] In a newspaper interview Somerset spoke of the distress the incident had caused him and argued with 'great earnest' that he was returned because he 'spoke for his rights'.[18] He complained that he had been deceived and that the officers who treated them with kindness locally had changed once they arrived overseas.

Somerset also complained about the poor quality and inadequate amount of food the soldiers had to eat and the insults he received when he protested. He claimed, for instance, that on one occasion, a group of 30 men had to share five tins of salmon and that on another, when he explained he did not eat mutton, he was curtly told that if he did not like it he could leave it. His complaints about the food may have been justified but, as we will see, this was a problem which most soldiers experienced, irrespective of nationality. Nevertheless, these problems, and especially the lack of redress, allegedly created a great deal of dissatisfaction among the men although, according to Somerset, they seemed 'too faint-hearted to speak for their rights'. As he was not prepared to submit to such treatment, he was repatriated.

This episode provides some insight into the manner in which fresh recruits at times struggled to reconcile the paradox of enjoying considerable personal freedoms and rights in civil society but inevitably and, perhaps necessarily, are deprived of these once they enter the military. The West Indians were not regular soldiers and hence had brought civilian perceptions into the army. Somerset and his followers mistakenly continued to express their grievances as though they were civilians. They seemed oblivious to the seriousness of their actions, which Barchard could well have classified as mutiny, which in time of war could be punished by death. In this regard, Lawrence James' study of mutinies in the British and Commonwealth forces between 1797 and 1956 is instructive.[19] He shows how even the 'mildest' of mutinies, often in response to genuine grievances, were suppressed with unwarranted cruelty. Barchard appears to have behaved in an unusually 'soft' and compassionate manner towards Somerset and his followers. It should, however, be emphasised that there were several similar cases of protest among British troops which were dealt with equally leniently by the Adjutant-General's Department, which engaged in negotiations with the recalcitrant soldiers.[20]

The Fragmentation of the BWIR

On January 21, 1916, the first battalion and part of the second embarked on the *Marathon* for Alexandria, Egypt, where on March 18 they were made part of the Egyptian Expeditionary Force. The rest of the second battalion were temporarily relocated to Crown Hill Barracks, Plymouth. By April, most of the other soldiers in England had completed their training and upon the urging of Woodhill, arrangements were also made for them to be transferred to Egypt. On arrival in Egypt, the battalion was ordered to proceed to the Western Desert to Sollum, near the Red Sea, where there had been trouble with followers of the Senussi. Woodhill, however, protested to the authorities because they had not been through a musketry course. Training, which consisted of drills, lectures and practice in the use of the various weapons, therefore continued at Mex Camp, which was located about six miles west of Alexandria. Detachments were regularly sent to attend the various courses at the Imperial School of Instruction, Zeitoun, located near Cairo. They often performed well in training. On one occasion, for example, the first battalion sent 43 officers and 243 NCOs and men on a training course and of these, 39 officers and 202 NCOs and men were successful and many gained distinctions.[21]

Throughout this period the Suez Canal was threatened with attacks from Turkish forces.[22] Consequently, in June, the three battalions were moved down to the Canal zone and stationed respectively at Staging Camp, Ferry Post and Serapeum, where they trained in constructing canal defenses, barbed wire entanglements, bombing and other aspects of trench warfare. Those soldiers who had been mechanics, electricians, blacksmiths, fitters and engine drivers as civilians were also attached to the Royal Engineers. In early July the fourth battalion, which included some of the men who had been involved in the Halifax disaster, arrived under the command of Lieutenant-Colonel G.V. Hart. Their arrival raised the hopes of the officers commanding the blacks for a unified regiment which would be used in combat but the War Office had other plans. With the arrival of the fourth battalion, a draft of 500 officers and men from the first three battalions was ordered on July 26, to East Africa as part of the East African Expeditionary Force at Mombasa.[23] The decision to send the West Indians to East Africa was prompted by the high rate of mortality, which white soldiers from British Rhodesia and South Africa had suffered as a result of disease. Within a few months of their arrival in that area in early 1916, approximately 80 per cent of them were no longer fit for active service.[24] The devastation of the white regiments, plus the fact that the Germans were using their African forces in East Africa effectively, convinced the military officials that sending more white troops to the region was wasteful.

A few weeks after the West Indian detachment left for East Africa, another 100 men were recruited from the first and second battalions in Egypt and transferred to Mesopotamia to be attached to the Indian Expeditionary Force. The proposal to move the West Indians to Mesopotamia and use them as pioneers for railway construction was first raised in June by the Chief of Imperial General Staff.[25] At this point, the general officer, Sir A.J. Murray, opposed the idea emphatically.[26] He argued that the West Indians were of poor physical stock and were not likely to stand the hard work and heat of the desert any better than his young and inexperienced territorials. He also warned that the West Indians saw themselves as representing the West Indies and were anxious to fight and that neither they or their supporters at home wished to see them turned into garrison troops or labour corps. The decision to send a small number of the West Indians in the first instance was thus a compromise as well as a trial to test their usefulness in Mesopotamia. The scheme was successful and hence in December 1916, another draft of 328, made up mainly of Honduran recruits, was also sent to Mesopotamia under the command of Captain (later Major) L.A. Jeffreys. A small draft of 42 Hondurans followed in August 1918. In Mesopotamia the blacks were employed on guard duties at the various Inland Water Transport camps, but about 100 served as clerks, carpenters, blacksmiths, and motor–boat drivers.[27]

A further break-up of the regiment occurred in the middle of July 1916, when the War Office ordered the third and fourth battalions to be transferred from Egypt to France for work as ammunition carriers.[28] Woodhill was informed of the decision by the adjutant-general, Major-General J. Adye, who explained that because the Bermuda Volunteer Artillery had done so well as shell carriers under heavy fire, the War Office had decided to employ two battalions of the BWIR on similar duties.[29] In spite of Woodhill's objections that the West Indians could not endure the cold climate in France, the decision was enforced and on August 28 the two battalions left for Marseilles in France. The fifth BWIR was retained at Mex as the reserve battalion for the first and second battalions. This decision to transfer the two battalions to France to be employed as labourers made it clear that the War Office intended to use the blacks as it desired. This was confirmed on September 28 when it raised the question with the Colonial Office of recruiting 10,000 West Indian labourers, such as those who had worked on the Panama Canal, to construct light railways in France.[30] The War Office made it clear that these men were to be organised into labour battalions.

This declaration by the War Office was reflective of the fact that for the first time since the war began, a coherent policy on the use of non–white colonial labour was being formulated. For the first two years of the war, the army had pursued an improvised and generally counterproductive system which resulted in the over-utilisation of its regular troops in support, rather than in fighting, roles.[31] During the early years of the war, as we have seen, the War Office perhaps, of all government departments, was most fiercely opposed to the employment of blacks on the Western front, and had continually raised doubts about the West Indians' ability and stamina to serve as soldiers in cold climatic conditions. It was now convinced that blacks from the West Indies and Africa could make effective labourers even in climatic conditions which were rapidly deteriorating with the onset of winter. In fact, by this time, the War Office had become the most ardent supporter of bringing blacks to the Western front, even though individual members of the general staff and some officers in the field were strenuously opposed to the idea.[32]

The War Office's dramatic conversion to the use of blacks so frustrated the Colonial Office that Bonar Law angrily suggested: 'I think it is high time that the War Office were told bluntly that the idea of collecting a huge force from the thinly populated West Africa colonies is chimerical ... In any case we could not agree to let a force of West African natives be murdered by France's winter climate simply to make a Royal Garrison Artillery holiday.'[33] It would not be accurate to suggest that the War Office's new attitude was solely a result of the crisis created by the battle of the Somme which began on July 1, 1916, because the manpower problem had been steadily developing since the war began. However, there is no doubt, as Robin Kilson has shown, that it was the 20,000 casualties on the first day and collectively the 420,000 losses between July and November which caused the War Office to resort to the large–scale use of blacks and other colonial troops on the Western front.[34] From 1916 onwards, approximately 193,500 non–white labourers from China, India, South Africa,

Egypt, the West Indies, Malta, Mauritius, the Seychelles and Fiji were employed on the Western front.[35] The War Office's declaration that the new West Indian recruits were to be used as labourers represented an attempt to resolve the anomalous position of the West Indians who, while officially categorised and trained as soldiers, were being confined almost exclusively to manual labour.

Although Bonar Law expressed concern to the War Office about the ability of the West Indians to withstand the winter and alluded to the bad experience of the blacks at Seaford, he nevertheless proceeded to probe the local governors about the possibility of raising further labour contingents for France.[36] Their response was generally sceptical. Governor Probyn of Barbados thought 2,000 men could be raised, provided that they were going to work 'absolutely' outside the danger zone, but warned that this recruiting should in no way interfere with local labour requirements.[37] He also warned that there was little chance of getting men experienced in canal construction as most of those who had returned from Panama were suffering from poor health. Governor Manning of Jamaica expressed concern about the climate in France and indicated that local men would not work for the army labour rates, which were below what the casual labourer could earn in the West Indies.[38]

The strongest protest was made by Governor Haddon–Smith of the Windward Islands.[39] He alluded to the prevalence of diseases such as malaria and venereal diseases, which he believed made the men degenerate and incapable of standing the winter climate. He told the War Office that it would be more economical to recruit 5,000 West Africans than 10,000 West Indians. He also warned that the West Indians were 'of a suspicious nature', especially when they thought they were being asked to do any task with an element of risk, so that it would be difficult to induce them to come forward. As a result of these discouraging responses, the War Office decided to use the West Indians mainly on ammunition supply duties rather than on railway construction, which was eventually done by the Chinese labour corps. The ambiguity of the West Indians' position therefore remained a problematic feature of their existence on the European front. While it was possible for the military officials to adopt various institutional constraints for the other labour corps brought to Europe, the status of the West Indians as soldiers with similar rights to British soldiers, meant that they had to be more circumspectly treated.

Cairo Conference

By late autumn the man–power shortage had become even more acute in both France and Egypt. Consequently, on November 20, 1916, a conference of senior army officials was convened at general headquarters, Cairo, to discuss further recruiting in the West Indies.[40] The meeting was attended by the Chief of General Staff, Major–General A.L. Lynden–Bell, Lieutenant–Colonel C. Woodhill, Major–General J. Adye, and Major–General W. Campbell. The conference was in favour of the idea but agreed in principle that the soldiers should be employed in a suitable climate. More important to the soldiers in Egypt, it was agreed that the first and second battalions should be moved forward and allowed to take a more active part in actual combat. It was also decided that a few selected men should be tested in combat and returned to their unit.

The decision to allow the BWIR to participate in battle was influenced by the discontent which was becoming increasingly evident among the soldiers. The meeting noted considerable dissatisfaction among those in the first and second battalions who had completed their training but were being confined to fatigues and guard duties. This frustration and anger was not surprising because the soldiers had been led to believe that combat was the ultimate way to prove their manhood and many had volunteered for this reason. Meanwhile, letters of complaint from the soldiers about their lack of combat and confinement to manual work were creating anxiety in the West Indies.[41] These issues were raised in the meeting by Woodhill, who argued that the use of the battalions in France as 'more–or–less' labour battalions was doing untold harm to recruitment in the West Indies.[42] In the light of these concerns the conference agreed that if the West Indian colonies were to be further exploited for labour, it was essential for the War Office to drop the idea that the only role of the BWIR should be to carry ammunition and do the general work of labour battalions.[43]

The principal significance of the Cairo Conference was that it cleared the way for those in the BWIR battalions in Egypt to get a limited opportunity to prove their ability as soldiers. Otherwise its impact was minimal because the War Office was determined to use subsequent contingents as labourers in France. Nevertheless, the fact that the officers commanding the West Indian battalions in France rejected the notion of a unified BWIR in Egypt may have been to some extent damaging. Once they received news of the Cairo

Conference, the BWIR officers in France immediately sent a letter of protest to the War Office stating that the blacks in France were happy and did not wish to return to Egypt on any account.[44] For the War Office, this division of opinion between the BWIR officers in France and Egypt proved most convenient because it left them free to make their own decisions.

Given the controversy raging at the official and public level about the use of black soldiers in Europe, it was clearly a psychological plus for blacks and their officers to be stationed on the Western front. Significantly, the assertion that some of the West Indians at Seaford were to be kept in England, while others were to be sent to Africa, had precipitated a fight in which Somerset, the recalcitrant recruit, was involved.[45] It is therefore not surprising that many of the blacks in Egypt envied those in France and wanted representation to be made by the West Indian authorities for some of the soldiers in Egypt to be transferred to 'fiery France' which they believed was 'the real thing'.[46]

As far as the War Office was concerned the opposing positions of the officers and men of BWIR battalions in France and Egypt did not present a dilemma. Manpower pressures and deep–rooted prejudice had made the use of blacks as labourers in France imperative. It thus seems that Woodhill's assertion, echoed unquestioningly by C.L. Joseph, that the want of unanimity practically destroyed the regiment, overstates the importance of the differences of opinion.[47] In fact, Joseph's more plausible assertion that the dispersal of the BWIR was 'possibly to forestall their eventual use as a fighting force on the Egyptian front', clearly contradicts the significance he attaches to this division.[48] It is unlikely that agreement on the part of the officers would have affected the War Office's decision on the matter significantly, since in addition to the manpower problems neither local governors nor the Colonial Office were keen on confrontation with the War Office. All subsequent battalions were therefore employed on the Western front, primarily in non–combatant roles, including building trenches, roads, stretcher–bearers, unloading and loading ships and carrying ammunition to the big guns.[49]

Like other troops who served in the war, the BWIR battalions experienced conditions which were arduous and often very dangerous. They were subjected to enemy artillery bombardment, sniper fire, exploding ammunition dumps and aerial attacks. In France, life was also made uncomfortable by the prevalence of fleas, lice and rats, while in Egypt there were problems with scorpions, lizards, snakes and especially flies. Nevertheless, in every theatre the West Indians consistently displayed courage and discipline and as a result, many won decorations.[50] Their invaluable service and the bravery with which they performed under dangerous conditions were highly commended by senior commanding officers.[51] Douglas Haig, for example, alluded to their fine physique, excellent discipline and high morale.[52] He also praised them for rendering valuable services during main campaigns, including the battles of the Somme, Arras, Messines and the operations near Ypres.[53] Colonial Office officials also expressed satisfaction at the performance of the BWIR and permitted the reports from France, Mesopotamia and Egypt to be published on the grounds that this would 'gratify West Indian sentiment'.[54] The reports generated some excitement in the colonies and the *West Indian* argued that it was vital, for political reasons of course, that the region write the history of its contribution to the war-effort.[55] What the official reports naturally failed to mention, however, was the extent of the suffering and hardship the soldiers were experiencing overseas.

Food and Diet

One of the most persistent complaints of soldiers during the war was that their food was inadequate in terms of both quality and quantity.[56] Although the BWIR were entitled to the same rations as British soldiers, their diet, like that of most soldiers, was often deficient and unsatisfactory.[57] The scale of rations for Europeans and BWIR troops in East Africa, for instance, consisted of: one pound (lb) fresh or frozen meat or one lb preserved or salted meat, one and a quarter lb bread or one lb biscuits or flour with baking powder, quarter lb bacon or two ounces (oz) milk and two oz bacon, five-eighths oz tea, quarter lb jam, three oz sugar (four oz for European troops beyond railhead), half oz salt, one-thirty-sixth oz pepper, one-fiftieth oz mustard, half lb fresh vegetables or two oz dried vegetables.[58] In theory, these rations might have constituted a reasonably balanced diet, but what the soldiers actually received was often far short of the amount stipulated. In France, the medical authorities soon realised that the West Indians required more satisfying and filling foods than the Europeans and hence rice and flour of approximate nutritive value were given instead of other less bulky foods.[59]

The reasons for the problems with the diet were numerous and varied according to region. In East Africa, for instance, the difficulties included the distance from the source of supply; problems with trans-shipment and unloading; the climate; inland transport problems; the rapidity of military movement; inadequate administrative preparation and the complexities of catering to the different and peculiar diets of Europeans, Indians, Africans and other troops.[60] In other areas like Mesopotamia, however, the difficulties with the food were at times partly the consequence of profiteering cooks and orderlies.[61] On board the transport ship *Magdalena* in 1916, according to one soldier, the meat was often 'unfit for human consumption', and the food 'far from palatable owing to the negligence of the cooks'.[62] However, at night plates of mashed potatoes and roast beef were sold at the galley for six pence and one shilling and upwards.[63]

The consequences for soldiers who ate deficient and improperly cooked food were likewise numerous and not always clearly identifiable. Among the earliest symptoms were indigestion and diarrhoea, but malnutrition and its related ailments, could develop in the longer term, thereby significantly reducing immunity to disease. It would not be accurate to suggest that most of the blacks suffered from major dietary deficiencies during their time in the army or even that those who were affected developed the problem solely because of conditions experienced overseas. The multiple problems which plagued the processes of examining and selecting the recruits in the West Indies, plus manpower pressures, contributed to the high incidence of disease overseas, by allowing men who would otherwise have failed a more rigorous selection procedure, to come overseas with the contingents.

Nevertheless, there was a relationship, however complex and unclear, between poor and irregular diet, insanitary and overcrowded conditions, neglect and inadequate medical care, warfare and the harsh climatic conditions, on the one hand, and the high incidence of diseases like measles, scabies, diarrhoea, pneumonia, dysentery, influenza and even malaria and typhoid, on the other. The available statistics do not indicate if these diseases affected officers and the rank and file differently. However, given that officers were usually better fed, housed and cared for medically than the rank and file, it seems likely that the latter suffered more. The devastating impact of disease on the 15,204 men who served in the BWIR is revealed by the fact that of total casualties, 185 or 1.22 per cent were killed or died from wounds, 697 or 4.58 per cent were wounded while 1,071 or 7.04 per cent died from disease.[64] The fate of the BWIR in this regard was by no means unique, for similar statistics exist for the black labour corps and carriers from West Africa and South Africa, but the incompleteness of these figures preclude systematic comparison.[65]

It is hardly surprising that the casualty statistics for the BWIR compare so favourably with those of the British Army in which 5,215,162 men were enlisted and of whom 673,375 or 12.9 per cent were killed and 1,643,469 or 31 per cent wounded, given that West Indians were mostly involved in non–combatant roles.[66] Although precise estimates are difficult if not impossible, any analysis of the casualties of the war must also address the issue of the long–term effects of active military service on the health of the ex–servicemen. Many died after the war as a result of the wounds or diseases they contracted, while others may have had their resistance lowered. In this regard it is worth noting that 1,772 BWIR men returned to Jamaica invalided and by 1920 it was reported that 'a not inconsiderable' number had died.[67]

Allegations that their diet had improved since they entered the army were frequently used to insult the West Indians. In one instance a Jamaican soldier who refused to drink milk from a jug which an Indian labourer had previously drunk from was informed by the medical orderly that the 'damned black bastards' were used to nothing better than that in their own home.[68] The orderly was clearly not prepared to tolerate the Jamaican's attitude of superiority towards the Indian. On the journey back to the West Indies after the war, one Lieutenant Roden likewise told complaining blacks that they were never as well fed as in the army and that at their homes they were accustomed to eating only plantain and yams.[69] The comments may have contained a strong element of truth, especially with regard to the lower–class recruits from the urban areas of the West Indies who did not normally have access to the range of ground provisions and livestock of their peasant colleagues, but this would not have made the assertions less provocative or insulting.

France

If the West Indians believed that their departure from the training camps in England marked the end of their misery they were mistaken. Likewise, later battalions were in for an unpleasant surprise when they arrived overseas.

When the ninth battalion arrived in France in August 1917, it was immediately placed in isolation because of an outbreak of measles which had occurred on board the ship. Reverend (Major) A.E. Horner who served as senior chaplain to the battalion described what ensued at this 'Rest Camp':

> Pouring rain, quite tropical in its violence, and cold winds and mud, such mud as we never see in the West Indies except in hog–pens, became our portion. The mud was quite above our ankles and as we had only our thin uniforms the inevitable result was cold, influenza, pneumonia, fever and ague ... Our tents were far from new, and I have vivid recollections of sleeping with a waterproof sheet over us and not under, to keep out the leakage from the thin canvas, whilst we lay in liquid mud, rendered more objectionable by the absence of the rubber sheet.[70]

After complaints were made, the battalion was provided with new tents with boarded floors which gave temporary relief. Unfortunately, once the battalion left the Rest Camp for its more permanent station outside Ypres, similar climatic problems were encountered, but this time with additional danger from German bombs.[71] Faced with such conditions, much of the enthusiasm and excitement which had marked their departure from the West Indies probably quickly dissipated and gave way to a more profound understanding of the harsh realities of war conditions.

During the winter of 1917, the weather in France deteriorated significantly, creating further problems for soldiers stationed there. The mud and cold pervaded the everyday life of the black soldiers and were commemorated in song and prose in an attempt to normalise and neutralise the horrible conditions by making fun of them.[72] Nevertheless, during the winters of 1916 and 1917, the West Indians suffered severely from the weather and lack of proper housing, heating and clothing which led to numerous cases of sickness and death. The third and fourth battalions suffered greatly from exposure on the first December 1916 and as a result had to be relocated to areas like Boulogne, France, where huts were available. At Boulogne, the sick were sent to the number two Canadian Stationary Hospital, where they were treated for respiratory problems, pneumonia and frostbite. In November, as many as 572 men were sick with sore feet and 333 with bronchitis.[73] Within one month of arriving at Boulogne approximately ten per cent of the battalions were ineffective. This was in spite of the fact that they had been provided with three pairs of socks, two pairs of drawers and vests, fur and leather undercoats, and extra pairs of ankle boots.

The tenth battalion which arrived in France on October 6, 1917, was likewise severely affected by the cold but their suffering began during the voyage overseas. Of the 1,024 men who embarked, four died at sea, 294 were reported on the sick list, and 180 had to be physically carried to camp on arrival in France.[74] Some who had not been accustomed to wearing shoes were unable to walk, and the damp and cold on board ship had led to many cases of 'dry gangrene' and 'trench feet'. In November there was also an outbreak of mumps. Between December 1917 and February 1918, there were ten cases of double amputations, and these continued throughout the winter. In the light of this, on April 20, 1918, the War Office instructed the director-general of medical services in France that all future cases of amputations among the blacks were to be transferred to the Western General Hospital in Liverpool, where the men could be fitted with artificial limbs before returning to the West Indies. Those invalids not requiring orthopaedic treatment were repatriated directly to the West Indies from France.

The suffering of the tenth battalion continued for some time after, as an inquiry resulting from a disturbing letter sent by Harry Brown, the chaplain, to the West Indian Contingent Committee revealed.[75] In his letter, Brown claimed that about 25 per cent of the unit to which he was attached were in hospital as a result of the cold. He further noted:

> I visited a barracks today and discovered German prisoners *warm* and *comfortable*, their rooms adequately heated by stoves and in the same barracks our West India boys on the *extreme* top floor without warming apparatus *of any kind*, cold and suffering. In every room where I saw West Indians there was at least *one* sick man, and in one room two men were stretched on a *concrete* floor both with high temperature and both huddled up trying to secure as much warmth as possible from a couple of blankets. The Officer who took me round described the room as the ghastliest and a perfect abomination. I asked about the stoves and was told that they had been promised. I had the same reply some weeks ago.[76]

On the basis of what he had seen, which in his view was as serious as the Halifax incident, Brown pleaded for an inquiry into the condition of the soldiers. The letter was forwarded to Grindle at the Colonial Office by Everard im Thurn, chairman of the West Indian Contingent Committee, who fully endorsed Brown's allegations and pressed for an investigation and remedial action.

The letter generated much concern among officials in the Colonial Office for both humanitarian and political reasons. The head of the West Indian section, H.T. Allen, regarded the sickness among the troops as regrettable, but was equally concerned that the claim that German prisoners were being treated better than the black soldiers, if found to be true, was likely to provoke 'strong, if not bitter feeling' among the public.[77] Based on discussions with Major de Boissiere, the commanding officer of the battalion, senior staff member E.R. Darnley, also concluded that the conditions did seem very severe for the black troops. Consequently, Brown's letter was shown to Lord Derby so that the matter could be investigated but the chaplain's name was kept confidential.[78] The allegations apparently annoyed Derby, who demanded the name of the Colonial Office's informant so that the War Office could start proceedings against him if they were found to be untrue. He argued that the War Office had frequently received similar allegations which when investigated, were found to be 'absolutely untrue'. Nevertheless, an inquiry was conducted by G.H. Fowke, the adjutant-general in France, who acknowledged that there was a good deal of sickness during the winter months but attributed this more to harsh climatic conditions than to neglect.[79]

When he was questioned by the adjutant-general, the medical officer of the battalion denied the allegation that sick men were lying on concrete floors and claimed that the huts had been provided with stoves, plenty of fuel and three blankets per man. Yet, these denials did not mean that Brown's accusations were untrue. The inquiry revealed that for a time a detachment of soldiers had been located in barracks which experienced delays getting stoves installed. The quartermaster-general who assisted with the investigation believed that this was probably the group that Brown had seen but insisted that the stoves were being installed on the very day that the chaplain visited. Whether or not Brown exaggerated the situation is debatable, but the high rates of sickness and death among the troops in France were to some degree indicative of the strength of his allegations, even though other factors such as fatigue, malnutrition and poor hygiene were probably responsible for the high incidence of bronchial problems and pneumonia. Many of the men may also have been weakened physically and psychologically as a result of their experiences during the journey overseas. Additionally, because antibiotics had not yet been discovered, the best efforts at treating bronchial ailments often proved futile. There were 103 and 150 deaths from pneumonia in 1916 and 1917.[80] It should be noted, however, that according to the estimates of Governor Manning and the Colonial Office, there were approximately 6,000 BWIR men in France in 1917, four or five times the number in 1916.[81] Although the West Indians suffered severely from the weather during both years, the lower rate of deaths in 1917, when climatic conditions had deteriorated, may have been the result of the troops being better clothed, fed, housed and nursed; they may also have developed faster immunity.

As is usually the case with such investigations, no one wanted to accept responsibility for the problems. Major de Boissiere was blamed by the officer commanding the labour group for not immediately indenting for the necessary supplies when the soldiers arrived. Since the major had also complained to the Colonial Office officials, it is difficult to establish who was more responsible. What is clear is that there was a great deal of neglect, bureaucratic inefficiency and procrastination on the part of a number of senior officers. The incident also showed that, as several of the BWIR commanding officers told Governor Manning when he visited them in late 1917, the battalions in France lacked administration and had very little communication and co–ordination with general headquarters or with each other. The War Office's decision to fragment the regiment had left it weak and unable to adopt a common approach to the many similar problems the various battalions experienced.

Nevertheless, in an effort to put the blame squarely on Major de Bois-siere, the adjutant-general reported the matter to general headquarters in Italy, where the battalion had moved, so that, as he put it, 'the question of the *Slackness*' of the major could be investigated.[82] It seems, however, that the matter was not taken any further because the Colonial Office was unwilling to press the issue. Grindle thought that the War Office was probably tired with inquires about 'this not important regiment', and that therefore there was no need to press the matter any further.[83] Meanwhile, West Indians in the Middle East and East Africa were experiencing conditions which in severity equalled or surpassed those of their comrades on the western front.

East Africa

The draft of 500 BWIR men from Egypt arrived at Kilindini, British East Africa, on August 8, 1916 and on the same afternoon left for Handeni, via Korogwe. Initially the authorities proposed that they should be attached to the second WIR, which had reached there two weeks before from Jamaica via Sierra Leone in West Africa but this immediately created a crisis.[84] Since the men of the BWIR viewed themselves as different and of superior status to those of the WIR, the proposal caused many to view the suggestion 'with alarm mingled with disgust'.[85] In the view of the men of the BWIR, the W.I.R was merely a second-class colonial force, whose inferiority was reflected in the lower pay of its members.[86] The men of the BWIR also regarded themselves as the official representatives of the West Indies in the war, since they had been specially raised for that purpose. Moreover, a strong regimental feeling had developed in the BWIR. The intensity of the objections was conveyed in a secret despatch from the officer in charge of the troops in East Africa to the War Office which warned:

> Amalgamation of BWIR with 2nd West India Regiment is found to be so repugnant to former unit that I have deferred. If it is carried out serious trouble will result involving riot and probable murder. Therefore propose to leave units as they are. Some disorder has already been threatened. Trying to discover ringleaders but think feeling so general that it is improbable to fix responsibility on individuals. The unit's well behaved in other respects.[87]

The War Office promptly instructed the general not to merge the units.[88] As a result, the draft of the BWIR-men was allowed to serve as a separate unit on lines of communications and other non–combatant duties, although the group was under the charge of Captain Porter, an experienced WIR officer.[89] The decision was probably also satisfactory to the WIR because some members of that regiment were equally contemptuous of the BWIR and tended to refer them as 'recruits', 'civilians', and 'squashies'.[90]

After their arrival at Handeni, the detachment was broken up into small parties and used to protect the hundreds of miles of road so as to keep open the lines of communication. The task was done under adverse conditions since heavy rains had flooded much of the country. When the various parties were brought together in January 1917, it was discovered that sickness had reduced the draft's effective strength to 300. Moreover, as a result of problems in getting supplies through to them, all ranks had to be put on half rations for three months. During this period an officer's supply for 15 days was 15lb. rice, eight oz. sugar and three oz. tea. Officers were of course better fed than the rank and file. Although wild animals were captured to supplement their diet, the men experienced severe deprivation.[91] Clothing was so scarce that when a man died, applications would be made for his boots and clothes within two hours. Few or no cigarettes were available but on occasion beer and tobacco were issued.

By the middle of June when the weather improved, casualties reflected the suffering the men had endured. On June 20, 1917 the total strength of the unit in East Africa was 18 officers and 587 other ranks, but at one point 207 of them were hospitalised, mainly with malaria.[92] Of the 700 men who had served in the region by October 1918, 44 or 6.28 per cent had died and 300 or 42.86 per cent had been invalided out as unfit for further service.[93] That the soldiers in East Africa were quite demoralised and depressed by this time was made clear by Corporal A.H. De Gannes who wrote home:

> I have never yet experienced such an unhealthy country as (East) Africa. It is absolutely a place of fever, dysentery, etc., and other diseases caused by the mosquitoes, flies and all sorts of insects that Nature can produce ... We are all quite anxious to leave this country as it is nothing compared with England, Egypt and Asia Minor.[94]

He also complained about the long marches, deprivation and soldiers having to sleep on wet mud floors with 'water–proof' sheets, which were at times more like 'blotting paper'. [95] The BWIR–draft was concentrated at Mikesse in December 1917, from where they were ordered to Dar–Es–Salaam to join the second WIR who were also being sent to Egypt. During August 1918, the BWIR–draft left Dar–Es–Salaam on the *Trent,* for the Suez Canal in Egypt. There is no evidence that the transportation of the two groups of soldiers on the same ship caused any conflict but it is possible that some measures were put in place by the authorities to minimise contact.

Palestine\Egypt

Early in July 1917, Woodhill requested and was granted permission from General E.H. Allenby, the commander-in-chief of the Egyptian Expeditionary Force, to attach a detachment of the BWIR machine-gun section to the machine-gun company of the 162nd Brigade, 54th Division, for a period of intensive training on the front line. Their courageous performance in subsequent raids on enemy positions led to the rest of the first and second battalions getting an opportunity to be engaged in combat in the months following.

During this period, the West Indians were severely affected by sickness. Between July 27 and the end of August 18, 4 other ranks and 22 officers of the first battalion were treated for sandfly fever. The fever usually took the form of a sharp attack with a high temperature lasting for about three days and left the patient very weak. The period of convalescence was about a week.[96] In September, six officers and 76 other ranks were sick, mainly with fever and although the health of the battalion improved in October, there were several cases of dysentery and septic sores.[97] In November when the battalion was moved forward to provide support services, many more of the soldiers fell sick. Due to transportation problems, the battalion was forced to leave all winter clothing and great coats behind. Consequently, they had no protection when the weather changed from extreme heat to rain, sleet, hail and ankle–deep mud in the mountains of Judea.

In January 1918, conditions deteriorated further and the battalion was forced to move north to a new camp but having completed three–quarters of the journey, they were forced by the mud, in some areas waist deep, to abandon the transport with all their rations, spare blankets and bivouacs until the following morning. The men had to spend the night under very heavy rains without any shelter.[98] As a result, 92 other ranks were admitted to hospital and of these seven died of exposure. In May, there was an outbreak of fever which caused 59 soldiers to be hospitalised. The most devastating effects of disease were experienced in July 1918, however, when the Spanish Influenza epidemic paralysed all three battalions in Egypt. Over 200 cases were reported among the first battalion, 500 among the second and the fifth also had to be placed in isolation.[99]

Early in August when the epidemic had abated the first and second battalions received orders to proceed to the Jordan Valley, a distance of 50 miles, where they came under the orders of Lieutenant-General Sir H.G. Chauvel, commanding the Desert Mounted Corps.[100] Shortly before the main campaign was launched in the Jordan Valley, the bulk of the troops of the Desert Mounted Corps were withdrawn from the area and a composite force consisting of a cavalry division and eight infantry battalions, of which the two BWIR battalions formed part, were placed under the command of Major–General Sir E.W.C. Chaytor. This force had the task of defending the Jordan Valley line and, more importantly, of driving the Turks from their position and then proceeding to Amman. At the conclusion of the campaign, the West Indians were highly commended by senior officers and their New Zealand colleagues for their bravery and good work. The most important commendation came from Chaytor who wrote in a message to them: 'Outside my own division there are no troops I would sooner have with me than the BWIs who have won the highest opinions of all who have been with them during our operations here.'[101] Such sentiments probably made the West Indians feel that they had finally vindicated themselves and proven their manhood but in view of their casualties, many others may have regarded this experience as a pyrrhic victory.

Again health problems arising from exposure in the field and outbreaks of pneumonia and malaria took a severe toll on the battalions. Of the 2,300 men and 40 officers who took part in the Jordan Valley operations, only 500 returned 'fit', and nearly 90 per cent of the men had contracted 'pernicious' malaria.[102] There was a reduction of 77 per cent among the officers of the first battalion and 73 per cent of the rank and file.[103] On September 20, 1918, the strength of the battalion stood at 35 officers and 1,152 other ranks, but on returning to Jerusalem on October 10, its strength had been reduced especially by malaria, pneumonia and dysentery to eight officers and 311 other ranks. Twenty-three officers and 693 other ranks had to be hospitalised, and 42 died immediately thereafter. The battalion was brought up to strength by large drafts from the fifth and soldiers returning from East Africa. The news of the West Indians' courageous role in the campaign was quickly communicated to the West Indian governors who in turn authorised the publication of the details in the newspapers.[104] The news may have helped to defuse some of the local anxiety over the fact that the blacks had been confined largely to non–combatant duties but by this time some of the soldiers had already written home threatening retaliation for their poor treatment overseas.

Mesopotamia

For those members of the BWIR serving in Mesopotamia the living conditions were just as bad. From this group we get, perhaps, the clearest picture of how the situation affected their attitudes. In his detailed evidence before the Commission of Inquiry into the Belize disturbances of July 1919, the ringleader of the rioters, Corporal S.A. Haynes stated of their experience in Mesopotamia:

> We arrived in the height of the winter season, and were ushered into mud huts without any flooring. We had two blankets, one rubber sheet, and one great–coat in our possession. We experienced trying times in the mud and rain. These huts were always leaking, the roofs not being strong enough to stand the weather ... The accommodation was rotten. In Tanoma, Khora Creek, Inland Water Transport Dockyard, houses were deplorable. It was strongly noticeable that in the huts in which British soldiers were quartered, electric lights, flooring, and winter stoves were introduced, but not in our camp in my time. There was no heat in the camp at all except in the galley. We went to the galley to get warm.[105]

Haynes' statements were corroborated by other witnesses like drummer D.N. McKoy, who stated that they were put into straw huts with mud floors.[106]

The complaints and allegations of discrimination by the black soldiers at Mesopotamia were probably partly justified but their situation was not unique. Conditions in Mesopotamia as in the other theatres of war were bad for all soldiers. The Commission which investigated conditions and services in Mesopotamia between 1915 and 1916 revealed a sordid story of widespread neglect and deplorable conditions which affected troops of every nationality.[107] Following the inquiry, improvements were introduced but British soldiers were the first to benefit while change was slower for the blacks and Indians. With their perceptions shaped by the communal experience of slavery and oppression on the one hand, and striving to secure equal rights with the British soldiers on the other, it was perhaps inevitable that the situation would be viewed as grossly discriminatory by the blacks.

Health Care

It is well documented that the medical treatment of soldiers during the war, especially when they were in the field, was usually quite poor.[108] The care given to black soldiers was similarly bad but some of them believed that it was 'exceedingly poor compared with that paid to British soldiers'. [109] However, prejudice as an explanation of their situation is probably less important than one which emphasises the exigencies of war, class discrimination, neglect and the military's pressing manpower needs. In Mesopotamia, Lieutenant J.D. Kapur of the Indian Medical Service not only absented himself from the patients until such times as he thought fit, but also, even more seriously, treated cases of heat stroke, dysentery, diarrhoea and malaria as trivial even though the blacks were employed on laborious work.[110] Moreover, the doctors often allowed the military officers to dictate who should return to duty or otherwise.[111] Lieutenant O.J. Schofield, for example, would instruct the orderlies not to report more than six men per day on the sick register, even though there were on occasion as many as 15 men suffering from dysentery.[112] Similarly, in Egypt an English doctor called Moseley had a reputation for being tough and constantly on the lookout for 'malingerers'.[113] At that time, army doctors were apparently more willing to accept the complaints of the officer class as genuine, but tended to be dismissive of the complaints of the rank and file.

Although prejudice was pervasive on the Western front, it seems that the West Indians enjoyed a level of medical care fairly comparable to that of white soldiers. In contrast to members of the labour corps who had their own 'native' hospitals, the members of the BWIR usually shared accommodation with white soldiers. Military and Colonial Office officials may have felt some unease with this arrangement but they did not prohibit it because West Indians were regarded as being more 'British' and 'civilised' than other blacks and coloureds. This was not uncontested. A. Fiddian, a senior clerk at the Colonial Office protested for instance: 'It is monstrous that coloured men should be treated in the same hospital as white men. I only hope white nurses have nothing to do with them.'[114] There is no evidence, however, to suggest that any of the other Colonial Office officials shared or approved of Fiddian's extreme views.

There may also have been some hostility from individual staff members to the presence of the blacks in the hospital with whites but significantly, some black soldiers were able to attract additional attention by capitalising on the novelty of their blackness and conforming to the Europeans perception that blacks were child–like and frivolous. Chaplain Horner recalled that if blacks in the hospitals were 'civil and obliging' they immediately became the 'pet and play–thing of both inmates and staff'.[115] In this way, Horner claimed, they were able to enjoy all the 'pleasures' of hospital society. Aubrey Williams, a Trinidadian 'yard boy' whose exploits will be looked at in more detail later, similarly recalled that, during his trip overseas to join the army, the fact that he was a 'nigger' made him the pet of all on board.[116] Although Williams may have ignored the possibility that this was partly because he was a shipmate of the whites, his observation was probably also partly correct. It may be, however, as Horner hints, that some black soldiers did not take too kindly to being treated as pets.

Black West Indian Doctors and Racism: An Example

Black West Indian doctors were at times subjected to the most blatant forms of racism from British officers, as can be seen in the case of J. McDowall, a Vincentian doctor who enlisted in England in November 1917 and was given a commission by the War Office. He served with the sixth and ninth battalions and later with the base depot of the BWIR but in September 1918, was attached to the Staff Marseilles Stationary Hospital and subsequently transferred to the Ambulance Transport, *Egypt*.[117] His placement was regarded as deeply offensive by Major F.F. Middleweek, the Officer Commanding the transport, who requested his transfer but this was refused. Undaunted, Middleweek sent a letter to surgeon-general, Sir William Donovan, which reiterated his objection to the presence of McDowall:

> I wish to let you know that when we left Marseilles on February 15, Captain J. McDowall, RAMC, – a West Indian Negro – was put on board by the Assistant Director of Medical Services, (Base) Marseilles for permanent duty. I greatly resent this and consider that an Ambulance Transport is not a suitable unit for him to belong to, where the limits of space are so circumscribed, and where his presence on deck and in the dining saloon is greatly resented. Moreover, it is not at all pleasant for Nursing Sisters in having to work with him in the

wards. I should feel greatly indebted to you if you would kindly transfer this Officer to another sphere of duty.[118]

Under the King's Regulations, Middleweek was obliged to show McDowall the report at some point before it reached the level of the War Office but this was not done.[119] McDowall only found out about the letter because the assistant director of Medical Services at Marseilles sent him a copy in an attempt to rectify what was probably not a procedural error.

Not surprisingly, the letter caused McDowall considerable distress particularly since, as he protested to the West Indian Contingent Committee, the report did not charge him with any lack of professional ability or conduct unbecoming of an officer and a gentleman.[120] He also could not understand why members of the Indian Medical Service were allowed to serve on the ambulance transports, while a West Indian holding the King's Commission was discriminated against. The West Indian Contingent Committee protested in turn to the Colonial Office and warned that the incident would generate much resentment among members of BWIR and people in the colonies once they learnt of it.[121] There was, however, very little that the Colonial Office could do because by the time these protests were being registered, McDowall had already been removed from the ship, after having made only two voyages. This experience was, however, just one aspect of the multiple and complex set of relationships which affected the West Indians overseas.

Military Relations

In all military institutions, a codified system of discipline, punishment and reward maintains conformity. For this reason, among others, the army often comes close to a 'total institution', that is, 'a place of residence and work where a large number of like–situated individuals, cut off from the wider society for an appreciable period of time, together lead an enclosed, formally administered round of life'.[1] The British army with its highly bureaucratic and hierarchical system, harsh methods of punishment and close surveillance therefore typified the total institution. However, even though there was a high degree of standardisation and regularisation in the disciplinary code structure, inequalities in attitudes towards and treatment of the different races, classes and ethnic groups did exist.[2] The major problems of discrimination, however, were not to be found here, but rather, in the practical application of army regulations in an environment in which stereotypes of race and class were prevalent. Even though the army structure and system of accountability did in many instances eventually vindicate the rights of all soldiers, adjustment into army life was usually more difficult and precarious for the black soldier than for his white counterpart.

Drawn rapidly from civilian life where they worked as teachers, labourers, clerks, and so on, this sudden venture into army life and discipline inevitably produced some difficulties of adjustment. Chaplain Horner recalled that: 'As long as soldiering meant bands and uniform and a certain element of mild heroism all was well; but when it meant smartness, neatness and, above all, punctuality – a thing the West Indian knows but slightly – and, again, not "answering back", for he loves to argue, it was not so well. There was "too much of rules" – as it was put.'[3] Another eye–witness, quoted in the *Manchester Guardian* marvelled when he saw some recruits from Demerara 'mastering the difficulties of the English words of command and suffering the agonies of having their feet confined within boots'.[4] Both observers were amazed at how in a short time, these 'raw recruits' were transformed by army discipline and war conditions into smart–looking soldiers. Other West Indian blacks like Aubrey Williams who joined English regiments complained that the physical aspects of their training were quite difficult.[5]

In this process of adjustment informal pressures were as important as the formal regulations of the army. Under the conditions of war it was critical that informal pressures rapidly induced conformity to military values and regulations. A central problem confronting the army was how to turn the great numbers of civilians required for the prosecution of the first 'total war' into persons capable of killing or dying on command. It was imperative that volunteers be made to understand that even though they were being called upon to sacrifice their lives in defence of 'civilised society', they were expected, in a major way, to abandon its most cherished humanitarian principles and the 'civilising' influences of civilian life for the duration of the war. To function competently, the soldier had to learn to suppress his own feelings of caring for the enemy. Perhaps more critically, there was no time for extensive schooling and indoctrination in the history, traditions, and practices of the army which would in peace-time have socialised recruits. Intensive 'shock treatment' was therefore a critical part of training and discipline. The process of mortification whereby the individual is harassed, deprived of his identity and forced into conformity by punishment, obloquy or ridicule in order to make him feel a close identity with the norms of the institution constituted a major aspect of the 'shock treatment'.[6]

Drill sergeants, described by Cynthia Enloe as, 'masters of military socialisation and psychological manipulation', were the persons mainly responsible for converting the civilian volunteers into soldiers.[7] In the military these sergeants are usually feared because of the intensity of the pressures they are able to inflict on the recruit. Dupuch recounts the terror tactics used by one such training instructor at Alexandria, Egypt:

> He told us he had heard there were some tough men in our lot. He wanted them to know that no one ever broke the British Army. It cost nothing to dig a hole in the desert and shove the body of a bad man in it. "If you play rough", he warned, "we will break you. All you can do is break your bleeding mathi (mother's) heart back in your mountains in Jamaica". I have forgotten his name, but the men called him Cock because, when he called the parade to attention, he tucked his swagger

stick under his arm and marched off until he found a mound on which to crow. This man seemed to have eyes in the back of his head. Every day, while marching away from the parade, he would suddenly spin around and shout: "Sergeant Ashley (this was the name of a Jamaican sergeant), that man fourth from the left in the rear rank moved; throw him in the clink and bring him before the [Commanding Officer] tomorrow morning". No one could figure out how, with his back turned to the parade, he could see a man move in the rear rank of one thousand men. It was only after the war, when I had become more worldly wise, that I figured it out. No one had moved. This was only a part of his terror tactics.[8]

These threats were important in inducing compliance. The fact that privates were painfully aware of their own vulnerability before authority was well expressed by one British soldier, who wrote that wherever one more rash and intemperate than the rest had rebelled against a superior officer, the wiser and more experienced would say to him: 'Don't be a fool, if you go against the army the army will break you.'[9]

While there is no doubt that this approach was vital in shaping the recruits into the type of soldiers the army desired, they were not sufficient by themselves to achieve that objective. Army officers also mobilised notions of masculinity in this process. Most armies project the image and are usually perceived by society as institutional spheres for the cultivation of masculinity. War, and in particular, combat, is seen as providing the social space for its validation.[10] As such, a major objective in the training of volunteers is to strip the trainees of most or all of their 'feminine' attributes, including sympathy. Thus, drill sergeants are notorious for their propensity to devastate and humble rebellious volunteers by contemptuously referring to them as 'women' or homosexuals.[11] Such imagery is vital in inducing conformity because although notions of masculinity and femininity are subject to different interpretations and reinterpretations, they are nearly always defined in contrasting relation to each other. In other words to be a 'man' means not to be 'feminine' or passive and gentle, but to be aggressive and possess all the other attributes of manliness.

Yet, paradoxically, recruits are expected to remain passive when the drill sergeant refers to them, as 'women' or verbally abuse and threaten them as in the case of the black soldiers in Egypt. It is this apparent contradiction which forms the basis of much resistance by recruits because by remaining submissive, the recruit is in fact not only taking on a typically 'feminine' role, but also, acknowledging his inferiority and loss of civil rights within the army's hierarchy and class structure. In the army, notions of masculinity are given more forceful and exaggerated expression, but this takes place within the context of severe authoritarianism. Significantly, however, most total institutions do not really look for complete cultural victory, but, instead, 'create and sustain a particular kind of tension between the home world and the institutional world and use this persistent tension as strategic leverage in the management of men'. [12] The tension, for example, in the sexual imagery used by drill instructors gives the army a powerful means with which to control the men because, as Sharon Macdonald argues, 'the insecurity it generates can be countered only by the man proving his masculinity along the lines laid down by the military ideology. Were he already assured of his manly status, he wouldn't have the same incentive to demonstrate it; his sexual status is always *on the line*.' [13] While the drill sergeants excelled in these demonstrations of power in order to enforce discipline, power within the military also functioned automatically at a more discreet level. This is often not grasped by military historians who generally emphasise punishment as the central reality of military discipline. As Michel Foucault has argued, however, power in modern Western societies operates not simply by means of physical punishment but also through procedures of examination, normalisation, observation, control and interrogation; these constitute the techniques of 'disciplinary power'. [14] In *Discipline and Punish,* Foucault shows how in both nineteenth-century prisons and the army, the functioning of power not only has an 'automatic' quality but also operates discreetly. [15] According to Foucault:

He who is subjected to a field of visibility, and who knows it, assumes responsibility for the constraints of power; he makes them play spontaneously upon himself; he inscribes in himself the power relation in which he simultaneously plays both roles; he becomes the principle of his own subjection. By this very fact, the external power may throw off its physical weight; it tends to be non–corporal; and, the more it approaches this limit, the more constant, profound and permanent are its effects; it is a perpetual victory that avoids any physical confront-ation and which is always decided in advance. [16]

In this way, he argues, 'the efficiency of power, its constraining force have, in a sense, passed over to the other side – to the side of its surface of application.'[17] Although Foucault's formulation probably understates the content of fear and physical coercion in the army's disciplinary strategy, his insights into the dynamics of the functioning of power are nevertheless important. His perspectives on power are equally instructive in understanding the processes by which primary groups are formed and function within the army.

The process of socialisation ensures that individuals are made susceptible to the requirements of the existing power structure, while the principle of 'hierarchy' functions to reinforce this ideological dominance by placing the imperatives of the formal command structure beyond their effective challenge.[18] However, the army's strong emphasis on loyalty makes the primary group the immediate and main focus of an individual's attention and loyalty. The formation of these primary groups is usually accompanied and facilitated by the more subtle process of male bonding normally expressed in a multiplicity of relationships, such as those between best friends, task peers, lovers, professional mentors, drinking partners and inhabitants of the same dwelling. During World War One, bonding was encouraged by the extensive periods the soldiers spent in the trenches in much the same way that seamen or the slaves being shipped from Africa to the Caribbean developed lasting friendships from the basis that they were 'shipmates'. The resultant group bonding, referred to as 'mateship' in the context of the Australian soldiers and diggers, was heightened by the distance from home in space and time, and the impossibility in many cases of home leave.[19]

In these primary groups, an inner-core usually decides, through a process of internal regulation, what is permissible behaviour for its members and ensures that they comply with this view of the social world by imposing a variety of sanctions upon deviant conduct. These may include mild ridicule or non-co-operation or even out-right rejection. Thus, as we will see, the less educated members of the BWIR were at times subjected to pressure from their more 'intelligent' comrades to function in a more disciplined manner as well as to speak 'proper' English. Peer pressure was also exerted to maintain group excellence and competitiveness during training. A BWIR officer explained that if a soldier could not endure the strain during marching he would experience ridicule from the entire battalion with such remarks as: 'But look he; is wha' you lef' you country fa'. Po' fellow; is the boots mek so.

He use to walk barefoot an' now they gie he boots he ent able.'[20] Such comments disciplined the men and forced them to conform with the goals and aspirations of the group by challenging their individual and collective 'manhood'. Crucially, however, the primary group also provides the individual with the knowledge of how best to cope and function within the strictly disciplined setting of the military.

The importance of primary groups in the military goes beyond merely facilitating adjustment and providing for the welfare of the individual. They also motivate members to fight and perform better as units in combat.[21] At the same time, these primary groups can also be dangerous to the army's stability and cohesion. Colonial leaders were always conscious that these groups represented a potential source of mutiny, particularly when loyalty to the sub–group persistently transcended allegiance to the army as a collective institution. It was for this reason that colonial authorities in Africa and India often mixed their 'native' regiments with men of different, even antagonistic, ethnic groups. This is reminiscent of the way planters in the West Indies would select slaves from different African groups to help reduce the possibility of insurrections.

These various tactics and constraining forces were critical factors in conditioning the attitudes of the black soldiers to their experiences overseas. Yet, their responses were not always muted by fear or restrained by existing power relations. This was particularly the case when they experienced verbal and physical abuses because of their colour. This racial discourse was rooted in and derived its potency from racist practices. Black soldiers were usually aware that racist language could readily be translated into racist violence, in spite of the army's emphasis on discipline. One veteran wrote of the 'consciousness of discrimination' against 'native troops', which they felt in the army.[22]

If black soldiers needed any reminder of how tenuous their position and status was within the army it was provided by the sight of Indian soldiers and officers being severely ill–treated and of Chinese labourers being driven at their work by British privates with sticks.[23] The abuse of an Indian sergeant by a British private led Dupuch, for example, to the painful realisation that, 'the lowest, dirtiest, scrubbiest Englishman was considered superior to the finest Indian.'[24] More importantly, such incidents acted as a catalyst to political consciousness. Thus, Dupuch became peculiarly aware that the British officials were 'insensible to the heartbreaks that the dark races had endured in patience for an incredibly long time', and began to dream of the time when he might be instrumental in helping to break down racial barriers in the Bahamas.[25] For this reason he considered the time he spent in the Bahamas legislature working towards this vision as the greatest achievement of his life; his accomplishments in this regard were by any standard remarkable.[26]

Although the West Indians considered themselves on a higher social scale than the West African, Indian and Chinese labour units, the abuse of these groups was a constant reminder that their own social position was also always under threat. Verbal and physical attacks on the black soldiers brought this home in a most powerful manner. On one occasion in Mesopotamia, four BWIR tally clerks bathing in an enclosed area reserved for British troops were driven out by a British officer who told them that 'no niggers' were allowed to bathe in that section.[27] Similarly, a major incident took place in August 1916 when a group of tired and hungry BWIR men marched into 'A' camp at Garbbary. When they arrived at the YMCA singing 'Rule Britannia', they were confronted by a number of British soldiers and rudely asked: 'Who gave you niggers authority to sing that! Clear out of this building; only British soldiers admitted here.'[28] This resulted in a fight involving 20 of the soldiers. When the matter was reported to the officer in charge, the only consolation the BWIR soldiers received was his assurance that steps would be taken to avoid similar disturbances.

These were by no means isolated incidents, for blacks in Egypt and Mesopotamia were frequently tormented and taunted by British troops attempting to make them lose their temper. Common racial slurs included 'nigger, nigger, what you've come here for' and 'Bloke, see a monkey in Khaki.'[29] Such insults were particularly hard for middle–class black soldiers who had taught many of these same British soldiers to read and write and who were then ridiculed by them.[30] The experiences of blacks who served in the military of other countries such as the United States and Canada were strikingly similar. For example, Private A.W. Stoute, a Barbadian, who complained that he was in 'a horrible state of hell' because of racial harassment in the twelfth Reserve battalion of the Canadian Expeditionary Force in England, was granted a transfer to the BWIR.[31]

One response adopted by the black soldiers was to write to local newspapers urging for 'something hot' to be written against race prejudice.[32] Their intention was to mobilise West Indian public opinion in the hope of getting proper representation and possibly relief from the daily harassment. In fact, soldiers sometimes accused the papers and the local public of getting them into these difficulties by having urged them to enlist. One soldier, writing to T. Albert Marryshow, editor of the *West Indian*, complained angrily:

> You have done a great deal to get us into this mess. Here we are, thousands of miles away from home, and what do you all care about us? Where is the interest in us? We wonder whether the folks at home know what we have to endure in a soldier's life? If they do, they should have shown us their sympathy.[33]

Although the *West Indian*, was sympathetic to the cause of the soldiers, and such complaints, according to the paper, often brought its editors to the verge of tears, the letters were often filed away unpublished so as not to embitter the local population or paralyse the local war-effort.[34] The danger that they might be prosecuted like the *Argos* in Trinidad was probably a deciding factor, even though the editors claimed that the threat of being jailed was, as far as they were concerned, the least of their troubles. But in the light of their struggle for political reform, it seems reasonable to believe that the overriding factor was the desire not to do anything that would jeopardise the movement for representative government.

The military authorities also made efforts to enforce segregation in the various areas where blacks served. In one instance in Mesopotamia, a BWIR sergeant and 30 men were refused entry into a tent where church services were being conducted and had to take seats outside.[35] Similarly, in France, attempts were made to exclude the BWIR soldiers from the YMCA tents. Army officials there tried to impose segregation regulations which had been specifically designed for the South Africans and other black corps on the West Indians. On this occasion, the white NCOs of the BWIR refused to enter the YMCA tents until the blacks were also permitted entrance.[36] This objective was only achieved when the West Indian Contingent Committee intervened, arguing that the West Indian soldier, 'though generally of colour' was of 'a very different educational and social status from the West African and some other soldiers from the Crown Colonies'.[37] The committee's argument reflected the manner in which the officials at times had to incorporate class distinctions into their discourse on race in order to resolve the paradoxes which occasionally surfaced in the discourse and practice of racism.

On some occasions, retaliation to these verbal insults was spontaneous and violent. In one case, a European soldier was given a sound beating by a black soldier for referring to him as a 'black son of a bitch'.[38] In another, a white soldier grabbed a piece of bread from a BWIR corporal named Willoughby, who snatched it back. The European then struck Willoughby in the face but he returned the blow. The orderly in charge of the hospital where the incident took place laid a charge against Willoughby for striking a white man. While the white soldier was set free, the BWIR corporal was demoted to the ranks.[39] These incidents suggest that while the system of punishment was heavily weighted against them, the responses of the black soldiers though circumscribed were at times far from passive.

Their responses may also have been manifested in a multiplicity of other forms such as screams, wails, grunts, scatting and wordless singing which are common to black culture and indicate the struggle to extend communication beyond words. The argument can be taken even further to include acts of non–verbal communication. Social psychologists have long recognised that in human social interaction, speech is accompanied by an intricate set of vocal and gestural non–verbal signals, which affect meaning, emphasis and other aspects of utterance.[40] These would also include acts of violence. It is thus possible to view the aggression of the black soldiers as a form of social and political protest. Violence resulted from and reflected their powerlessness to change a racially hostile environment, which was only partly mitigated by the rules of the military. Violence could create the social space for these soldiers: there is little doubt that the white soldier who was soundly thrashed by his black colleague for calling him a 'black son of a bitch' would have quickly received the message. However, such action was potentially dangerous, as it could have invited retaliation.

Not every soldier was willing to press his case with such aggression. Some sought a form of quiet accommodation within the system. One Barbadian soldier, when questioned about racism denied ever having experienced any racial insults; in his view 'anything you looked for is the same thing you got'.[41] Quiescence may have been the product of centuries of colonialism and the feelings of inferiority which it engendered because legal emancipation had not brought about a corresponding psychological liberation. A more immediate, and perhaps more realistic explanation, suggests that it was simply a way of avoiding trouble, particularly as the system of discipline was not often enforced in their favour and was often fairly arbitrary. There is a certain similarity to the way that the inmates in the mental institutions studied by Erving Goffman attempted to cope with and preserve their identities within the institutional setting. Goffman found that in appearing to conform, inmates were able to hide behind the rules and regulations and thereby preserve an area of private space in which they maintained a degree of self-respect.[42] Similar strategies were adopted by slaves in the Caribbean and America to cope with and resist the dehumanisation implicit in the institution of slavery.

The problem with such postures was that in the various theatres of war, race prejudice was pervasive and ever–present. Consequently, trouble and confrontation were inevitable for their colour remained the fundamental issue, and as one soldier noted, the major distinguishing thing about them.[43] Therein lay part of the problem, for as Marryshow dramatically warned his audience at a meeting of the Representative Government Association in Grenada, the average English public man knew nothing 'of the West Indies beyond visions of half–naked savages grinning under palm–trees, or hiding in ambush in a jungle of sugar–cane, and white men making the best of fitful slumbers in armed bungalows for fear of savage attack'.[44] Marryshow may have exaggerated and failed to reflect the range of impressions of blacks held by the English public, but in general the British were ignorant of black culture and racial stereotypes, such as the myth of the lazy negro, were prevalent. His powerful contrasting imagery which suggests that the British impression of blacks was generally unfavourable whatever form it took was equally valid. It was caricature rather than truth that was the hallmark of the English impression of the negro.[45] Crucially, as Marryshow was suggesting, it has been these caricatures and stereotypes which historically have provided much of the rationale for the unrelenting subordination and persecution of blacks by whites.

In a situation where blacks were seeking to assert their equality with whites, there was a certain inevitability that these adverse stereotypes would be conjured up as the basis for denial and rejection. The problem was compounded by the fact that many West Indians had been so intensely indoctrinated that they not only regard themselves as 'British' but had even come to view England as their 'motherland', which every loyal citizen dreamt of visiting. However, to many white soldiers, the notion of being black and 'British' was inconceivable, unpalatable and unacceptable. At the same time, black–white encounters in Europe have been informed by a complexity of other factors, including class considerations so that the antagonistic relations cannot be reduced to any single explanation. Nevertheless, racism had a powerful potency in the encounter and daily relations of black and white soldiers but functioned within the specificities of the military environment.

The antagonism was not merely because of the conflicting ways in which both groups perceived themselves and the other, or the fact that the heritage of slavery and the felt presence of racism made the blacks view many things in racial terms. Conflict was also related to the fact that racism in its various forms had the effect of undermining or threatening the 'masculine' identity of the black soldiers by seeking to categorise them not only as less than human, but also as less 'manly' than white soldiers. It is instructive in this regard to note that Jonathan Rutherford has argued that violence is a common response when masculine identities are under threat.[46] This is significant because, as noted previously, in the military extraordinary emphasis is placed on proving masculinity. Some confrontations may therefore have reflected the attempts of black soldiers, as one noted, to protect their 'manhood'.[47] Feminist scholars have also argued that, 'in racial, ethnic and nationalist struggles, oppressed groups tend to stress "manhood" themes, rationalised on the basis of the minority male's lack of power within patriarchal societies.'[48] Yet, white soldiers were also socialised in the norms of heterosexual masculinity and some probably felt that they were exercising or protecting their white 'manhood' by launching verbal and physical attacks, especially on the more confident and assertive black soldiers.

Although antagonism between black and white soldiers was common, there was also friendly intercourse. Friendships often sprang up during the discussions and interactions which accompanied work, such as loading and firing of the big guns. In France, for example, conversations generally initiated by the black soldiers during work or at the guns were cemented later on by a visit to the regimental canteen where experiences were exchanged and opinions expressed.[49] Male bonding and the development of 'comradeship' also contributed to more amicable relations. Norman Manley's experience among a group of British recruits at East Deptford, in London, illustrates the manner in which these processes helped to overcome racial barriers.

> I got to know them very well and a great affection developed between us ... If you were broke and did not have a cigarette to smoke they

would not hesitate to give you one if they had two. They showed an innate courtesy, I suppose because we liked each other, and soon found out that I did not like being called "Darkie" as came natural to them, and I have heard a real tough guy get hold of a new arrival, a casualty replacement, who automatically called me "Darkie", and take him aside and say, "Don't call him that; he doesn't like it. We call him Bill and we like him."[50]

The situation varied, of course, and Manley was to suffer very rough times when he joined another unit in France. Nevertheless, Manley's experience on this occasion is instructive not least because it suggests people were not necessarily being racist when they used racist language; yet this unconscious use of insulting language could have led to a great deal of mutual misunderstanding. The diminution of white mistrust, misunderstanding and even dislike and the establishment of mutual appreciation was often facilitated by the high level of literacy and fluency of many black soldiers, particularly the former school teachers, although sometimes it had the opposite effect on less talented whites and may have been why they abused their black teachers in racist language.[51]

While racial prejudice frequently characterised black-white relations, it seems to have been less important as a factor generating antagonism, between the black soldiers and their comrades from New Zealand, Australia and France. There is some limited evidence to suggest that the relationship between the BWIR black soldiers and these white soldiers and particularly the New Zealanders and Australians were more amicable and friendly. This was noted by army officials, the press and the black soldiers themselves.[52] One black soldier even credited the Australians with being instrumental in getting the BWIR men at Egypt to 'do something else than pushing wheelbarrows'.[53] In fact, the Australians on occasions assisted the West Indians in their fights with the British troops.[54] It is however very difficult to make a general argument about or differentiate between British and Australian racial attitudes towards the West Indians out of scattered anecdotal evidence.

It would most certainly be an over simplification to attribute the Australians' apparently better relations with the West Indians to an absence of racist tendencies. Indeed, Governor Eyre Hutson of British Honduras was quite surprised at the allegations that blacks received much better treatment

from the Australians than from the British. He recalled that while he was
serving in Fiji, it was the Australians rather than the British, who usually
ill–treated the Fijians.[55] E.R. Darnley at the Colonial Office minuted in
support of the governor that he knew of instances where Australians abused
blacks.[56] Both the governor and Darnley were correct in suggesting that
racism was also imbedded in Australian society. Avner Offer has also documented the extent to which Australian society and government adopted a
policy of exclusion to prevent non–white and especially Asian labour from
entering the country.[57]

Acrimony and violence, however, characterised the encounters between
the West Indians and the white South African troops. The relative freedom
of the West Indians and their assertiveness represented major areas of irritation and contradiction for many South Africans, who generally considered
all blacks as 'niggers' who had to be 'kept in their place' socially, politically,
economically and if possible, psychologically. On several occasions, according to Cipriani, the South Africans refused to play cricket or take part in
athletics with the West Indians because of the colour–bar.[58] Consequently,
conflict often developed when their intercourse was not regulated by the
army.

This was very evident in Egypt where West Indian and South African
contingents were stationed at Ismaelia as peace keepers during the outbreak
of the Egyptian revolution.[59] The intensity of the animosity and violence in
their encounters was succinctly expressed by BWIR Sergeant Percival
Vasquez, who recorded that both groups were 'deadly opposed'. [60] They
clashed frequently in 'serious free fights'. Significantly, because the black
soldiers had generally amicable relations with the Egyptians, they were at
times assisted if they were outnumbered by the South Africans.[61] As a result
of the conflicts, both groups were confined to barracks and, following an
investigation, had their leave days alternated in order to avoid further
confrontation.

The relationship between the black soldiers and the German prisoners of
war was, not surprisingly, also often strained and contentious as a result of
pervasive British anti–German propaganda. Moreover, the black soldiers
were quite aware of the Germans antipathy towards them. Sergeant A.
Headley of the second battalion BWIR recalled that the Germans usually
referred to the West Indian soldiers as the 'Black Devils'.[62] Indeed, from the
onset of hostilities Germany had, for racial and manpower reasons,

expressed horror and indignation at the fact that France had brought its black battalions to the Western front and charged that this was a serious violation of international law.[63] Not only were the black South African troops on that front shelled by the Germans; propaganda leaflets were also dropped during these raids warning blacks that they would be singled out for special destructive treatment since they had no reason for being involved in a European war.[64] It is thus not surprising that Norman Manley recalled the terror he felt at the prospect of being taken as a German prisoner–of–war on an occasion when it appeared as if the Germans were going to invade their position: 'I loaded my rifle, the rifle I had thought never to use, with care and prepared to sell my life dearly, not in the cliché sense, but for the practical reason that I was half–Negro and the stories of what happened to coloured men taken prisoner of war were very grim and of course believed by all of us implicitly.'[65] Fortunately, his detachment was able to elude the advancing German army.

Close encounters between blacks and Germans were therefore likely to be contentious and violent. On one occasion in France a group of German prisoners encountered a party of BWIR Bahamians carrying colleagues for burial and made some derogatory remarks in German about the dead soldiers. Given the mutual antagonism, and the rage and sense of loss that soldiers in the war feel over the loss of a comrade and the respect accorded a burial, the German prisoners could not have made a more serious blunder. Their comments were quickly translated by one of the black soldiers, who unfortunately for the Germans understood the language. The result was that the Germans received a severe beating from the West Indian soldiers.[66]

Crucially, the West Indians' perception of themselves as being 'British' was often a major cause of conflict and misunderstanding with the Indians, Chinese, Africans and other officially classified labour battalions. In their efforts to assert their perceived and real rights and claims to being British and members of the King's army, the West Indians often resented being forced, whether by circumstances or deliberate intent, to interact with the labour corps. In Egypt and Mesopotamia they objected strenuously to being forced to live in huts or to being treated in hospitals with 'Africans and Asiatics, who were ignorant of the English language and Western customs'.[67] Slavery and British cultural hegemony had led many West Indians to view Africa as 'uncivilised', and Britain as the epitome of civilisation.

During slavery the process of creolisation and the conflict it created between African and 'creolised' slaves had not only made it easier for planters to practise divide–and–rule strategies but also served to undermine slave rebellions. This misunderstanding persisted after slavery and in 1860, Anthony Trollope claimed that: 'The West Indian Negro knows nothing of Africa except that it is a term of reproach. If African immigrants are put to work on the same estate with him, he will not eat with them or drink with them, or walk with them. He will hardly work beside them, and regards himself as a creature immeasurably the superior of the new comer.'[68] In the light of research by Patrick Bryan and other historians which has established that throughout the nineteenth century there was a strong 'Africanist' tradition in the West Indies, Trollope was clearly exaggerating, but deep divisions between creoles and Africans did exist.

In France the conflict was also present because the West Indians had an irritating habit of 'rubbing in' the fact that they, as soldiers, were on an 'immeasurably higher social scale' than members of the labour corps who were merely wage labourers with very little status.[69] West Indian self–esteem depended on a conception of themselves as soldiers, rather than labourers, whatever the actual nature of their work. They found it psychologically important to differentiate between themselves and those classified as labourers, and to distinguish between 'civilised' and 'uncivilised' blacks. This profoundly affected the relationship between the BWIR and the colonial labour battalions. In fact, in Mesopotamia West Indian soldiers were in charge of gangs of Indian labourers.[70] At the same time, members of the various labour corps contributed to the bitter relations by objecting to the West Indians' freedom in the use of cafes, and by 'standing outside such places and making rather heated remarks as the West Indians, with an unnecessary amount of "gusto", retired from their refreshments'.[71]

Although the evidence is rather limited there is also some indication that tension and conflict marked the relationship between white officers, particularly the NCOs, and black NCOs. There is little in the primary sources about the specific nature of the relationship between these groups in the BWIR but given the experiences of some West Indians NCOs in British regiments, it is possible to suggest that relations may have been at times contentious. Some British NCOs felt threatened by the presence of blacks of equal rank. Manley wrote of his tumultuous experience in one such regiment:

When I joined, I joined a mounted unit and I was part of the most mobile part of it, the ammunition supply. I had grown up with horses and horse–drawn vehicles, and knew more about them than miners and town–bred Londoners, so naturally enough within a month I was a Lance–Corporal or Bombardier as they were called in the Artillery, and by the time we left for France I was promoted Corporal. Here I came up against violent colour prejudice. The rank and file disliked taking orders from a coloured N.C.O and their attitude was mild by comparison with that of my fellow NCOs. Corporals and Sergeants resented my sharing status with them. They were more spiteful and later conspired to get me into trouble. It was only the Officer class that I could expect to behave with ordinary decency and both aspects of this phenomenon I fully understood.[72]

In France this conflict persisted and intensified, so that Manley finally decided to give up his stripes and proceeded to another regiment where he was made a gunner. He was subsequently awarded the Military Medal for bravery. Manley's experiences clearly suggest that army stripes had little effect in the face of colour prejudice, or in fact exacerbated it.

That senior officers accorded Manley, and presumably other black officers, more respect is not surprising, and not merely because distinctions of class, status and privilege meant that they were less or perhaps not at all threatened by Manley's rank. Like other white soldiers, they were often caught between the values of the military and the prejudice of the wider society. However, as senior functionaries they adhered more strictly to military principles, its code of conduct and the need to get the job done. Respectable behaviour by senior officers was also a result of the long–standing tradition in the British army that an officer should have the honour, integrity and other attributes of a 'gentleman'. Adherence to these standards of behaviour was regarded by the army as necessary for maintaining the harmony of the officers' mess and a prerequisite in earning the respect and obedience of the rank and file. [73]

Although these assumptions were increasingly questioned during the late nineteenth century as the army felt the impact of social and technological change, the officer–gentleman tradition remained pervasive.[74] But this did not preclude the occasional display of racial hostility. Indeed, notions of black inferiority and their child–like mentality informed the War Office's selection of officers for the black troops.[75] Thus, senior officers were exclusively of white West Indian or British extraction. Some officers had been commanders of the older WIR and C.L.R. James has argued, with some bitterness, that a number were a handicap to the BWIR since they had originally been recruited from Sandhurst failures. In his view officers like Colonel Barchard should have been placed on the retired list long before the war started.[76]

In all armies, issues of power and prestige are major concerns among officers. Consequently, white officers commanding black soldiers were often considered inferior in status by their colleagues in charge of white troops. At the same time, these officers of black troops were imbued with notions of class and race superiority and these informed their relationship with the black soldiers. On the one hand, they were at times insultingly patronising. Horner, for example, recalled that officers viewed the black West Indian not only as a soldier, but also a 'very interesting character study, full of quaint humour and cheery friendliness' and 'simple wisdom'.[77] On the other hand, race and class prejudice was coupled with British military discipline which placed heavy emphasis on strict control from above, even at the cost of alienating the rank and file. Thus, soldiers were at times upbraided in a 'manner which was positively sulphuric', and at other times even physically abused.[78] Such displays of naked power may not have been unrelated to their attempts at gaining self–gratification and compensation for their inferior status within the officer core. Instead of ensuring discipline, these hostile attitudes probably undermined morale. For instance, Captain George Dawson, an Englishman who had been superintendent of a large cane–plantation in Jamaica, was on one occasion, subjected to 'every variety of dirty cuss–word that came out of the West Indies', by the men of the fourth battalion.[79]

There were, however, white officers who were able to win the admiration and respect of the black troops. A number of Grenadian soldiers who served at Egypt publicly expressed praise for white Barbadian officers like Lieutenants G. Challenor, E.K.G. Weatherhead and others.[80] Personality and style of leadership thus affected the relationship between white officers and the black rank and file. Although junior officers shared a good deal of responsibility with the senior officers for implementing official army policies, as enlisted men they were also subject to the informal pressures of the rank and file. As such, they could choose to side consistently with army officials, and risk alienating the rank and file, or to be more indulgent and sympathetic, thereby gaining their appreciation and liking. In this situation, the question of colour was generally of secondary importance. Thus, relations between the black NCOs and the black rank and file was also determined by personalities, style of leadership and professional competence. When asked whether he preferred to take orders from black officers or white officers, one BWIR veteran candidly replied that it did not matter.[81]

Nevertheless, the quality of leadership overseas was severely affected by the pervasiveness of the colour factor, which made officer–ship largely the special reserve of whites. Some of the NCOs sent from the West Indies were, according to Woodhill, marked by 'an entire absence of any soldier–knowledge, or knowledge of handling men, and simply by force of circumstance were given command of battalions and made temporary Lieutenant–Colonels'.[82] In addition, the lack of a proper regimental system of promotion among officers meant that officers who joined up with the first contingents in 1915 were still subalterns at the end of the war, whilst others who joined in 1917 and 1918 were made colonels, majors and captains.[83] Many of these were the former draft resisters who had been made officers by local authorities in order to get them to enlist. This not only had an adverse effect on the efficiency of the battalions but also created much discontent among the black officers of the early contingents. Although they had been fully trained, they now had to take orders from the recently arrived, untrained but more senior officers.

The anomalies in the selection of officers may also have been due to the massive casualties the British army suffered during the war, which were disproportionately high among the officer corps.[84] This meant that a high proportion of the officer corps came to be made up of non–public and grammar–school boys who had little knowledge of soldiering. Despite the severe shortage of officers however, army tradition still made it difficult initially for a ranker to be commissioned, even though many suitable candidates were promoted from the ranks and given 'temporary' commissions as the war progressed.[85] The BWIR thus could not depend on English regiments for its officers but had to look instead to the West Indies and the middle–class draft resisters. Of the approximately 168 Jamaicans appointed as BWIR officers after April 25, 1916, only four had any previous military experience.[86] The extent of the dismay and shame felt by the older group of Jamaican officers was expressed by one member who asked: 'Should the war end in the near future, and we be sent home, would it be pleasant (to say the least of it) to find ourselves, through no fault of our own, on the same ship, junior and having to take orders from men (through no ability on their part) who did not even belong to a home defence force when we held the King's Commission?'[87] Meanwhile, whites from the West Indies who had been made NCOs locally but had opted to join British regiments, also proved a nuisance to senior British officers on occasion. They were useless as leaders, but with recommendations of various degrees of informality and value, they nevertheless wanted to be given commissions although even some of the privates in their regiments were more qualified.[88]

At the same time, a rigidly enforced colour–bar prevented blacks from gaining commissions as officers. These restrictions were clearly codified and outlined in the military regulations, which stated explicitly that aliens, including blacks from the empire, should 'not be capable of holding any higher rank in His Majesty's regular forces than that of a warrant officer or Non–Commissioned Officer'.[89] The blacks did not take kindly to the fact that they could not move up beyond the rank of NCO In a letter to the Barbados government one group of middle–class black soldiers strongly protested against the anomaly that the BWIR were subject to the full penalty of military law but were not entitled to the privilege of promotion based on merit.[90] Another protested to the Jamaica officials over the filling of senior positions in the second battalion with English officers no better qualified than themselves.[91] Worse yet, a number of black NCOs were used to train whites for commissions, while they were deemed ineligible for such promotions.[92]

Nevertheless, the attainment of a sergeant's rank was a major achievement for blacks and they viewed it with great pride. It meant being on the threshold of an illusive commission, so that sergeants were noted for their air of 'dignity and aloofness'.[93] Importantly too, the sergeants' mess in the different British forces as well as the BWIR, was known for its intellectual atmosphere, for it was there that 'weighty discussion and learned discourses would take place'.[94] This intellectual vibrancy resulted in attempts by the sergeants to grapple with the problems confronting blacks not only in the army but also back in their various countries. As we will see, this encouraged a sense of West Indian identity and had political implications for the West Indies.

By 1918, the Army Council had quietly conceded that commissions in the BWIR might go to 'slightly coloured persons' at the discretion of the governors of the West Indian colonies.[95] Ivan Shirley, a black from Jamaica but a former pupil at Dulwich College, London, was made a lieutenant in the ninth BWIR.[96] At the same time, manpower shortages in the army also encouraged the lowering of the colour–bar. Dupuch remembered, for example, that as the war progressed, the army began to run short of doctors and as a result, coloured doctors were commissioned with the rank of captain.[97] It was not, however, until the 1940s that blacks 'of clearly discernible colour', such as Arundel Moody, the son of Dr Harold Moody, a Jamaican long resident in London, were given commissions in the British army on a regular basis.[98]

Within military institutions many of the distinctions of status are replaced or at least over–shadowed by the army's own system of hierarchy, especially below the officer core. Thus, during the war, soldiers commonly lost most of the status symbols – job, family, address, clothes, prestige, property – which previously distinguished them in their respective societies. This was not an automatic or quick process, as it took time for the divisions of civilian life to be broken down. Nevertheless, this meant it was possible for West Indian labouring–class blacks to upgrade their status if they got promotions in the BWIR. On the other hand, the status of some middle–class blacks was to a large extent reduced once they entered the army, although their education afforded them greater possibilities for promotion. The case of Sergeant W.H. Mitchell of Grenada represented just one case out of many. He was a 'planter and man of means' when he enlisted as a private in a Grenada contingent and 'saluted and obeyed those who were in lower social stations than himself'.[99] Similarly, a number of 'junior public officers, smart government clerks, lawyers' clerks, mercantile clerks, dispensers and other fine gentlemen, marked time or formed fours at the bidding of those who lived in humbler walks, but who were selected as their superiors in military training'.[100] This frequent reversal of status at times created class antagonisms and contradictions within the army.

Dupuch was one of those middle–class blacks who were forced to come to terms with the impact of army life on status. 'Normally', he wrote, 'NCOs and Privates didn't mix, but I had some warm friends among NCOs from the other islands, especially Jamaica ... Bahamian NCOs were not too friendly. They seemed to resent me, apparently because I had some kind of background in Nassau while most of them had come from nothing. For example, a man who had been a messenger boy on the staff of our family newspaper, the *Tribune*, was a full Corporal. He enjoyed lording it over me.'[101] Another soldier who recognised the problems, urged those middle–class and intelligent men who were to join them overseas to come prepared to drop former social relations of class, friendship and association in favour of the army's ethic. He explained:

> It may well irk a man who has occupied some responsible position in the old life to find himself under the command [and] compelled to obey the orders of a Non–Commissioned Officer intellectually and socially his inferior, but here again, he has to employ the large vision. If you want to learn motor–driving or swimming or horsemanship, your main consideration would be to get the best teacher; you would neither consider the question of intellect nor of social position; you would want to have a man directing you who knew the job and could teach you as much as he knew himself. You are not in the Army for your health or to improve your social status, or to enlarge your circle of intimate friends ...[102]

Thus, middle–class blacks who joined the regiment in the lower ranks suffered humiliation not only because they were, like blacks of the lower–class, subjected to racial harassment from English soldiers; at times they, like some British middle–class and educated soldiers, also had to put up with pressure from comrades who had formerly been their social inferiors but were now their superiors in the army.

Relations in Egypt within the battalions which were most representative of the West Indian colonies were normally quite friendly, but this was not automatic or immediate. Amicable relations developed over time through interaction and communication, induced by their common experiences. On arrival at Seaford and later in Egypt, the inter–island rivalry, distrust and notions of inferiority and superiority based on island origin which character-ised West Indian societies after centuries of colonialism, did not disappear immediately. At Seaford, a nascent West Indian identity began to emerge and was alluded to by one English journalist, who claimed: 'All local jealous-ies have vanished, and the men no longer say I am a Jamaican, Barbadian, Trinidadian, or Honduran, but always, I am a West Indian.'[103] The journal-ist's observation reflected the extent to which a West Indian consciousness had emerged at this early stage in terms of how blacks viewed themselves in relation to Europeans, and how the Europeans regarded them. It seems, however, that the actual development of a similar consciousness and identity in relation to each other was a more difficult and protracted process.

Reflecting on those early days overseas, one veteran recalled that conflict persisted until they sat down under the trees and talked.[104] Inter–island conflict was also evident in the Grenadian complaints that while Grenada was supplying men, other colonies like Jamaica and Barbados provided the officers.[105] Although there was a great deal of co-operation, a strong element of antagonism remained. This prompted one Jamaican soldier to write:

Contrary to the accredited belief that the Westies love each other dearly I soon discovered that Trinidadians look down their noses at Barbadians and all the other inhabitants of the various islands of the Caribbean, and they all look with considerable disfavour on the products of Jamaica. After a little study of their characters, one soon discovers that as much jealousy and pride of race exists in the inhabitants of the microscopic little islands dotting the West Indian waters as there is amongst Irish, Scotch, Welsh and English folk. I am afraid to admit that sometimes this rivalry is not always for the best, and envy, hatred and other uncharitable evil exists. Many of the men seem to miss the point that we are all out for one common purpose, and if we are to obtain the best results we must pull together and be one happy family.[106]

This letter itself reflects the rivalry which persisted among the soldiers of the different colonies and reveals the extent of the difference which existed between the Jamaicans and the others. But conflict among the troops was not only a product of historical forces specific to the region. It was also in part, created or at least fuelled by notions of masculinity, which encouraged fierce competitiveness. One soldier, for example, attributed much of the antagonism at Seaford to every man trying to 'out–do' his comrade in competition.[107]

The regimental chaplains of the BWIR performed an important but at times ambiguous role as officers and confidants of the soldiers. As officers, they enjoyed many of the privileges which the black soldiers were denied and this was apt to create a divide between themselves and the soldiers. On the other hand, chaplains were compelled by their moral and religious duties to work closely with the soldiers. This intercourse was most intense and intimate when they tended to the sick and wounded, administered last rites, handed out cigarettes to the men or took messages for relatives from the dying.[108] In addition, many chaplains found themselves in a moral bind, in that as loyal citizens they tended to put forward the official view of German barbarism and cruelty, but their calling dictated that they articulate the gospel of love. Their dilemma was quite apparent to some of the black soldiers who questioned the chaplains about the contradiction between what they preached and the life of killing other people.[109] Although the inconsistency was not immaterial to the soldiers, the question of racism in the church, however, seems to have generated greater concern. On one occasion in Mesopotamia, for instance, the chaplain administering Holy Communion deliberately first served only the whites before offering the chalice to the blacks. Naturally the latter were deeply offended by the incident.[110]

Chaplains also participated in the educational classes organised in the evenings for the soldiers. An inquiry into education in the army during the war concluded that interest in these classes was because they brought together so many people of different class backgrounds and perspectives, and because of the issues which the war involved. These factors it argued, 'led many who previously thought but little about the larger problems of life and society to seek knowledge and understanding'.[111] In the BWIR a similar trend existed, for as one veteran remarked, education was essential in moving one beyond the level of an idiot.[112] Moreover, the classes had a practical advantage in that the qualifications received were integral to getting promotions as NCOs and facilitating interaction and bonding among some of the soldiers. The classes were mainly taught by chaplains and regimental schoolteachers, many of whom had been teachers in the West Indies before the war.

Subjects taught included reading, writing, divinity and geography, which were all important to the blacks in their soldiering capacity. Army education was not intended to create too intellectual or inquisitive soldiers. In fact, as the report noted, military training over a long period tended to make men less responsive to intellectual stimulus because of its monotony and rigid discipline.[113] This is not surprising, since the army has historically stressed 'practicality' and fiercely despised those who were intellectually or theoretically inclined.[114] For this reason, Lord Lugard was very opposed to those he derogated as 'book worms' being sent to Nigeria to fill officer positions in the colonial forces.[115] Furthermore, given the historical emphasis on obedience and social control in West Indian education, fears within the Colonial Office of unrest in the West Indies and the inherent distrust and suspicion among army officials of veterans, it was not politically expedient to teach the black soldiers anything radical or progressive. Indeed, the belief among officers in the British army, many of whom held Victorian attitudes and social Darwinist ideas, was that the working classes needed to be taught self–discipline, manliness and a sense of duty to the state, as these were the key to national success.[116] Yet, it is likely that the acquisition of basic literary skills in the army contributed to blacks' analyses of their situation. At the same time, their multiple experiences and interaction with the various societies overseas naturally added another dimension to these analyses.

Civilian Relations and Recreation

During times of war, stricter, measures of control and surveillance are usually imposed by military officials on intercourse between civilians and soldiers but this relationship nevertheless forms an integral part of a soldier's recreation and leisure experiences. This was especially critical for the soldiers of World War One, since the majority had only recently been drawn into army life. Indeed, even Jamaican officials who contemplated confining BWIR recruits during the week prior to departure in order to control venereal diseases could not implement this radical solution because, as the commanding officer realised, confinement beyond a day or two would have had to be enforced by the 'butt and bayonet' of the WIR, and would have led to 'more than resentment'.[1] Interaction between the black soldiers and civilian populations overseas took place within the prescriptions of army regulations but at various emotional and physical levels and in a variety of overt and discreet forms. This chapter examines these relationships, looks at other forms of leisure and recreation among the soldiers and shows that in spite of a variety of adjustment mechanisms, by late 1917 their morale had seriously declined.

Intercourse with civilians began almost immediately on a soldier's arrival in England. The reception of the black troops was generally warm, at times even ecstatic. As the soldiers passed through England for France, people cheered and brought them refreshments.[2] Every time the trains stopped girls flung parcels of sweets, cigarettes and apples at the soldiers and chucked 'kisses from every side'.[3] This warm response was particularly appreciated by the black soldiers as Private L. Malabre wrote: 'One thing that really strikes me is the manner in which we are appreciated and respected by the English people. You can just imagine how it makes us darkies feel at ease in our minds.'[4] At the Lord Mayor's show of November 1915, a BWIR contingent under Major G. Golding of St. Lucia and Captain H. Cavenaugh of Trinidad paraded along with other forces from the empire. The West Indians were favourites with the crowds lining the streets of London.

In an interview with a British newspaper, Private Peter Lambert of Jamaica reflected: 'I was proud to be cheered by the people of London, for I've come a long way to fight for them ...The people in the streets cheered us black boys more than the white boys. "That's because you're black", said someone to me. But we are English really; it's only the climate we've lived in that makes us black.'[5] It is not inconceivable that the black soldiers marched more smartly than their white colleagues but the observer was probably partly right, for in 1915 a black man in London and especially in the rural districts of England was a novelty. During the early years of the nineteenth century, the black population in London had been large and prominent but by 1914, blacks had to a large extent disappeared from London for social, economic and political reasons although small communities existed at various seaports like Cardiff.[6] In the country areas where the people were generally courteous and hospitable, the soldiers were constantly stared at and subjected to subdued whispers of 'here's a Blackie'.[7] While many black soldiers enjoyed the attention, it is also likely, as was suggested by a Sergeant of the eighth BWIR, that the more sensitive may not have found it pleasant.[8]

For the various press observers from England and the Dominions, black soldiers were as much a spectacle as they were for the British public. Some papers like the *Daily Telegraph* were particularly interested in the fact that blacks had responded to the empire's plight and viewed their presence as evidence 'that loyalty under the English flag [was] no matter of race'.[9] Others found fascination in the fact that these 'mighty men of valour', with their 'white teeth flashing' were 'black as night'.[10] The fact that many blacks spoke English well elicited an even greater appreciation and acceptance from the white press. The *Natal Witness*, while noting their 'remarkable resemblance to the African', was equally quick to add that they spoke English fluently.[11] The *Daily News* also observed that they spoke excellent English.[12]

The fascination of the press with black fluency in English derived from their amazement that blacks could have attained such a 'high level of civilisation' – meaning English attributes and the values embodied in the language. As Fanon puts it, nothing was 'more astonishing than to hear a black man express himself properly, for then in truth he [was] putting on the white world'.[13] For this reason British troops were also often astounded that many West Indian soldiers had such a good grasp of the language.[14] For many West Indian soldiers being able to demonstrate their knowledge of the English language to the British soldiers, press and officials was their way of dealing with their inferiority complex relative to whites and proof that they had 'arrived'. It was against this background that Private C.A. Card complained that some of the men who had come overseas lacked discipline and intelligence, and were not particular in their use of English.[15] He pleaded with intelligent men of the colonies to volunteer.

The blacks knowledge of the empire and the English language likewise astounded the British public, as one Sergeant writing in 1919 recalled: 'I spent a couple of days in the county of Durham and the miners as they expressed themselves were awe–stricken to hear a coloured man speak English as good, and in the majority of the cases, more correct than they, and they seemed more puzzled to know that you were conversant with the history of their own country more than they themselves. I make bold to say that our average elementary school boy who leaves school in 6th class has a greater general knowledge of the world than a boy leaving an English Board School in the same standard.'[16] In the light of the above comment it is possible to understand why many West Indians who came to England during and after World War Two were shocked and annoyed when whites asked them if they spoke English.[17] Similar consternation was expressed by the Jamaican workers when they were asked by whites if they wore clothes at home and if the girls in Jamaica wore grass skirts.[18]

When on furlough in England, the soldiers moved about relatively freely and mixed with the British public and other soldiers from the empire; some developed friendly, sexual and marital relationships with white women, as did blacks from the West Indies and Africa working in the munitions factories.[19] For example, one Charles Bryan of Jamaica married and had a child with an English woman while he was working in a munitions factory in Sheffield, but when they returned to Jamaica after the war, she discovered he had several other children and was not prepared to support her, so she went back to England.[20] A military officer from Manchester was appalled one night to count as many as eleven 'niggers', four of whom were with white women.[21] That he was incensed at black men being involved with white women was not surprising. At a subconscious level, the notion of black inferiority often went hand in hand with the belief that blacks were primitive and possessed an uninhibited sexuality; sex was regarded 'as that thing which, *par excellence*, is a threat to the moral order of Western civilisation'.[22] It is likely that relationships between black soldiers and white women were partly the result of necessity, as one black veteran argued, for at that point there were few black women in London.[23] The sexual imbalance created a pressure on black males to seek relationships with white women, particularly of the lower class, who were more accessible and whose class status was more roughly comparable.

It is also arguable, however, that such relationships represented the achievement of full status and psychological equality with whites for some blacks as Fanon has argued.[24] Fanon maintains that a dominant concern of Antilleans arriving in France was to go to bed with white women as a means of initiation into 'authentic' manhood.[25] This seems to explain the declaration of a Carib volunteer from British Honduras that he intended to bring back a French woman with him from overseas, much to the consternation of the *Clarion*.[26] It is, however, difficult to unravel the soldiers' motivations without being able to interview them and most are now deceased. Thus, while the arguments of Fanon, and others who have theorised about intimate relationships between blacks and whites, may be relevant in analysing the behaviour of the black soldiers, it seems more reasonable and empirically sound, to accept the view that the soldiers became involved with poor white women simply because they had little alternative.

At the same time, however, it seems that their blackness and military uniform made them sexually attractive to white women. This was explicitly and enthusiastically expressed by one recruit who wrote from Seaford: 'Plenty of girls. They love the boys in khaki. They detest walking with civilians. They love the darkies!'[27] Apart from the general white abhorrence at these unions, they also created disciplinary problems for the army. A diary entry of one member of the second Jamaican contingent reads: 'On account of mutual attachments formed between the Milbrook and Plymouth girls and the "darky boys" a strong picket of between 40 and 60 men had to be despatched tonight to capture every battalion man found within the borders of those towns.'[28]

These relationships, especially the marriages, were important to the black soldiers, not only because they helped reduce problems of isolation, boredom and sexual deprivation, but also because they facilitated their adjustment into British society and enabled them to resist racism. An African who enlisted in England during the war related stories of how white women sympathetic to the blacks, came to their rescue when they were being attacked by mobs of white men.[29] Likewise, many black male immigrants who came to England after World War Two, often spoke warmly of how their white female partners fought against racial discrimination.[30] The fact that many British women experienced class and gender oppression, perhaps made it easier for them to sympathise with black men facing racial abuse.

BWIR battalions serving in Italy were also well received by the public. School children welcomed them with songs such as, 'Way down upon the Swanee River', and 'Pack up your troubles in your old kit bag, and smile, smile, smile'.[31] In France, the initial reaction of the civilians in the villages to the black soldiers was often one of suspicion, 'strangeness and aloofness'.[32] But this attitude was quickly transformed. Chaplain Horner recorded:

> It was perfectly astonishing how our boys managed to wheedle themselves into the hearts and homes of the civil population. I remember well a little row of houses very close to our camp in everyone of which, during the evening, BWIR boys might have been seen huddled round the stove, for it was cold, doing odd jobs for the lady of the house, regaling themselves with coffee, and so far as they were able, carrying on a conversation .... Frequently, after necessary duty was over, one would see a boy doing some totally unnecessary piece of work, such as for example laying in a stack of firewood, or feeding the pigs, or some other activity about the place. Upon enquiry, it would be elicited that it was "just a little job to help the madame".[33]

While some of these relationships, in part facilitated by the massive removal and dislocation of the European male population, which left many women lonely, remained at the level of friendship others became intimate and sexual.[34]

In Egypt and the surrounding areas, black soldiers were also engaged in various relationships with the civilian population. Gambling, prostitution and drinking all represented important forms of leisure and recreation among troops. While recognising the negative effects of drinking and drunkenness on troops, drinking can also be regarded as an important form of male bonding and therefore a positive social activity.[35] During war, drinking becomes even more important to the soldiers in overcoming boredom and releasing stress, and like the use of coarse and vulgar language, in asserting their virility and masculinity. Drinking, and more generally the use of drugs, may represent a desperate attempt to overcome the discrepancy between a soldier's personal identity and the stereotypical demands, such as aggressive behaviour and bravery, of heterosexual masculine identity.

However, drinking, gambling and prostitution were regarded by the officials as the sources of venereal diseases which adversely affected the health, strength and discipline of the battalion. By the end of the war, the Allied forces had registered approximately a million and a half syphilis and gonorrhoea casualties.[36] To be sure, these problems were not new to the British army in 1914; the military and society in general, had been grappling with these issues for decades before the outbreak of war.[37] The Contagious Diseases Acts of 1864, 1866 and 1869 were designed to reduce the alarming incidence of venereal disease amongst the British forces in particular, although their supporters hoped that their provisions would be applied to the entire country.[38] During World War One, women were again subjected to a range of oppressive regulations in order to protect the soldiers, so the officials claimed, from the multitude of infected women who infested military camps.[39] The army believed that sexual activity was vital to a soldier's happiness but simultaneously regarded women, and especially prostitutes as a source of pollution and a threat to morale and military efficiency. Moreover, the army felt it had a moral and patriotic responsibility to protect the soldiers so that they could return home healthy, and reduce the risk of their families and communities being 'innocently' infected. In this respect, the army was partly responding to the great concern expressed in the United States and England about soldiers returning home and infecting the civilian population.[40]

The army's policies also reflected the historical construction of female sexuality as 'dangerous' and the way in which working–class sexuality was brought under increasing scrutiny and stigmatised during the nineteenth century. Women were seen as morally responsible for sexual relations and therefore the spread of sexual diseases.[41] These attitudes were also evident in the West Indies and were expressed by the *Gleaner,* which argued that sailors from the warships and local volunteers were frequently the 'victims' of women who spread infectious diseases in and around Kingston.[42] The sailors, volunteers and members of the military forces being male, were not held responsible for their actions. It was as if they had a right to engage in prostitution without risk.

The measures adopted in Egypt, Palestine and France, as elsewhere, were therefore both stringent and extensive. In Palestine and Egypt, restrictions were placed on the existence and location of 'Disorderly Houses', described as houses or rooms frequented by 'two or more women for the purpose of prostitution', outside specially designated areas of the towns.[43] Pecuniary penalties and\or jail terms of up to six months were prescribed for the owner or occupier who knowingly permitted their 'premises or any part thereof to be used as a Disorderly House'.[44] A loophole in the legislation meant that a house used by one woman for prostitution was technically outside the law. At the same time, however, prostitutes were liable to be jailed or charged for loitering in any public place or, by word or gesture, soliciting any soldier or displaying themselves in doorways, windows or balconies. The regulations also stated that any woman suffering from venereal disease in a communicable form who had sexual intercourse with any member of His Majesty's Forces, or who solicited or invited any member of the army to have sexual intercourse with her was liable on conviction, to up to two months imprisonment.[45] In France, soldiers were given numerous leaflets and pamphlets warning them of the dangers of venereal diseases, and a system was established whereby soldiers were required to identify the women who they believed infected them.[46] The women were then taken to a hospital and medically examined, and, if found to be infected were removed from the locality.

The treatment of soldiers with venereal diseases, however, created a dilemma for the army. Given that during the war, soldiers lived very closely together, and under conditions adverse to personal cleanliness, the risk of cross infection necessitated the segregation of infected soldiers, especially during acute stages of the disease. Army officials also feared that if infected soldiers were allowed complete freedom this would inevitably lead to more widespread infection. However, the army was against prolonged hospitalisation of the soldiers, since it was felt that this would lead to enforced idleness and the wastage of much needed manpower. Officials believed that hospitalised men would become 'slack in mind and body' and that their disease would become an obsession which interfered with their recovery. Thus, the tendency was to keep infected soldiers in hospital for as short as time as possible.[47] A variety of drugs was used to treat syphilis in the army but the main ones were Salvarsan and its derivatives, as well as mercury.

While army policies for combating venereal diseases focussed heavily on the women, penal measures were also adopted for soldiers who became infected. Generally, the army did not punish the soldier unless he was discovered to be concealing his sickness. Many years of experience in dealing with venereal diseases convinced the army that punitive measures only increased concealment. Nevertheless, an officer or soldier who became infected had to pay hospital stoppages of two shillings, six pence and seven pence respectively, but these fines were payable in all cases of sickness requiring hospitalisation, except where it was directly attributable to service in the field. All illnesses, with the exception of venereal disease and alcoholism, were usually regarded as contracted through service. As in times of peace, the infected soldier could, at the discretion of the commanding officer, lose his proficiency pay. Infected officers and warrant officers also forfeited field allowances for the duration of their stay in hospital, just as they would if they were on furlough.

The problem of illicit sexual association between civilians and soldiers of the various armies of the empire had, by 1917, become serious enough for the army to reiterate its illegality.[48] Under new regulations for British troops in France, issued on January 27, 1917, infected soldiers were also made ineligible for leave for 12 months after they left hospital. This measure was intended as a deterrent and a means of preventing diseases being carried back and transmitted to 'innocent' family members. However, it soon became inoperative, since most soldiers were usually evacuated to England because of other diseases or wounds long before the year was up. Clearly, the measures instituted for soldiers were very mild compared to those for women. The Canadian, Australian and New Zealand forces did, however, impose fines on soldiers who contracted venereal diseases.

Collectively, the army regulations for soldiers and prostitutes sought to reduce their interaction to a minimum. But while these measures may have created obstacles to relationships between prostitutes or girlfriends and the soldiers, the problem remained an intractable and illusive one. This was inevitable, since in the all–male military setting great value was placed on sex, not only as a means of proving virility and masculinity but equally as a way of releasing erotic tension. Black soldiers in Egypt would periodically 'break barracks' at night to look for women to get their little piece of 'dirty sex', as one symbolically expressed it, even if it meant contracting diseases like 'leak' or gonorrhea.[49] If they were caught, they were likely to be put in the guard room until the next morning when punishment was delivered.[50] A murder inquiry in Italy also revealed that it was common for women to visit the black soldiers in their dug–outs at night.[51] Punishments varied but the King's Regulation and Army Act provided for a maximum of 28 days Field

Punishment no. 1 – popularly known as 'crucifixion' – which allowed offenders to be shackled to gun wheels or railings for up to two hours a day.

Although there are few statistics on the incidence of venereal diseases in the BWIR overseas, it appears that the strength and efficiency of the regiment were seriously affected. The black soldiers were subject to the same punitive measures as English soldiers but in some cases, the authorities adopted more drastic procedures to control the venereal disease problem in the regiment. Early in 1916, on the request of the National Council for Combating Venereal Disease, the army instituted a system whereby each unit was provided with a compartment which had an irrigator with 1:3,000 potassium permanganate solution and calomel ointment.[52] Soldiers were strongly encouraged to disinfect themselves after exposure to infection. Although the use of these facilities varied among the different army units, it was generally believed to be unsuccessful because of the length of time which usually elapsed between exposure and disinfection. Moreover, men were reluctant to be seen entering the urinals where the irrigators were located. At Taranto, Italy, the system was enhanced by the employment of trained orderlies to disinfect men on their return to camp. However, because the military officials believed that venereal diseases were 'particularly rife' among the BWIR, their disinfection on return to camp was made compulsory. This may have had some positive effect because admissions reportedly fell from 80 per week to four per month.[53]

Claims about the efficacy of the system are, however, suspect and not merely because of the general confusion surrounding the treatment of venereal diseases in the army. It is true that some blacks arrived overseas already infected and that many were forced by circumstances to find sexual partners among prostitutes and this might have increased the likelihood of infection. At the same time, it is probable, as Allan Brandt has argued in respect to blacks in the American Expeditionary Force in France, that army doctors were predisposed to diagnose many of the ailments among blacks as sexually transmitted.[54] Very high rates of venereal diseases were also reported among blacks in the American forces and as a result many divisions ordered compulsory prophylaxis for all blacks regardless of exposure.[55] At one base, for instance, a wire stockade was erected around the camp and all black stevedores were forced to enter and leave through certain check posts. Four–hour passes were issued and all returning men had to undertake chemical prophylaxis. As in the case of the BWIR the rate of venereal diseases reportedly fell dramatically. The drastic measures instituted for blacks and prostitutes, and the numerous experiments to which infected soldiers of all nationalities were subjected, not only cast doubts on the efficacy of army treatment at the time; they also reveal the extent to which questionable statistics and Victorian assumptions about race, class and gender, provided the rationale for the methods to be employed in the fight against these diseases.

Significantly, as in the United States and England, there were those in the West Indies who worried greatly about the effect infected soldiers would have on the local population on their return. Reports that hundreds of BWIR men who had contracted venereal diseases in Egypt and England were to be returned to Jamaica created panic at the *Gleaner,* which questioned worriedly: 'What is to be done with these men when they arrive? Are they to be taken in hand and cured or are they to be let loose on the community to add to the poison that is already working such havoc in our midst?'[56] Fortunately, the reports were false.[57]

As among British and other soldiers, black soldiers' responses to their sexuality included carrying obscene pictures of women, and probably homosexual activity, though the evidence is limited.[58] Homosexuality may have been a response, as one veteran claimed, to the fact that some black soldiers could not 'get' women or because they had a preference for other men.[59] Even though the army recognised the need for the release of sexual tension, it was particularly averse to what it saw as 'unnatural offences', like masturbation and homosexuality. Such acts were perceived as problematic for discipline, efficiency and morale.[60] Moreover, homosexuality offended basic Christian sexual taboos, was medically categorised as symptoms of male psychological sickness, and was contrary to the 'manly' ethics of the army. The authorities realised that temporary or 'deprivation homosexuality' represented a common form of male bonding among soldiers but were not prepared to tolerate it. A soldier found guilty of homosexuality was liable to be imprisoned and then dishonourably discharged.

During the war, military officials were worried that the close–packed trenches of the Western front would lead to an epidemic of homosexual behaviour and the Germans, who were particularly sensitive on this issue, periodically launched witch–hunts in regiments where it was suspected to be common.[61] Yet, as several studies of gender and sexuality have shown, homosexuality is often one of the complex responses to tightly–regulated, all–male environments.[62] More important perhaps, because of the aggressive emphasis on masculinity and the army's categorisation of homosexuality as deviant, any soldier caught engaging in it was likely not only to face disciplinary actions but also to experience shame and humiliation. When a soldier from Trinidad reported that one of his colleagues had committed an 'unnatural offence', it led to his murder.[63] Before the offence could be investigated, the accused escaped, armed himself with a rifle and shot the Trinidadian and another comrade.

Lack of leave constituted a grievance among the BWIR soldiers, since many who enlisted in 1915 served until the end of the war without adequate holiday.[64] Nevertheless, many soldiers were able to experience the culture and social life of the countries in which they served. Some officers and men visited Buckingham Palace, went on formally arranged visits to British homes and formed part of the guard of honour at the opening of Parliament.[65] On several occasions those who were members of the Ancient Order of Foresters were invited by their British counterparts to grand receptions at some of the leading courts in England.[66] Others marvelled at British buildings and the political system.[67] Egypt and its environs also had special cultural and historical significance. One soldier enthused in a letter about the museums, a wedding and funeral of 'the Oriental type', which were, in his view, both 'naturally attractive to strangers'.[68] Others visited the Pyramids and the Sphinx and one soldier marvelled: 'All around us is history; every stone or tree has been used by somebody.'[69] These numerous experiences overseas helped to broaden and alter the perspectives of the BWIR on life in general and of different cultures, societies and politics.

The story of Aubrey Williams, the former 'yard boy' from Trinidad illustrates this. His experiences began with the two–week journey to England, during which, he wrote proudly, he was able to consume more eggs, creams, ham and bacon and radishes than he had eaten throughout his entire life in Trinidad.[70] It is not surprising that he regarded this experience as noteworthy because it signified a degree of improvement in his class status. While these foods were consumed regularly by the middle and upper classes and symbolised their elite status, the lower class only ate them on very rare occasions because they could not afford such 'luxuries'. Williams' reflections on food would doubtless have been shared by many British soldiers from marginal rural and the urban slums, whose diet, and hence weight and height, improved once they joined the army.[71] Williams provides an even more vivid account of the impact of life in England after he arrived in Liverpool on May 31, 1915:

> When I left the station and went into the thoroughfares I almost went mad; I never saw such confusion in my life. I saw about 30,000 people in one street; trains running, not by steam but by electricity; not only on the ground, but also above and under the ground for miles; trams with people packed on the top going in all directions. Motor cars flying, actually flying in the street; vans and wagons as big as houses, and then the big stores and the market. The market in England is not like the market in Trinidad. In Trinidad Mrs. Nobody scorns the idea of going to the market. In England the best time you can spend is in the market. There you see English life at its best; fashion to make you crazy ...When you leave the market you go over to the big store opposite; you see so much things you are obliged to close your eyes. There, sun shines till half past nine and England is at her best at 8 o'clock; not to talk of the theatre, the pretty faces and fat legs and fine voices and wonderful acting that you see ...I have been so lucky that a white lady has adopted me and the life I am living is too grand to describe.[72]

Williams' experiences probably went beyond his wildest expectations of the 'Mother Country'.

The military bands of the various battalions also provided opportunities for recreation and intercourse with civilians. Although its primary function was to provide music for its battalion, the band was often required to play at social functions, including sports meetings and concerts. [73] In France the band of the ninth became a prime favourite of the children, villagers and even the ladies of the village elite, who turned out in 'full array' to its concerts. At these concerts the band also served as an instrument of cultural transmission by playing various 'Jamaican and other West Indian' tunes, such as 'And in my sleep I'll dream of thee, my home, my sunny home'.[74] These songs also linked the soldiers psychologically with home, helping them overcome their feelings of isolation and loneliness. One soldier in Egypt wrote to the *West Indian* urging that on Intercession Sundays in Grenada, songs like 'O God our Help in Ages Past', 'Oft in Danger, Oft in Woe' and 'Onward Christian Soldiers' be sung, since these old favourites would enable the folks at home to get into 'spiritual touch' with the soldiers.[75] These concerts probably provided a way for the West Indians to express their identities and also assert their equality with whites. But if these cultural and religious activities had positive effects, they may also have helped at times to disadvantage them socially by reinforcing English stereotypes of blacks, especially the myth that blacks were peculiarly musical and carefree.

Letters home were a means of complaint and political protest against conditions overseas, as well as another way soldiers attempted to maintain psychological ties with their communities in the West Indies. The *West Indian* with its regular articles championing the cause of the Grenadian and other West Indian soldiers and its black nationalist agitation, was, for these reasons, very popular among all West Indian soldiers.[76] Not surprisingly, the persistent non–arrival of letters and newspapers from the West Indies was a serious concern. Part of the problem stemmed from the disruption and occasional destruction of mails service by enemy action.[77] The sheer volume of mails received from the West Indies, incorrect addresses and the constant moving about of battalions, especially in France, further complicated the problem.[78] The sense of loneliness felt by the soldiers was conveyed in a letter from a Honduran soldier in Palestine who complained bitterly that it was heart–rending not to receive letters from those who should remember them.[79] Private Cyril Lougheed of Grenada likewise questioned plaintively: 'Why don't people at home write us? We get no answers to our letters. If they have nothing to send they can still write. We feel lonely.'[80] In response to these complaints a committee was established in Grenada to facilitate communication between Grenadian soldiers overseas and their families.[81]

Sports also played a critical part in providing relief from stress and boredom and helped to keep the soldiers physically fit and boost morale. Sporting activities included regimental football matches, boxing, athletics and horse racing.[82] Individual sporting activities, like boxing and athletics, functioned to reinforce attributes like competitiveness and aggressiveness, which the army regarded as crucial to the soldiers' ability to perform their duties effectively. Moreover, by engaging in these 'masculinising' sporting activities, the soldiers were able to reduce the 'feminising' processes, such as compassion, of the wider society. At the same time, the army had to ensure that the individual's need for identity and self assertion did not undermine its collective ethos.

Team sports like cricket and football helped to redefine and reinforce a soldier's identity and loyalty to his battalion. Through team sports the values of comradeship and the individual's need for identity and security are exploited simultaneously. Wherever they were stationed, the BWIR soldiers excelled at sport, particularly cricket. During the 1918 cricket season in Egypt, the West Indians played 34 matches of which they won 31, drew two and lost one.[83] The *Palestine News* reported on matches involving the West Indians, which 'created much interest locally' and of competitions between BWIR battalions, which 'produced much speculation' and marked 'the event of the week'. [84] Their prowess in cricket especially, was not simply a question of recreation and good sports; there was also a measure of psychological importance attached to their victories.

In the colonial context, cricket, like music, was not merely recreation, but also an arena where players struggled to decide the results of social proselytism and cultural power. To be able to adopt this British game, as several Caribbean historians including, C.L.R James have argued, represented another way in which British colonial ideas and institutions were reinterpreted by the black population to assert their humanity, equality and cultural identity.[85] In the face of racist insults and the denial of their rights, victory in cricket was a major psychological achievement and proof that they reached the heights of 'civilisation'. Critically, however, their sporting activities were restricted because of racism.

At Basra, Mesopotamia, the BWIR were only allowed to compete against Europeans in cricket, perhaps because unlike in football, in cricket there is minimum physical contact between players.[86] It may also have been related to the British love for cricket; they were unable to resist a good game. This made it difficult for the colour–bar to operate in that branch of sport, since the West Indians were always considered to be among the best cricketers. It is not unlikely that cricket assisted in improving race relations. Nevertheless, the 'invidious distinction' usually made between the West Indians and the British troops caused at least one soldier to decide that, in spite of his fondness for athletics, it was better to keep out of the games.[87]

Another way soldiers overcame their feelings of isolation and as a form of leisure was to 'gather outside' their tents and 'have a chat about home' and dream about their return.[88] As H.A.S. Hurley recalled:

Our life in Egypt and Palestine has not been easy. We have been through the mill in real earnest, we have endured much and suffered much. When days seemed darkest and everything seemed to be going wrong, the thought of our dear friends and relations back ... in the homeland, longing and praying for us, has gone a long way to cheer and smooth our path, and the welcome which we knew awaited us upon our arrival has ever been our happiest anticipation.[89]

These conversations were also to be important for the societies to which the soldiers would return. Newspapers served to keep the soldiers informed of political developments in the region and more particularly, of the movement for representative government, which gained support among the soldiers because of their ordeal overseas. According to a Grenada soldier writing to Marryshow:

> Your article in the *West Indian* on Representative Government for Grenada has met with most warm and splendid congratulations by her sons on this side of the seas, and we must confess that since we've been out here we've never felt so happy as when we read the roaring speeches given by our able countrymen on the good cause ... it was our intention to invite our countrymen to take that step as soon as we returned home. Our present experience has opened our eyes more widely to the disadvantages which our little colony has to contend with. When the papers reached us out here they were lent to the men of different islands and often [when] reading the speeches they were filled with great enthusiasm.[90]

These discussions also helped to spread and concretise unrealistic expectations of what the local societies owed the soldiers. One Barbadian veteran recalled that he would say to the others: 'If I ever get back to Barbados they got to give me what I ask them for; they can't tell me what they like!'[91] S.A. Haynes, who later led disturbances in British Honduras, expressed in song the nature of the demands the BWIR men were planning to make once they returned home. This warned the civilian population and the authorities that, regardless of their objections, the soldiers were coming home to collect their 'Military Pay' and to live in comfort.[92] Although civilians on the home front were doing their 'bit' through the local war–effort, the black soldiers, and indeed, soldiers of every nationality, felt and were encouraged to believe by recruiters that their sacrifice was superior. They felt that society owed them a considerable and permanent debt.[93]

Declining Morale and Revolt at Taranto

A morale–boosting visit by King George in the middle of 1917 produced tremendous cheers and enthusiasm from the West Indian soldiers in France but this did not last long.[1] The inspection of the West Indian forces had been arranged by the Colonial Office in the belief that such a visit would be, 'very gratifying to West Indian sentiment, besides having excellent political results'.[2] Yet by late 1917, there was a marked decline in morale among the black soldiers not only in France but also at the different locations where they were stationed. This was in part reflected in cases of serious criminal acts and more extreme forms of resistance which led to what seems to have been the only four executions to have occurred in the BWIR. In December 1917, 18–year–old Private J.A. Mitchell was executed in Egypt by firing squad. He had been found guilty of murdering a local inhabitant.[3] On January 20, 1919, Private Albert Denny of the fourth Trinidad contingent, but formerly of St. Vincent, was executed at Taranto, Italy, for the murder of Private A. Best of Barbados.[4]

The incident was referred to in the West Indian press as 'painful and humiliating news'.[5] Best had worked in Panama and had plenty of money. On the night of his murder he had visited a brothel in Taranto where he stood the other soldiers to drinks and displayed his 'wad of notes'. Later that evening he was found mortally wounded. At trial, Denny was defended 'with conspicuous ability' by Austin Cooper of the Jamaica contingent, 'a coloured gentleman', who in civil life had been a clerk of peace. Although Denny was found guilty, it was believed by the officials that four or five others had assisted him; he, however, never revealed their names. He received the announcement of the death penalty calmly and as a last request asked not to be blind–folded at his execution but the authorities refused. He was subsequently executed along with a European who had been sentenced for desertion.

Desertion from the army represented both a decline of troop morale and resistance to intolerable conditions, but the punishments, especially in war–time, were severe; a soldier could receive the death penalty.[6] It seems that there were only a few cases among the BWIR, and these occurred mainly from late 1917. While some deserters received prison sentences, at least one was executed. In France, Private H. Morris attempted to desert via a seaport but was caught by the military police. His capture was not surprising because it was difficult for deserters to remain at liberty behind the line in France for long and it was even more difficult to escape to England.

There were military police continually checking passes and travel documents and patrolling the roads, villages, towns and the railway stations in the vicinity of the battle areas. In addition, strict surveillance was maintained over all the soldiers entering the Channel ports of Le Havre, Boulogne, Rouen and Dieppe and the Allied and neutral vessels in these ports were inspected periodically to ensure that there were no deserters on board. This was not the first time Morris had tried to escape and warned about the severe nature of the punishment for 'being absent without leave'.[7] He was court–martialled and sentenced to be executed at 6.00 a.m. on Thursday September 20, 1917. Chaplain Ramson recounted the events of the day of the execution:

At 5 a.m. we were on our way through the damp morning mist, and a drizzling rain ... We were admitted at once to the cell, and again lifted up our hearts to God in earnest supplication for the condemned man. He was quite calm and told us he was prepared to die. The guard came; his hands were hand–cuffed behind his back: a thick cloth wrapped over his head, and a white cardboard disk pinned on his tunic over the heart: and he was marched out of the cell into the courtyard and tied securely to a post a few feet from the wall. On a small barricade of sandbags, some 20 paces off, were 10 rifles loaded, and with bolts drawn back ready for firing: one had a blank cartridge in it, as is customary, and no one of the firing party knew into which rifle it had been placed. While the prisoner was being secured to the post, the ten men, seven of whom were men of the BWIR and three white, were marched in and knelt behind the rifles: the attendants stepped back: the Captain raised his hand: aim was taken: the Captain's hand dropped smartly, and the 10 rifles rang out as one shot. The body at the post gave one convulsive shudder and was still ... Seven shots had passed through the heart and body into the wall behind, one through the neck, and one missed.[8]

He was buried next to a white soldier who had also been executed for desertion only five days previously.

Undoubtedly such demonstrations must have been, as they were intended by the army to be, sobering experiences for the black executioners as well as for those observing the incident.[9] Yet the efficacy of these executions as a means of inducing obedience should not be overestimated. The carnage of the war dulled the senses of many soldiers, producing indifference to death *en masse*.[10] In addition, some soldiers found life in the trenches so ghastly and 'hellish' that they actually wished for death to release them from their earthly torment.[11] Private Denny's last request not to be blind–folded for his execution may have been both an act of courage and indifference to death.

Desertion was not always or simply a matter of cowardice or the soldier's response to poor treatment and working conditions. It may have been related to the psycho–sociological problems connected with the world's first industrialised war and the immobilisation inherent in trench warfare. In his study of World War One, Leed argues that the consensus among British soldiers was that the 'deafening sound and vibration of the barrage, which defenders were required to suffer for hours, even days' created neuroses.[12] West Indian soldiers had similar reactions. As one wrote:

> We spent about thirty–five days more or less in the same position. During this period our experiences were innumerable, and very grave, for at any moment anyone of us could have been hurled into eternity. We were face to face with high explosives and Wizbangs and Shrapnel too, bursting over trenches which could have cut any of us to pieces at any moment. One of the first awful sights I witnessed was seeing one of the high explosives fall in a dug–out and blow two of my chums from British Guiana to pieces; another was severely wounded and another driven mad.[13]

By the winter of 1914, it was reported that cases of 'shell–shock' in the army accounted for as many as 40 per cent of casualties in the battle zones and by the cessation of hostilities 80,000 cases had been examined by army medical facilities.[14]

As a culturally constructed concept, madness had historically been considered as an essentially female malady. Men regarded women as constitutionally prone to irrationality and weak nerves. Consequently, this vast number of 'emotionally incapacitated' men represented a shocking contrast to the heroic visions and masculine fantasies that had preceded it.[15] The enforced passivity soldiers experienced in the trenches confounded heterosexual notions of masculinity, which army training had reinforced and intensified. This 'gender shock', which was manifested among the soldiers in a particular form of 'madness' called 'neurasthenia', was similar to the neurosis suffered by many Victorian women like Virginia Woolf, who were forced to grapple with extremely limited domestic, vocational and sexual spaces.[16]

The response of the army to shell–shock and madness may have given some individuals an additional incentive to abscond; indeed desertion may have represented an attempt at all cost to avoid madness. This was evident in the case of a Jamaican soldier executed for desertion. In a last message to his mother he explained that he could not 'stand the soul–searing noise made by exploding shells'.[17] Such cases were often viewed as displays of cowardice and indiscipline.[18] Many army officials and medical officers for a long time believed that to treat these cases as illness would undermine the structures of discipline that kept soldiers in the war; because of the class bias in army medical treatment, however, a more sympathetic attitude was adopted towards officers with 'shell–shock'.

Crucially, however, psychological problems often persisted after the war. Under the strain of war, of seeing his brother Roy killed and financial problems, Norman Manley had a nervous breakdown, although he had recovered sufficiently to enter Oxford in 1919. For others, the problems were more permanent. As the war came to a close in 1918 several West Indian soldiers in the BWIR and other regiments went mad.[19] Some were temporarily confined in various lunatic asylums in England before being repatriated home. Private E. Shaw, a Jamaican who enlisted in the BWIR, was held, for instance, at the criminal lunatic asylum, Broadmoor, from October 23, 1918 until he was sent back home in late December 1919. Apparently his condition had improved because the superintendent of the asylum felt he did not require any special attention during the voyage home. It was, however, not clear whether he had to be put in the local asylum on arrival in Jamaica.[20]

Another case was that of Private Ernest Archibald Nembhard. He enlisted in New York on August 9, 1918 but on arrival in England was posted to the King's Own Yorkshire Light Infantry. In April 1919, he was charged with a criminal offence but was declared insane and sent to Rampton Lunatic Asylum, Retford, Nottinghamshire.[21] In Hull prison, where he was previously held, he was dangerous, noisy, destructive and irrational, and often violently assaulted officers and stripped himself naked.[22] By the time he arrived at Rampton Asylum he had become confused and apathetic although on one occasion he wrote an incoherent letter to his wife in Jamaica. Later he was able to write more coherent letters but remained apathetic, until it was recommended by the asylum authorities that he be sent home to Jamaica as an ordinary lunatic.

The total number of West Indians and, more specifically, BWIR men who returned 'mad' from the war is not known but between 1918 and 1919 the Jamaica asylum received 22 men suffering from 'shell-shock' and between 1919 and 1920, it admitted 49 members of the BWIR suffering from 'war excitement', a term used to describe shell–shock and other forms of mental disturbance; other patients were sent to their respective countries.[23] Dupuch remembered visiting a fellow Bahamian veteran at a mental hospital in the Bahamas: 'I went to see him. He was in a padded cell. I looked at him through a peep hole in the door. He was crawling around the room on all fours like a caged tiger. As soon as he became aware of my presence at the door, he raised up on his legs and charged violently at the peep hole.'[24] The process of readjusting in postwar society after much pain and disillusionment was thus a major problem for some veterans, as well as for members of their family and the wider community. After striking one of his sisters with a stone, veteran Henry Kirby inflicted 'terrible injuries' on a policeman, giving him a five–inch cut across the face.[25] While serving overseas, Kirby had been sentenced to three years penal servitude for striking a senior officer but had arrived in Grenada in 1919 suffering from 'recurrent mania'.[26] At the magistrate's court in Grenada, Kirby was pronounced insane and sent to the lunatic asylum but by March 1920, the medical officer reported that he had recovered.

The return of these mentally disturbed soldiers raises numerous questions about mental health care and psychiatry in Jamaica and the West Indsies at the time which this study did not, because of space and time limitation, investigate. Nevertheless, it is worth pointing out that the quality of care in local asylums probably left much to be desired, and not only because restraint was the main therapeutic tool, or because this form of mental illness was new to West Indian societies. Mentally ill persons in the Jamaica asylum, for instance, were often treated more as criminals than as patients.[27] Moreover, the asylums were overcrowded and frequently severely infected with diseases, such as yaws, syphilis, tuberculosis and dysentery. Care for the mentally ill in the community was not likely to be much better, because relatives were usually not keen on caring for a family member who had been in the asylum. It is also likely that, as was customary, relatives would have sought cures from bush doctors, 'French woman', obeah men and religious healers who, many believed, were more effective than the medical doctors. Significantly, however, the medical superintendent of the Jamaica asylum in 1918 concluded that some of those returned because of 'shell–shock' were of 'unstable mental organisation' and should never have been sent overseas.[28] His comments may be interpreted as an indictment of the medical examiners who allowed them to go overseas; his comments also point to the irregularity which characterised the selection process during recruitment.

Pay Discrimination

During the last months of the war discontent intensified among the black soldiers. The boredom, anxiety and anger against being confined to non–combatant work and against discrimination in housing, promotion and treatment, led to much resentment. This was evident in the rebellious attitudes among soldiers of the second WIR and others from the BWIR returning from East Africa to join their colleagues in Egypt for demobilisation.[29] Several were tried by court martial for using insubordinate and threatening language to superior officers and engaging in conduct 'prejudicial to good order and military discipline'. Some were imprisoned with hard labour, while others received up to 90 days Field Punishment No. 2, which was a less painful form of punishment than Field Punishment No. 1.

The speedy demobilisation of British troops, due to pressure from the servicemen and the British public, angered some of the West Indians who felt that Englishmen were being rushed to the region to take away their jobs.[30] Black soldiers in Egypt also furiously insisted: 'We have done our bit already and now we want to go home.'[31] This developed into a serious protest, which necessitated a senior officer coming to explain the situation to them. At the same time the Egyptian revolution was rapidly developing and this led to further delays as the West Indians were used as patrols and escorts.[32] Similarly in France, there was considerable restlessness and discontent among blacks detained at Marseilles prior to their repatriation. Although, according to the officials, they were 'treated more liberally than other patients in the matter of diet, extra rations of sugar and comforts, such as chocolates', they were all craving to be placed on board ship to take them home and 'this alone would satisfy them'.[33]

The situation was worsened by discriminatory pay. Recruited under the regulations governing British troops, the men of the BWIR were promised and officially entitled to the same scale of pay as British soldiers once they embarked for overseas. Consequently, the black rank and file received the same one shilling per day which was then paid to British troops. Nevertheless when special pay rates were given for particular jobs, attempts were made to exclude the BWIR In Mesopotamia, for example, a special bonus was given to all ranks attached to the Inland Water Transport who worked in a clerical capacity. Yet Sergeant–Major F.H.E. MacDonald of the British Honduras contingent, who worked as chief clerk in Baghdad, only received six pence a day, while his white subordinates drew about one shilling, four pence.[34] The most blatant form of pay discrimination occurred when the entire BWIR were denied a pay rise granted to other imperial troops under Army Order No. 1 of 1918. Under these regulations, British soldiers were given an increase of six pence per day, bringing their new rate to one shilling, six pence per day. The War Office ruled, however, that this increase was not applicable to the BWIR because they were classified as 'natives'.[35]

Black soldiers protested quickly and angrily. In a letter to the various governors in the West Indies, they insisted that this discrimination was not only an insult to those who had volunteered the fight for the empire but also an insult to the whole West Indies.[36] By this time a clear pattern of protest had emerged: soldiers were expressing their grievances in a West Indian context and petitions were usually signed by representatives from all the colonies. This suggests that their common experiences overseas were crucial in encouraging them to adopt a 'West Indian' outlook, instead of the narrow and parochial views which were then pervasive in the West Indies. This development of a more inclusive perspective among the soldiers appears quite congruent with the more general experience of West Indians overseas.

The celebrated West Indian novelist, George Lamming has, for example, written that 'no Barbadian, no Trinidadian, no St Lucian, no islander from the West Indies sees himself as a West Indian until he encounters another islander in a foreign territory.'[37]

Discontent and disillusionment were very evident in other letters of protest to West Indian governments and to the secretary of state signed by hundreds of soldiers. In one such letter the sergeants of the third BWIR objected that the circumstances encountered by the battalions serving in France and Italy did not 'tend to engender the most cordial feelings for the empire in West Indians'.[38] Another group angrily concluded: 'We have been deceived. We like to think the deception was not intentional. The fact remains conditions are not as we expect.'[39] In response to this letter, Governor O'Brien of Barbados pleaded with the Colonial Office to consider the complaints, because the signatories were all men of good character and standing in the colony and their petition was respectfully worded and 'differed considerably in tone' from other such letters received by members of the public.[40] The churches too came under serious questioning from the disgruntled soldiers. Chaplains were accused of failing to put into practice the 'simple teachings of Christ' and not rectifying the situation whereby the blacks were, 'treated neither as Christians nor British citizens, but as West Indian *niggers*'.[41]

The letters of protest and especially the show of cohesion among the West Indian soldiers caused much anxiety among the members the West Indian Contingent Committee. In an ominous letter signed by several former West Indian governors to the Secretary of State for the colonies, Walter Long, the committee pointed out the hypocrisy and impossibility of the situation. They alluded to the inadequacy of separation allowances in view of the great increases in the cost of living in the West Indies.[42] The letter pointed out the anomaly that West Indians who had been recruited in the United States and posted to British regiments were granted the pay increase, while those who were transferred to the BWIR found their pay and separation allowance reduced. In the light of these grievances, the committee felt compelled to warn the Colonial Office that this differentiation would have a serious effect on public opinion in the colonies when the West Indian contingent was demobilised. In a follow–up letter, the committee again warned the Colonial Office of the 'most serious effect' pay discrimination would have in the West Indies.[43]

In response to these numerous protests, on January 31, 1919 the Colonial Office held a meeting with the War Office to discuss the pay issue. At this meeting, the War Office officials withdrew somewhat from the claim that the West Indians were 'Natives', and argued instead that one of the main reasons for excluding them was that if the BWIR received the increase, similar concessions would have had to be made to other non–white units.[44] However, during the discussions, it emerged that 'a clear line' could be drawn between the BWIR and the other units. According to George Grindle, the War Office seemed oblivious to the 'grave political issues' involved in their decision to exclude the West Indians.[45] He feared that if the men of the BWIR were discharged with 'a rankling sense of injustice due to their colour', the British connection in the West Indies would be weakened, just when they needed to secure the loyalty of the blacks against American aggressiveness. It was agreed at the meeting that efforts had to be made to resolve the dispute in order to avoid serious disturbances in the West Indies and especially Jamaica. Grindle was convinced that if riots resulted from the War Office's decisions, the Colonial Office would be blamed.

As a result of these concerns, Lord Milner, who took over as secretary of state for the colonies on January 9, 1919 and who was firmly committed to the preservation of the empire, instructed that a cabinet memorandum be prepared outlining the reasons why the West Indians should be granted the pay increase.[46] The draft memorandum, prepared by senior clerk, E.R. Darnley, pointed out that the BWIR was raised on the specific promise that the men would be paid at British rates, and that the local governments had supported this.[47] Indeed, this had led the government of Barbados to decide that if the imperial government were not disposed to give the pay increase, it would. The fear was expressed that if other local governments followed the Barbados example, it would place the imperial government in the very invidious position of refusing to honour what the best colonial opinion regarded as a promise. Milner probably thought that this was put too crudely and hence suggested that the latter statement be omitted from the final draft.

The second main point of the memorandum was that the battalions in Palestine had earned distinctions in battle, while those in Europe had received high praise from their senior commanding officers. They had been subjected to the rigours of several European winters, although they had never previously been out of the tropics and had suffered severe casualties as a result, and they had been near the front line where they were constantly under shellfire. The regiment was entirely composed of volunteers, many of whom were of a 'superior class', and had incurred much private loss by their patriotic services.

The third and most important point of the memorandum was that the exclusion of the BWIR from the pay increase would have serious political repercussions. The War Office was made aware of the numerous protests and warned of the consequences of not treating the BWIR fairly. The memorandum concluded that Lord Milner was 'clearly of the opinion' that differentiation upon racial grounds was not only unjust and inexpedient, but would give rise to serious disorders in the West Indies and would also cause an exacerbation of racial feeling which might prejudice the future of the colonies for a generation. Although Milner was not prepared to pledge that if the concession was made there would be no disorder, he was convinced that there would be no comparison between such minor difficulties that might occur in any case, and the grave consequences which were to be expected if the pay increase was not granted.

While Milner thought that the memorandum contained the substance of the case to be put to the cabinet, he felt it was too long and the issues could have been put more simply, emphasising the political considerations.[48] It was only after these protests and warnings by soldiers, local officials and the Contingent Committee that the War Office, on the urging of the Colonial Office, decided to extend the benefit under Army Order No. 1 of 1918 to the BWIR.[49] Clearly, the same fears of disturbances and attacks on property, which influenced West Indian participation in the war, were again at work over the pay controversy. Thus, the decision over equal pay was not so much the triumph of fair–play and justice, as an effort to prevent unrest in the West Indies. However, as we will see, the decision came somewhat late because a major disturbance had already erupted among the black soldiers at Taranto, Italy.

Taranto Revolt

After Armistice Day, the eight BWIR battalions in France and Italy were concentrated at Taranto, Italy to prepare for demobilisation.[50] They were subsequently joined by the three battalions from Egypt and the men from Mesopotamia. As a result of severe labour shortages at Taranto, the West

Indians had to assist with loading and unloading ships and do labour fatigues. This led to much resentment and December 6, 1918 the men of the ninth battalion revolted and attacked their officers. On the same day, 180 sergeants forwarded a petition to the secretary of state complaining about the pay issue, the failure to increase their separation allowance and the fact that they had been discriminated against in the area of promotions.[51]

During the mutiny, which lasted about four days, a black NCO shot and killed one of the mutineers in self–defence and there was also a bombing. Disaffection spread quickly among the other soldiers and on December 9, the 'increasingly truculent' tenth battalion refused to work.[52] A senior commander, Lt-Colonel Willis, who had ordered some BWIR men to clean the latrines of the Italian labour corps was also subsequently assaulted.[53] In response to calls for help from the commanders at Taranto, a machine–gun company and a battalion of the Worcestershire Regiment were despatched to restore order. The ninth BWIR was disbanded and the men distributed to the other battalions, which were all subsequently disarmed. Approximately 60 were later tried for mutiny and those convicted received sentences ranging from three to five years but one man got 20 years, while another was executed by a firing squad from the Worcestershire Regiment.[54]

Although the mutiny was crushed, the bitterness persisted, and on December 17, about 60 NCOs held a meeting to discuss the question of black rights, self–determination and closer union in the West Indies. An organisation called the Caribbean League was formed at the gathering to further these objectives. At another meeting on the twentieth, under the chairmanship of one Sergeant Baxter, who had just previously been super-seded by a white NCO, a sergeant of the third BWIR argued that the black man should have freedom and govern himself in the West Indies and that if necessary, force and bloodshed should be used to attain these aims.[55] His sentiments were loudly applauded by the majority of those present. The discussion eventually drifted from matters concerning the West Indies, to one of grievances of the black man against the white.[56] The question of white officers being appointed in place of blacks who were not inferior was also discussed and subtle threats were made against those white officers who were to be sent back with them. The soldiers decided to hold a general strike for higher wages on their return to the West Indies. The headquarters for the Caribbean League was to be in Kingston, Jamaica with sub–offices in the other colonies.

Details of the meeting and the formation of the Caribbean League were related to the officials by Major Maxwell Smith of Trinidad, the commander of the eighth battalion, whose informant was a sergeant in his battalion who had attended the meeting. On learning about the Caribbean League, the general officer at Taranto, Major–General Thuillier, considered bringing the Jamaican organisers of the meeting, Sergeants H.L. Brown, A.P. Jones and C.H. Collman, all in the third BWIR, to trial for conspiring to cause sedition[57]. Finally, however, he decided that it would be 'useless and inadvisable' to do so because of the difficulty of inducing loyal witnesses, whose personal safety would be endangered, to give evidence in court. He feared, moreover, the defence was likely to produce witnesses who would deny that any seditious words were uttered.

When the men from Egypt and Mesopotamia subsequently arrived at Taranto, they had to perform the ordinary daily camp and kitchen fatigues at transit camps occupied by European units of the Egyptian Expeditionary Force passing through on their way to demobilisation.[58] This was regarded by the men of the first and second battalions as a gross insult because they had been engaged in direct combat. In addition, at Taranto unlike in Egypt, all YMCA huts and cinemas used by British troops were placed out of bounds to the West Indians by order of the base commandant, Brigadier–General Carey Bernard, a white South African who had served for two years with the Egyptian Expeditionary Force.[59] The men of the BWIR were also made to go to the Native Labour Hospitals. Woodhill alleged that several men 'died from sheer neglect' at the No. 6 Native Hospital and that 300 West Indians died at Taranto.[60] The dread the West Indians had of this hospital was made clear by the private who wrote: 'Thank God I was not one of the unfortunates who had to go to the Native Hospital for treatment, oh! oh!, it is awful to think of it.'[61]

Although Major J.B. Thursfield of the BWIR protested that the West Indians should be treated the same as British troops, Bernard took no notice, saying 'that the men were only niggers and that no such treatment should ever have been promised to them, that they were better fed and treated than any nigger had the right to expect, that he would order them to do whatever work he pleased, and if they objected he would force them to do it.'[62] There was also much discontent among the fifth battalion due to irregularities in court–martial procedures, which led to some West Indians being punished for allegedly beating three men of the Gloucester Regiment who had called them 'Sambo', which meant 'a son of a bastard'.[63] Subsequently, senior BWIR officers tried to get the events at Taranto investigated but after a superficial inquiry, the Army Council concluded that a full investigation was not necessary.[64]

Not surprisingly, events at Taranto produced much anxiety in the Colonial Office and impelled it into pressing the War Office to grant the BWIR the pay increase. Grindle confessed that he had 'considerable apprehensions' about demobilisation, especially in Jamaica and felt that some rioting was inevitable.[65] His fears were intensified because the main body of the garrison in Jamaica was black. Darnley also thought the men's knowledge of arms and discipline made them much more dangerous.[66] In the light of these concerns, the Colonial Office warned the governor of Jamaica to make arrangements to provide the ex–servicemen with employment and 'direct his attention to the problem of keeping order', and preparations were made to have a warship stationed in Jamaica when the men arrived.[67]

Race\Class Riots in England (Seamen and Ex–servicemen)

The cessation of hostilities quickly led to a profound change in white attitudes to the presence of blacks in the United Kingdom. As white seamen and soldiers were demobilised and the competition for jobs intensified, so too did the level of race and class antagonism, especially in London and the port cities. It was difficult, perhaps impossible, for blacks in England not to feel unwanted. Manley, for instance, recalled the great increase in race prejudice on his return to civilian life in England. In London, according to him, he was a 'constant and almost continuous' user of Gray's Inn and its common room for nearly three years but 'never came to know a single white man there or to speak to any except to say "Good Morning" or "Good Day"' and he felt 'race hostility or suspicions' as he moved around in lodging houses and shops.[68] The more serious aspect of this intensification of race and class conflict was the numerous riots which erupted and the assaults on blacks in the United Kingdom. Similar disturbances developed in the United States, and a number of black soldiers who had served in the Canadian forces were also brutally assaulted by whites who resented the presence of a black camp in their locality.[69]

One of the earliest outbreaks of violence took place in September 1918 at the Belmont Road military hospital in Liverpool, where there were about

2,000 wounded soldiers recuperating. Among them were about 50 black soldiers, many of whom had had single or double amputations. Conflicting details of the incident were reported in the *London Times* and the black edited *African Telegraph*. The latter was the official organ of the Society of Peoples of African Origin formed in London in 1918 to further the interests of all blacks, bring their grievances to the notice of the British public and promoting closer commercial ties between the United Kingdom and the colonies of Africa and the West Indies.

According to the *African Telegraph*, amicable relations existed between white and black soldiers until the arrival of some whites who had served in South Africa.[70] The newcomers started to taunt the blacks and this led to a fight in which a sledgehammer was thrown at a group of blacks, which included two legless men. After being harassed in the concert room, two blacks decided to leave but as they were passing a white soldier called out 'make room for the swine to pass'.[71] Following this incident the concert room was put out of bounds for the blacks. Later a rumour circulated that the ban had been lifted but when a legless black sergeant, John Demerette, alias Demetrius, attempted to ask the guard if this was true, he was seized and thrown into a cell. His yells for help brought ten other crippled blacks but this in turn led to a rumour among the whites that the 'niggers' were attacking the guards.

A serious altercation ensued in which 50 blacks engaged about 500 whites soldiers in combat; bottles, sticks, crutches, pots and pans were used as missiles. Significantly, some British soldiers who had served with the blacks in the trenches allegedly assisted them in the struggle, and when the military police arrived on the scene there were many white soldiers seen standing over crippled black limbless soldiers, and protecting them with their sticks and crutches from the furious onslaught of the other white soldiers until order was restored. A nurse was caught up in the action and although she was not seriously injured, went into shock and fainted. She subsequently developed pneumonia and died. An official investigation concluded that she died through misadventure.[72]

The *London Times'* version, allegedly based on information from William Henry Taylor, the officer in charge of the hospital, also indicated that the 50 West Indians were attacked by over 400 whites, but blamed the disturbance solely on the blacks.[73] Demetrius was accused of attempting to leave the hospital illegally, and of drawing a razor and slashing wildly with it when he was stopped. However, an investigation by the War Office found that the blacks were not entirely responsible for the riot.[74] Sir Everard im Thurn, chairman of the West Indian Contingent Committee, who had tried unsuccessfully to be at the inquiry, was deeply concerned that such a serious racial row should have taken place and feared that a great deal of the loyalty to empire created in the West Indies by the acceptance of their war services would be cancelled out when large numbers of aggrieved men were repatriated.[75]

The subsequent riots were far more extensive and involved thousands of whites who unleashed a series of brutal attacks on non–white groups in many cities including Cardiff, Glasgow, Hull, Liverpool, London and Newport.[76] In these disturbances white seamen and ex–servicemen often made common cause against the blacks. In one not unusual incident in Liverpool, a 24–year–old Bermudan or Trinidadian, Charles Wotten, who had recently been discharged from the navy, was thrown off a pier into the water and pelted with stones.[77] After his dead body was dragged from the water, no arrests were made. Some ex–servicemen were assaulted, although wearing their uniforms on the streets afforded them limited protection. On one occasion in Cardiff, a black ex–serviceman pleaded with the crowd in 'perfect English' not to molest him, but they nevertheless gave him several blows before the police escorted him away.[78] It was widely claimed that these attacks were partly a consequence of white–male resentment at black men having relationships with white women.[79]

Because of the large–scale onslaughts on blacks, and in an attempt to appease the British public, the government decided to repatriate as many blacks as they could and by the middle of September 1919, about 600 had been repatriated. However, in Cardiff and elsewhere, some blacks described as the 'militant section' by David Williams, Cardiff's chief constable, 'would not entertain the question of repatriation' and 'were insistent in claiming as British subjects their right to equality of treatment and freedom to remain' in England.[80] Other militants agreed to be repatriated, but openly stated that it would only be for the 'object of creating racial feelings against members of the white race domiciled in their country'.[81] Black seamen in Hull sent a delegation consisting of two West Africans and several West Indians, including one G. Steede, to see George Morley, the chief constable. According to Morley, they complained bitterly that they did not receive the same treatment as whites and that they were victimised even by the officials; they threatened that similar treatment would be given to the white men in their home colonies.[82] Steede made a 'particularly virulent speech' and indicated that the repatriated West Indians 'would become centers of disaffection' and that if England was to be 'a white man's country, the West Indies should be a coloured man's country'.[83] He also talked extensively about the rights of man.

While Morley did not attach much importance to what they were saying, contemptuously surmising that it was 'due to the delight which the half–educated coloured man take in hearing his own voice pouring out long words', [84] Lord Milner was more fearful of the effect of the return of these disgruntled men on the white minorities in the colonies.[85] He pointed out that many of the blacks had served in the army, navy and merchant service, and bitterly resented their treatment. His fears would have increased had he known that the radical section of the West Indian press was angrily publicising the abuse of the blacks in England. The *Federalist*, for instance, declared that the lowest classes of England were no more refined nor endowed with altruistic sentiments than the wildest savage in the darkest parts of the earth.[86] Against the background of the British free–passage emigration schemes to settle British ex–servicemen overseas, the *West Indian* saw the riots as even greater reason for closer scrutiny of the type of Englishmen, even if they be ex–servicemen, permitted to enter the colonies.[87] Organisations like the St. Kitts Universal Benevolent Association also protested against the 'barbarous treatment' of black soldiers and seamen in England.[88]

Meanwhile the wives of the black seamen and ex–servicemen also experienced difficulties as they waited to be repatriated with their husbands. On one occasion the secretary of the West Indian Contingent Committee, Algernon Aspinall complained to the Colonial Office that during a visit to the Maddox Hotel in Liverpool, he found 18 wives and 20 children of black ex–servicemen crammed into two or three small rooms awaiting repatriation.[89] He warned that the conditions were such that if an epidemic or illness broke out it would be serious. He urged that they be urgently sent home to Jamaica in order to prevent a 'fresh scandal' developing.[90] In response to representations from the Colonial Office, the War Office investigated their situation and agreed to provide additional food but better accommodation was difficult because the Maddox was fully occupied and no other hotel would accept blacks.[91] The unsanitary condition in the rooms was, however, partly because the women usually took their food into the rooms where they apparently felt more comfortable socially, and because they also objected to the European cleaners entering their rooms.

The question of European women accompanying their black husbands home proved an even more formidable difficulty for British officials, since West Indian authorities were not keen on having mixed couples in the colonies. In Jamaica, as in the other colonies, the integrity of marriage and the family was associated with the preservation of class, colour and caste boundaries and while individual choice was permitted, this was usually within the confines of race.[92] Marriage between blacks and whites was regarded by colonial authorities and elites as a threat to white hegemony. It was against this background that the acting governor of Jamaica, H. Bryan, informed the Colonial Office that while there was no objection in principle to white wives of blacks being admitted to the colony, such a course was 'most undesirable in the interests of the wives'.[93]

Governor Haddon–Smith of the Windward Islands likewise reluctantly agreed to accept the white wife of a Vincentian seaman, but warned that this would lead to the public degradation of white women, in view of the racial ill–feeling in the colonies.[94] His fears were later justified when the white wife of seaman C. Robinson of St Vincent had to be hurried back to Europe by the authorities after being publicly jeered and harassed.[95] Since there was little the Colonial Office could do to resolve what Grindle described as 'this insoluble problem', it simply opted to warn the women of the conditions they were likely to encounter in the colonies; several nevertheless resolved to go with their husbands.

The Climax

The Home Front

The fears of the local and British officials over the return of the BWIR men were intensified by the social and economic troubles which affected the West Indies between 1914 and 1919, partly as a consequence of the war. The extent of the suffering caused by the war was revealed in a series of reports to the West Indian department of the Colonial Office from the colonies. They all indicated that prices of staple food items and especially clothing had risen sharply, while wages had failed to do likewise. In Jamaica, for instance, foodstuffs rose by an average of 126 per cent and clothing by 216 per cent but wages, which varied regionally, only increased by 33.5 per cent for men and 26 per cent for women.[1] Likewise in Grenada, food prices increased by an average of 122 per cent and clothes between 200 per cent and 500 per cent but wages for men only increased by 50 per cent to 75 per cent and 60 per cent for women.[2] Conditions in Grenada were somewhat dramatically summed up in the *Federalist*:

> Grenada is in a state of siege. Food prices are rising every day. Wages continue stationary or are a diminishing quantity. Everybody is complaining and everybody is suffering. The shilling can scarcely purchase six pence worth of food. It can't buy a four pence worth of clothing for the working man. Samples of stuff which formerly sold here at two pence half–penny a yard are priced first cost at from twenty to twenty six cents. Clothing will scarcely just now be obtainable. Fig leaves may be available, but the poorer classes may have to feed on them. Government must do something.[3]

A government commission to investigate the conditions of the labouring classes in British Guiana during the war similarly revealed that most items of food and clothing had become prohibitively costly.[4] The effect of the war was, however, not consistent across all classes or even colonies and this needs to be looked at in more detail by Caribbean historians. In several colonies, including Grenada, Barbados, and in particular Montserrat, small farmers and peasant proprietors were reported as doing well and making good profits from the cultivation of crops like cotton, sugar cane and especially ground provisions.[5]

The sharp increase in the cost of living was also the result of the uncertainty, if nothing else, of the shift which the war, and more precisely the battle in the Atlantic, caused in the import trading patterns in the West Indies. In 1915 the Royal Mail Steam Packet Company terminated its contract for the transatlantic steamer service and the inter–colonial service was also brought to an end. From that time, most West Indian colonies were almost entirely dependent for communication with Britain on a contract service with Canada and on the steamers of the Scrutton's Direct Line. The irregularity of the service with Britain forced West Indian importers to look elsewhere for goods, and while Barbados turned mainly to Canada, most of the other colonies looked to the United States.

Whereas Britain supplied 38.4 per cent of the value of Jamaica's imports in 1913 by 1919, the figure had fallen to 19.9 per cent although it had risen to 29.7 per cent by 1920. On the other hand, the value of imports from the United States rose from 46.8 per cent in 1913 to 66.2 per cent in 1919. Although this percentage fell to 58.6 per cent by 1920, Jamaica remained much more dependent on American than British imports.[6] The change in Trinidad was also significant. British goods accounted for 31.5 per cent of the colony's imports in 1913 but had been reduced to 16.6 per cent by 1919, while American imports increased from 28.8 per cent in 1913 to 38.9 per cent by 1919.[7] Significantly, however, the difficulties in obtaining imports forced the colonies to establish intensive programmes of local food cultivation, but while these did fairly well in the Windward Islands, Jamaica and Trinidad, for example, in other islands like Barbados, drought conditions in some areas seriously limited production.[8]

The situation of the merchants, and especially the planters, represented a sharp contrast to the hard times being endured by the labouring classes. It was popularly believed that the merchants and planters were making 'super profits' and profiteering as a result of the war, while refusing to increase wages significantly. Whether the merchants were actually profiteering is a difficult and complex question and not only because the issues were clouded by adverse public opinion, which tended to generalise about all merchants, but because in England, the term profiteering remained imprecise and, as the commissioners in British Guiana discovered, establishing what constituted 'unreasonable profit' was not an easy task.[9] However, after examining numerous witnesses and the invoices of 19 of the leading merchants, they concluded that, contrary to popular belief, there was no evidence of profiteering by merchants in that colony.[10] The major causes of the price increases were the significant escalation in the cost of imported goods at their place of origin and freight rates as well as the high rates of exchange with the United States. Governor Haddon–Smith likewise examined the invoices of the merchants in Grenada and concluded that there was no evidence of profiteering.[11] This did not mean that some merchants in the region were not making considerable profits and engaging in dubious practices. One John Smith who owned a business called Bonanza, which was apparently on the verge of bankruptcy when the war started, died in 1919 leaving £250,000.[12] Shopkeepers and other retailers were also responsible for increasing the misery of the poor by engaging in illegal and dishonest selling practices.[13] Similarly, a number of shopkeepers in Antigua were convicted and fined for selling goods at a higher rate than that prescribed by the Food Control Committee.[14]

In the case of the planters, it was very clear to officials and the public alike that in spite of increased taxes and operational costs they were making considerable profits as a result of greater production and increased prices for their products. For example, cocoa which had been selling in 1914 on the London market for less than 60s. per hundredweight (cwt.), by 1919 was fetching over 130s. per cwt.[15] Thus, while Grenada's cocoa export valued £248,398 in 1909, by 1919 the figure had jumped to £539,740.[16] The prosperity of the exporters was also reflected in the fact that whereas before 1914 the number of motor cars in the island was less than six, by the end of 1919 there were over 200 in use in the colony in addition to other motor lorries.[17] The sudden importation of motor cars had a disastrous effect on the roads and as a result, a loan of £100,000 was secured by the government in 1917, mainly to improve the roads but also for the extension of pipe–borne water to the various districts. A similar situation developed in British Honduras where the sudden influx of cars forced the government to borrow £10,000 to repair the streets of the town.[18]

In Barbados, where sugar accounted for 93 per cent of exports in 1914, planters made massive profits as a result of the destruction of a large section of the world's beet–sugar fields, whose rise had caused a serious crisis in the West Indian sugar industry.[19] Ideal rainfall and more intensive cultivation in Barbados led to huge production during the war years, while sugar prices rose from 28s. per cwt. in 1915 to 60s. by the end of the war. Between 1916 and 1917, records were established in revenue and trade; money was subscribed for loans, and estates were for the most part cleared of debts, thus enabling profits to be invested in improved machinery and general estate improvement.[20]

The high prices for sugar led in part to the abandonment of the system of crop rotation and the neglect of the cultivation of ground provisions. Given that Barbados in sharp contrast to, Jamaica and the Windward Islands, for example, had historically always depended heavily on imports to feed its population, this further reduction in local food production increased the price of food items and caused greater hardship for the labouring population. As a result, the planting of food crops had to be enforced by the government and the control of reaping and sale was supervised by a committee appointed under the Vegetable Produce Act. By 1918, sugar had displaced bananas as Jamaica's main export but the colony was never really able to capitalise on the lucrative market conditions because drought conditions in some areas resulted in a fall in production of 6,000 tons from the comparatively small figure of 1917 to 26,000 tons in 1918.[21]

Influenced by the parallel debate in Europe about the relationship between labour and capital, the West Indian press and its radical section in particular, became perhaps even more assertive than in the pre–war years in their condemnations of the government and planter/merchant elites and in championing the cause of the poor. In one of its customarily scathing articles, the *Federalist*, for instance, observed:

Our Governor! What a kind friend he is to the poor people of Grenada. He and his councilors are allowing the community to be fleeced by a set of heartless shopkeepers and merchants. The merchants and shopkeepers – glorying in the war, reading the telegrams voluptuously, awaiting every word of the prices current with eagerness, like the satyr they blow hot and cold at the same time; with one breath they wish that the war would soon be over, while in their innate conscience wish it will continue – are unscrupulously raising the prices of their goods.[22]

The usually conservative *Gleaner* revealed that it too had a liberal strand and could champion the cause of the labouring classes when it thought necessary: 'We have only to glance at the profits made on many of our exportable products, at the rates of wages obtaining throughout this island and at the abnormal prices of nearly all articles of food and clothing, to have it borne in upon us that a few persons in Jamaica are profiting by the war and the vast majority are suffering sorely.'[23]

Because of the hardship caused by the war, many parents in Grenada and British Honduras, and probably in other colonies also, had to keep their children from school.[24] The reports of the Wesleyan Methodist Missionary Society for the years 1914 to 1919, indicate that attendance at church services declined significantly because people could not procure the clothing and shoes which they considered necessary for public worship.[25] Newspapers in Grenada also reported that the incidence of begging in the streets had increased significantly and there were several prosecutions for this offence, which the officials regarded as vagrancy.[26] That even the most destitute were liable to prosecution was revealed by the case of one Frank Ford in Antigua, described by the *Sun* as having a terrible deformity, who, convicted under the Vagrancy Act, was sentenced to two weeks' imprisonment.[27] In Trinidad a sentence of three weeks was passed on a mother for allowing her son to go about begging in the city.[28]

Crime rates also spiralled in most of the colonies and this led to fierce debates, especially about the ways to combat praedial larceny. In Jamaica, for instance, convictions for this offence in the resident magistrates' courts increased from 2,009 in 1914 to 4,787 by 1917, while for the same period, convictions in these courts for other offences against property increased from 1,652 to 2,663.[29] It should be noted that convictions for praedial larceny were often difficult to obtain because stolen items of food were quickly consumed. Planters did not hesitate to call for the 'Cat' as a remedy, since it was believed to have a 'moral effect' on thieves.[30] The drastic sentences which were frequently imposed on those convicted, reflected the hysteria surrounding the issue. In one not unusual case, a magistrate in Grenada sentenced a 61–year–old man to three months in jail and 15 strokes with the rod for stealing three pence worth of potatoes from a plantation.[31] The decision provoked much criticism in the colony and the *Federalist* condemned it as being 'monstrously stupid'. [32] In Barbados a noted fowl stealer Percy Sobers was even shot.[33]

Unlike in England, where infant mortality rates declined during the war years as a result of the improved standard of living, in the West Indies, the usually high rates persisted and it was not until the 1920s and especially the 1940s that there was a decline, for instance, in Jamaica.[34] However, an organisation called the Child Saving League was established in Jamaica in 1916, and like similar bodies in England, it sought to provide care for children. The crisis in the West Indies was also reflected in other more dramatic ways, including migration, especially to the United States and Cuba. Between 1911 and 1920, approximately 123,424 West Indians mainly from the British areas entered the United States. This level of migration was certainly significant but it should be pointed out that some 107,548 people had also migrated to America during the period 1901 to 1910.[35] What was more significant about the figures for the war years and what alarmed the local press and officials was that this increased migration, which included a large number of women, was taking place in spite of the economic hardship caused by the war and despite the fact that fares had increased significantly. For example, the cost of a passage from the West Indies to England increased from £25 single and £40 return in 1916 to £50 single and £100 return by 1920.[36]

Both the Grenada papers regarded the steady migration from the colony as a quest for better wages and an indictment of the government and the elites. The heavy migration, according to the *West Indian*, represented 'one of the historic methods of the silent protest of a people against tyranny, economic slavery, the governmental authority of dirt and disease, and the privileged systems of starvation under which young men and women are expected to live from hand to mouth, subsisting on their finger–nails'.[37] Governor Haddon–Smith, clearly out of touch with reality and misunderstanding the West Indian extended family structure, disagreed and argued instead that the heavy migration was caused more by the desire of men to escape the responsibility of providing for the numerous 'human parasites', which included aged aunts, cousins and families of deceased brothers and sisters, than by hardship.[38] He ignored the important role of remittances in the development of West Indian societies.[39]

Even more alarming to the authorities was the fact that between 1916 and 1919, a number of colonies including St Lucia, Grenada, Barbados, Antigua, Trinidad, Jamaica and British Guiana, experienced a series of strikes in which, in the case of Antigua, Jamaica and Trinidad, several strikers were shot and killed.[40] Significantly, women workers in Jamaica also organised a number of successful strikes during which they loudly sang popular army songs like 'Tipperary'.[41] In the light of these developments in the region, the *Globe*, in characteristic alarmist fashion, called for drastic measures against agitators in Barbados, and warned the authorities: 'These are days of strikes, burglaries, midnight maraudings and general unrest; our masses, directed by any silvery tongued leader in whom they might trust, are like kerosene, easily inflamed.'[42] In Trinidad in early 1917, a detachment of BWIR recruits who were awaiting transport overseas were sent under Cipriani, along with men from the naval patrols to guard the properties affected by the strikes.[43] Likewise a group of recruits from the Bahamas on their way to Jamaica did not hesitate to load the ship's cargo at Ragged Island where there was a dispute between the dock labourers and the shippers.[44]

These two episodes of strike–breaking suggest that at this point, the soldiers, imbued with a new sense of importance and identity, may have had little sympathy for the labouring classes from which many had recently been recruited. More importantly, the strikes reflected the extent of the economic and social malaise in West Indian societies and the increasing confidence of the labourers in asserting their rights to better wages and working conditions in spite of the fact that the authorities were likely to responded with disproportionate violence to suppress their demands. In many cases, the labourers were able to gain concessions. In Barbados and other colonies, there were also frequent clashes between police and large groups of the urban poor, whose numbers had increased significantly in many of the colonies during the late nineteenth century, partly as a result of the crisis in the sugar industry.[45] In fact, in British Honduras a determined effort was made in August 1918 to destroy the entire town with a fire which did extensive damage to the property of the elites and government.[46] According to the acting governor, R. Walter, the general attitude of the public to the fire was 'let it burn'.[47]

With the end of the war in Europe and the realisation that conditions locally were getting worse, the debate about labour and capital escalated and was accompanied by a more relentless and vicious assault from the radical press on the ruling classes and warnings of severe social unrest. The Grenada papers were among the most vociferous in this respect. In an article symbolically and prophetically entitled, 'Run to the Precipice', an angry *West Indian* questioned:

> How long are we going to shirk and put off the solution of the labour problem? We have put it off for years but cannot afford to elude it much longer. The time has come when the question must be faced squarely and some arrangements made for the better life of the masses. We have reached a point where we cannot run very much further from the labour question. We are on the brink of a yawning precipice over which are active discontent, economic ruin and the very social prostitution of the people as a whole.[48]

The paper went on to call for a new economic order, principally because it argued in a determinist manner, 'the moral, social or intellectual order takes its cue from the economic'.[49] It also accused the church of lacking any moral conscience.

These arguments by the paper show how quickly the radical section of the local press had begun to incorporate some of the more ideologically explicit ideas and rhetoric of the Russian Revolution and of socialists in Europe to bolster their attack on Crown Colony Government and the socio-economic situation in the colonies, although G.K. Lewis doubts whether Marryshow or any of his contemporaries were socialists in anything other than their domestic paternalism and the rhetoric they borrowed from the British Labour Party.[50] He argues, for instance, that Marryshow was, in spite of all his noble gifts, 'at most a West Indian Fabian, a Royalist–Loyalist whose staunch Whig constitutionalism never permitted him to fight the colonial power except on its own polite terms'.[51] Nevertheless, the paper's sentiments reflected the uncertainty, class divisions and conflict which characterised West Indian societies by early 1919 and, in retrospect, clearly pointed to the impending social catastrophe.

It was into this turmoil that the disgruntled seamen and ex–servicemen were about to return and many people in the region were hoping or anticipating and, in the case of the authorities, fearing, that their arrival would bring the conflict to head. In Barbados, for instance, there was according to Governor O'Brien, 'considerable amount of local excitement' over the disbanding of the soldiers, some of whom had sent threatening letters to various people in the community.[52] Although the strikes in Barbados had been settled, the labourers were sullen and there were hints that trouble would arise with the return of the ex–servicemen. Moreover, there were, he warned, agitators on the island who were desirous of 'stirring up strife and raising the racial question'.[53] He requested naval support should trouble arise.

Fears were also expressed in a letter to Lord Hankey, secretary of the War Council,[54] from one Colonel Homfray, whose job involved travelling to the various West Indian colonies.[55] The letter was passed on to Milner by Hankey, with the warning that Homfray's opinion was not one to be neglected. In it Homfray claimed that throughout the colonies there was 'a good deal of uneasiness' as to what would happen when the black troops 'imbued with revolutionary ideas' returned home *en masse*. He pointed out that they had already given trouble at Taranto and that all the returned soldiers he had met seemed to think that they would not need to work any more but would be supported by a grateful country. He thought that as the number of white volunteers in the colonies was small and the black ones unreliable, it was probably necessary for three cruisers to be sent out to the region with Royal Marines equipped with machine guns and stationed at Trinidad, Barbados and Jamaica where most trouble was expected. While he shared Homfray's concerns, Darnley thought that to send three cruisers to the West Indies 'would look like panic'.[56] Nevertheless, Milner warned the local governors to take 'every precaution to maintain order during demobilisation'.[57]

Similar concerns were expressed by Governor Probyn of Jamaica, who observed that the strikes and violence of 1918 had revealed that the military force in the colony would be inadequate if labour disturbances were to occur in more than three parishes simultaneously. He feared that such an outbreak might occur because of the ex–servicemen bringing back a form of 'Russianised unrest'.[58] He therefore appointed a select committee of the Legislative Council to consider how best to strengthen the local forces; as a result of its report, a sum of £10,000 was voted for this purpose.[59] The local authorities also attempted to raise a force in preparation for the landing of the ex–servicemen but found that there was a 'decided disinclination' amongst the civil population to join such a force.[60] Probyn also made arrangements for assistance to be given to those ex–servicemen who desired to migrate to Cuba.[61]

The legislature also passed an Act giving each ex–serviceman, except those dishonourably discharged, the right to vote in the next election only, in order to get them to put forth their case in a constitutional manner.[62] In addition, a food controller was appointed in 1919 to deal with the question of retail prices.[63] These measures had as much or more to do with the prevention of unrest among the ex–servicemen and the maintenance of social order locally, as with the desire to express any appreciation to the men for their military service overseas. Indeed, the prospect of the local forces of the law encountering rioters more skilled than themselves in the art of suppression and the use of weapons, terrified nervous local officials and white elites.

Arrival of Ex–Servicemen and Seamen

British Honduras

On July 8, 1919, the main body of the British–Honduras contingent which had been stationed in Mesopotamia returned to the colony on board the transport ship *Veronej*. After landing, the contingent marched through the town, which had been well–decorated with flags and banners with greetings such as, 'Welcome home', 'You have done your duty', and 'We have kept the home fires burning'. The parade ended at government house where Governor Eyre Hutson spoke to them, shook their hands and urged them to consult their senior officer whenever they had a problem. He also assured them that they would receive the main portion of their pay as soon as possible and encouraged them to put their money in the savings bank and be thrifty. Getting them to save their money was crucial if they were to be convinced to participate in the government's land settlement scheme for ex–servicemen. The scheme was outlined to the men and Hutson urged them to become agriculturalists, since this would help alleviate the colony's labour shortage and help make the country prosperous. The following day sports were held in their honour and they were entertained by the Returned Soldiers Welfare Society.

This grand welcome may have put the contingent men and the civilians in good spirits temporarily but the eruption of a major disturbance in the capital Belize, on the night of July 22, soon made it clear that all was not well. The disturbance was started and initially led by contingent men who, armed with sticks and acting under the orders of a leader, marched through the streets breaking shop windows. They were quickly joined by other comrades and thousands of civilian men, women and children. Shops of the most prominent merchants were systematically looted by the crowds which had quickly increased to between 3,000 and 4,000 or between a quarter and a third of the town's population. Looting lasted throughout the night and continued until the morning of the twenty–third. Women played an active part and carried away tremendous loads of loot in their dresses and returned for more.[64]

During the riot, threats were openly made against whites and persons acting in support of the law. Many of them, including P.E. Matthews, the captain and adjutant of the Territorial Force, Robert Wyatt, the superintendent of police, Percy George, editor of the *Clarion*, W.H. Hoar, the keeper of prisons and several of clerks from the leading stores, were ruthlessly beaten with sticks. The story each told of his ordeal emphasised the determination of the contingent men and civilians to devastate the local white population. Robert Wyatt, for example, related of his experience with one group of rioters:

> They were carrying sticks and shouting ... My intention was to prevail on the contingent men. I went right amongst them and appealed to them to stop, something like this: "For God's sake men do not do this, you will get a bad name". No sooner were these words out of my mouth than Tony Hamilton (a contingent man) struck me with a stick right on the left shoulder or upper part of the breast, and somebody, I am almost prepared to say it was Hamilton, shouted out: "Beat it, you white bastard, to the station; beat it to the station". A number of contingent men then set about me with sticks immediately ... During the time I was being beaten by the contingent men, the civilians standing by jeered and laughed and danced.[65]

E.A. Baber, the acting chief clerk in the colonial secretary's office was convinced that the rioters were determined to destroy anything and everything white.[66] It is not difficult to see how he arrived at this conclusion because the contingent men were shouting comments like, 'We are going to give them hell tonight', 'This is not Mesopotamia, this is not Egypt, this is Belize', 'We are with the civilians and the civilians are with us', 'We are going to kill the white sons of bitches tonight', and, 'This is the black man's night.'[67] Moreover as J.A. Gardiner, a barber, observed, the civilians were just as involved in the beatings as the contingent men.[68] In fact, J. Blades the acting assistant superintendent of police, claimed that he heard many civilians yelling, 'this is our country and we want to get the white man out'.[69] The brutal assaults on whites prompted some to desert their premises, while others found refuge on board a Spanish barge in the harbour.

Of all the local officials who were assaulted, none was more psychologically devastated than the acting chief justice, G.O.D. Walton. He and several other whites had been staying at the boarding house of I.F. Staine, a coloured woman who refused to board blacks, when a group of over 200 protestors began pelting the residence with stones, sticks and other missiles.[70] An axe was also used in an attempt to destroy part of the wooden foundation of the house. Realising that matters were getting quite serious Walton put on a steel helmet, went outside and informed the crowd that he was the chief justice and asked them what they wanted. He was greeted with a barrage of missiles and 'filthy, insulting expressions' abusing whites, and a bottle was smashed against his helmet forcing him to beat a hasty retreat.[71] Later in the evening he met the governor at the police station and in very violent language demanded that drastic action be taken at once to shoot down the rioters.[72] Fearing that Walton's language was likely to cause more trouble if overheard, the governor begged him to refrain from such remarks.

Attempts to summon members of the Territorial Force to quell the riot were unsuccessful because, although the call to assemble was sounded continuously in each direction, only about 35 of the almost 200–strong force turned out. Since the bugle was not audible everywhere and the rioters were noisy, some may not have heard it. Yet, the failure of most of the men to show up could hardly be attributed to this problem because as the governor rightly maintained, it was very unlikely that any person in the town that night did not know there was a riot in progress and that the police were unable to suppress it.[73] It therefore seems likely that many members of the Territorial Force deliberately ignored the call or were discouraged from responding. Indeed, on the eve of the riot, the officers had observed an attitude of lukewarmness on the part of some of the men despite attempts to win their loyalty. Some ex–servicemen remained loyal but they were too few to be of any significance.

Realising that the local forces were inadequate to quell the disturbance, early in the evening of the twenty–second, the governor sent a wireless message to the naval commander at Bermuda, which fortunately was intercepted by H.M.S. *Constance*. The disturbance continued until just prior to day–break when the crowds finally dispersed. The following day the town was in a state of tension as it was expected that the rioting would resume after sunset. There was even talk of burning down the town.[74] However, the police remained in their station and no arrests were attempted because the authorities feared that such action would precipitate further violence.

A meeting was organised by Lieutenant-Colonel James Cran of the local Territorial Force and Captain G.W. Hulse of the contingent in order to give the ex–servicemen an opportunity to discuss their grievances. A committee which included Corporal Haynes, the initial leader of the rioters, was subsequently formed to present their grievances to the governor. It raised five main issues. Firstly, it wanted information as to the function of the Employment Sub–committee of the Returned Soldiers' Welfare Committee. Secondly, it wanted further discussion on the grant of land to returned soldiers. Thirdly, it desired to discuss the refund of certain deductions made from the men's pay in respect to separation allowances. Fourthly, it raised the question of the government acting by legislation or otherwise to fix the price of the ordinary necessities of life, other than food. Finally, it was decided at the meeting that the contingent men would maintain order in the town. The governor's 'sympathetic' attitude towards their demands successfully established the basis for further dialogue and negotiations.

Even after the meeting, the civilians were, according to J. Blades, 'just as bad' as before and their activities continued up to midnight of the twenty–third.[75] This suggests that the civilians had only depended on the ex–servicemen for initial leadership and were willing to continue their onslaught without their support. The decision of the contingent to act as a force of law and order was thus significant in bringing the looting under control. It also reflects the way the ex–servicemen had exploited the civilian struggle to bolster their own cause, and were prepared to abandon the civilians once the alliance was no longer convenient. Although relieved that the meeting had produced good results, the governor nevertheless regarded the influence and power of the ex–servicemen as humiliating.[76]

The *Constance* arrived off the coast of Belize at 7 a.m. on the twenty–fourth and immediately landed an armed party of 100 men with machine guns to take over strategic positions of the town. This action was carried out against the will of the contingent men who objected fiercely to the landing of the sailors from the *Constance,* and at one point seemed as if they were going to attack. With this new support, the governor promptly dismissed 140 men of the Territorial Force who had failed to assemble on the night of the twenty–second. Although the arrival of the *Constance* discouraged further outbreaks of violence, there continued to be much anti–white hostility. Tension in the colony again escalated on the twenty–fifth when a fracas occurred at a public meeting as a result of an aborted attempt to arrest Claude Smith, whom the governor described as a man of bad reputation and a dangerous agitator.[77] As a result of the fiasco, Wyatt, whom the governor felt had lost his nerve as a result of the beating he had received on the twenty–second, was relieved of his post as superinten- dent of police. The job was given to BWIR ex–serviceman quartermaster sergeant, F.H.E. McDonald, partly in appreciation for his loyal services on the twenty–second and in his subsequent patrolling of the town. McDonald and a group of special constables enlisted from among the loyal ex–service- men captured Smith a few days later.[78]

On July 26, martial law was declared in order to protect the white popu- lation and by the time the United States gun–boat, the *Castine,* conveniently showed up for coal on the twenty–ninth, the tendency of the town popula- tion to insult whites openly in the streets had subsided. The disturbances had prompted the United States Consul to ask and gain the governor's permis- sion to telegraph for help and the *Castine,* which intercepted the message after clearance from Washington, quickly proceeded to British Honduras.[79] As the *Constance* had already arrived it was not necessary for the *Castine* to send men ashore but its presence may have further inspired tranquility in the colony.

The arrival of the *Castine* reflected the increasing policing role of the United States navy in the Caribbean by 1919, as *Pax Americana* began to replace the old *Pax Britannica* in Caribbean waters.[80] This was greatly facilitated by the problems Britain faced by January 1919 in apportion- ing its severely limited financial, manpower and military resources in the defence of an empire plagued by widespread nationalistic disturbances in the aftermath of the war.[81] Moreover, the threat of Bolshevism and revolution loomed large in Britain as did the fear of a major rebellion in Ireland. These circumstances meant that resources could not easily be allocated to the relatively unimportant West Indies. Sir Henry Wilson, the chief of the Imperial General Staff, believed that defence of the empire had to be strictly prioritised.[82] The situation was made quite clear to the Colonial Office by the Admiralty and War Office during negotiations over defence measures for the West Indies.[83] However, while the presence of the United States navy may have provided some comfort to the authorities in the colonies, the Colonial Office was, as we have seen, seriously concerned over the increasing role and presence of America in the Caribbean. Governor Hutson requested the *Constance* to remain in Belize until a Commission headed by Frederick Maxwell, a former chief justice, had completed its investigation and the trials of those arrested were over. Because of trouble in Jamaica, the *Constance* had to leave but a company of the Sussex Regiment subsequently arrived in British Honduras and they in turn were replaced by a detachment of the WIR from Jamaica.

Although it is impossible to know all the factors which led to the outbreak of the disturbances, several main causes and the manner in which they interacted and influenced each other can be identified. Among these causes there can be little doubt that the numerous grievances of the ex–servicemen related to their alleged gross ill–treatment overseas were critical, although the commissioners objected that none of this justified their 'lawless acts' during the disturbances. Not surprisingly, the *Clarion*, whose editor, Percy George, had been severely beaten, likewise dismissed the arguments of the ex–servicemen and condemned their actions.[84] The paper argued that the colony had done all it could for the contingent men but that instead of being grateful they wanted more. It also claimed that some of the men acted like savages during the riot.

The ex–servicemen's reply came in the form of a letter in the *Independent*, a paper which was not only more popular than the pro–government *Clarion*, but was edited by Herbert Hill Cain, a black radical. Like his counterparts in the other colonies, Cain systematically championed the rights of blacks and made disparaging attacks on Crown Colony Government.[85] They pointed out that Percy George was not in any position to understand the people of the colony because he and his 'continental friends' consistently shunned the locals. The *Clarion's* assertion that only a minority were displeased with their treatment overseas was denied by the ex–servicemen who claimed on the contrary that it was the majority who were disgruntled. They promised to produce an 'extensive' account of the details of their ill–treatment, but it seems they never did. They also expressed bewilderment at the assertion that the conduct of the rioters was not that of British subjects. They reminded him that after several attempts on their part to take their place besides British units on the battlefield, they were finally informed of the 'shocking truth' that 'it is against British tradition to employ aboriginal troops against a European enemy.' They also cited the incident in Egypt when a group of West Indians was rudely asked who gave 'niggers' permission to sing 'Rule Britannia' and was driven out of the building because it was reserved for British soldiers. Finally, George was contemptuously reminded of the strafing they had given him during the disturbances.

The upsurge and influx into the colony from the metrople of literature promoting ideas of black consciousness and black nationalism also helped to precipitate the riot. Many of the ideas articulated in, for instance, Garvey's *Negro World* were appropriated, developed and disseminated by the Belize *Independent*, which also carried details of the riots and atrocities committed against blacks in England. The commissioners regarded this influence as a 'very important' factor in causing the disturbances. To them, the rioters' cries of 'this is our country', and 'we want to get the white man out', their agitation against recent importation by certain firms of European clerks and the dissatisfaction that a native of the colony was not appointed postmaster in Belize, when that office was last vacant, were all seen by the commissioners as the effects of 'noxious' foreign literature. This tendency to blame outside influences for local unrest had also been evident in the arguments of the *Clarion*, which editorialised in response to the fire in August 1918: 'That there is a dangerous and ugly spirit abroad has long been apparent to us, but never could we have believed that the infection was so widespread.'[86] The hostile and at times hysterical reactions by local and Colonial Office officials to churches like the Jehovah Witnesses and to the strikes during the war years also indicate the great importance attached to 'foreign' ideas as the basis of disturbances in the region.

The extent to which these ideas were responsible for the disturbances is, however, difficult to assess. Numerous studies of radical literature like the *Negro World* have shown that these 'foreign' influences were important in generating political unrest in the West Indies, but this importance is often inflated by insufficient examination of the role of local factors in such disturbances. The problem of assessing the role of outside ideas is further complicated by the tendency of some of the literature to adopt, perhaps unconsciously, the official view that because the 'masses' were mainly apolitical, it had almost inevitably to be 'foreign' influences which were largely responsible of unrest. Although the officials tended to see the ex–servicemen as bearers of foreign 'revolutionary' ideas, it seems likely that these fears were largely unfounded, since army education and training, as we have seen, tended to have the opposite effect. At the same time, however, it is perhaps impossible to disentangle economic and ideological motivation precisely; people may have suffered intense economic deprivation without being able to formulate their opposition in ideological terms until someone like Garvey arrived with an 'explanation', which made sense of their situation. Of course, the ruling classes always tended to believe that the under-classes would be perfectly satisfied were it not for outside 'agitators', but there is, nonetheless, a grain of truth in this perception.

Nevertheless, the influence of dangerous foreign ideas cannot adequately explain the nature of the broad–based alliance between the ex–servicemen and the civilians, or the large–scale participation of the civilians in the disturbances. It seems more reasonable to believe that the riots were largely the result of the economic crisis precipitated by the war, and the ill–treatment and discrimination which the ex–servicemen experienced overseas. To a large extent, class antagonisms were played out through race conflict and each in turn intensified the other. Historical trends in British Honduras and the rest of the West Indies since emancipation and the stingy nature of British–colonial financial policy during the period, also provides grounds for an economic interpretation of the riots, although this does not exclude other factors such as race and ideology.

One of the main consequences of the disturbances was mass support for Garveyite institutions and philosophy in the colony.[87] Among the leaders in the Garveyite movement were H.H. Cain and ex–serviceman Benjamin Adderley, who was to become a prominent figure in the labour disturbances of the 1930s. However, the key person and general secretary of the Universal Negro Improvement Association (UNIA) of British Honduras was former BWIR Corporal, Samuel Haynes, who was regarded by Governor Hutson as 'a troublesome agitator' and very intimate with Cain. Haynes was also the secretary of the Contingent Committee, and in that role he tried unsuccessfully to negotiate the release of the ex–servicemen who were imprisoned after the riot. He was later recruited by Garvey and taken to the United States where he became the convener of the Pittsburgh branch and a 'prolific and vociferous' contributor to the *Negro World*.[88]

Unfortunately, his departure from British Honduras was partly responsible for the UNIAs loss of impetus and sense of purpose in that colony. Meanwhile the majority of the other ex–servicemen either returned to their former employment or migrated to neighbouring countries or the United States.[89] Others remained in the colony and persistently applied to the government for assistance.

Barbados

Against the background of their experiences overseas, it was not surprising that the journey of the main body of ex–servicemen back to the West Indies was marked at times by intense acrimony and some violence. The situation was often exacerbated by the presence of seamen who were being repatriated after the disturbances in England. On September 12, 1919, the *Orca* departed England with about 120 black ex–servicemen, 75 military prisoners of the BWIR, mainly from the Taranto mutiny and 200 seamen and other civilians.[90] From the time the ship left Cardiff there was trouble and insubordination. Five of the prisoners were in a state of open mutiny throughout the voyage and repeated attempts were made to rescue the prisoners from their cells. The seamen also continually threatened violence to all whites on board and tried to incite the soldiers and convicts to mutiny. Believing that direct disciplinary action against the seamen would probably result in serious rioting, the master of the ship and Major H.W. Hemsley, who was in charge of the troops, tried to adopt a conciliatory attitude but the bitter feelings persisted.

On September 15, the prisoners prevented the military police from carrying out their duties but after the excitement had died down, the ringleaders were confined to their cells. Since the prisoners persisted in wrecking the cells and tearing out the iron bars and planking, they were hand–cuffed. However, because they broke the hand–cuffs, their hands were manacled behind their backs. This generated further discontent among the civilians and the other soldiers. The manacles were removed on September 19 but on the morning of the twentieth the convicts had again become violent and the guards had to shoot one in the wrist before he could be subdued. When the convict was being manacled again he became violent and Private C. Lashley of Barbados, who tried to interfere on his behalf was shot dead. As the ship approached Barbados on the twenty–second the captain sent a telegram to the authorities informing them of the mutiny and requested an armed guard when the ship arrived.[91] When the ship docked on the twenty–third the captain wanted the five mutineers removed.

Governor O'Brien refused to accept the prisoners, however, as Barbados had no military prison, and claimed that he had been advised that the chief justice would be compelled to release the prisoners on habeas corpus proceedings. These arguments were largely a camouflage for the more deep–rooted fears of the ruling classes at having 'dangerous' military prisoners in the colony. Fortunately, the captain of the *Yarmouth*, which was then in port, agreed to take them. O'Brien's attitude had already been shown during a previous incident involving over 80 repatriated seamen from the *Santille* who had sojourned in Barbados on the their way to Jamaica, British Guiana and other colonies. Throughout the voyage, the men had been unruly and had freely expressed their resentment towards the white passengers on board.[92] Although the ship's master was convinced the seamen were armed he made no attempt to search them because he feared there would be serious bloodshed. Before they disembarked at Barbados, the men wrecked all the electric light fittings and destroyed the stores on board.

When they landed on July 15, 1919, they immediately besieged the treasury building and demanded their advances in a truculent manner. Although their request was promptly granted in order to avoid further disturbance, much delay and trouble was experienced before the last phase of the journey, and the crew refused to sail with the seamen unless they were given an armed guard to maintain order. This was not done and so the *Santille* left without the prisoners who had to be taken to Jamaica on another ship. Given the nervous state of the officials in Barbados, the situation was regarded by O'Brien with deep concern and he was adamant that it should not be repeated. He warned the Colonial Office: 'I need not labour the point that the presence of men in the frame of mind of the late arrivals, with no work to do, is a source of possible mischief, particularly in the present day when there is a great deal of latent unrest throughout the world from which we are not free in Barbados.'[93] In the light of this experience, O'Brien mustered up every objection to prevent the military prisoners from the *Orca* from landing in Barbados, although a Colonial Office official thought that he was merely pettifogging as the prisoners could easily have been kept in the prison there.[94] The Barbados officials were determined not to have prisoners from the BWIR, however, and as a result, early the following year a serious row developed with the Trinidadian officials over the keeping of military prisoners.

Of greater concern to the Barbadian authorities was the question of resettling the ex–servicemen. To deal with this problem, a Returned Soldiers' Committee was established and given the task of finding jobs for them but it was discovered that many desired to emigrate, especially to Canada.[95] The Canadian government promptly indicated that since it had to deal with its own ex–servicemen, their emigration should be discouraged.[96] The Canadian decision was probably influenced by the government's determination at the time to prevent more blacks from entering the country.[97] Instead, many Barbadian ex–servicemen went to Cuba to work in the sugar industry. By October 1920, no less than 422 ex–servicemen had left for Cuba and many more went subsequently.[98] Their departure was greatly facilitated by the desire of the authorities to get rid of them, so the committee contributed generously to their passage and ensured that they got first preference in the scheme to recruit labourers for Cuba. Also, although most of the men received between £25 and £60 on being demobilised, they invested little and spent the money extravagantly in the belief that they were entitled to more. Some of those who remained in Barbados found employment in the police force, fire brigade, civil service and many once again became labourers.

Others became involved in organisations like the UNIA and the Workingmen's Association but this form of activity was not countenanced by the authorities. For example, when ex–serviceman Joseph Garner became involved in these two organisations, he received no further consideration from the Returned Soldiers' Committee because of his activities.[99] The most outstanding Barbadian ex–serviceman was Clennell Wilsden Wickham, who, as writer and later editor of the radical newspaper the *Herald*, engaged in a relentless assault on the barriers that protected the privileges of the narrow and selfish minority in that colony.[100] In 1930, however, the *Herald* was forced to close down as a result of a libel case brought against it, and although Wickham started a periodical called the *Outlook,* he was doomed for several years to a life of frustration and great hardship.[101] Fortunately in 1934 Marryshow recruited him to work in Grenada, first as lead writer and later as editor of the *West Indian.* He died a few years later in Grenada.

Jamaica

The authorities in Jamaica were also very concerned about ex–servicemen and seamen joining together to seek revenge for their treatment overseas. As a result, the first main shipload of returning soldiers was met by a warship and a military guard on the wharf.[102] Because many people believed, perhaps correctly, that these measures were intended to intimidate the ex–servicemen, the authorities were forced to publish a statement claiming that this was not the case.[103] If these security measures disturbed the soldiers, the warm reception they received on landing may have, as in British Honduras, made them temporarily forget their grievances. The town was gaily decorated, the streets were packed with cheering crowds and several prominent persons made speeches.

Importantly, however, the authorities did not wish the ex–servicemen to remain in Kingston too long, as it was feared that this could lead to disturbances. Thus, those from other parishes were usually despatched within 24 hours to their hometowns where they were paid off.[104] The strategy seems to have worked, especially with the first groups to arrive. In June 1919, the governor concurred with an article from the *Gleaner,* which noted that the behaviour of the ex–servicemen had been favourably commented on by all classes.[105] Although the news that the ex–servicemen were planning to form an association to improve their condition did raise some doubts, the local authorities were fairly convinced that their intentions were honest. A Colonial Office official was less impressed, however, and minuted: 'This appears to correspond very much with the "Caribbean League" we have heard so much about', [106] but another cautiously observed that the proposed society had on the face of it very laudable aims.[107]

Nevertheless, the Colonial Office did not wish the Jamaican officials to be lured into a sense of false security and warned them that the Caribbean League had discussed the possibility of a black uprising which was to involve the elimination of the whites in Jamaica and the other colonies. The inspector–general of the police reported, however, that there was no evidence of the league in Jamaica and no sign of unrest.[108] Nevertheless, in the light of local fears of unrest, the arrival on July 5, 1919, of the Trinidadian, F.E.M. Hercules, the general secretary of the London-based, Society of Peoples of African Origin, was viewed with much concern by the authorities, especially when he addressed a group of strikers.[109]

The confidence of the Jamaican authorities was shaken two days later when a riot erupted in Kingston. On the night of July 18, a crowd, which included ex–servicemen and seamen shouting 'kill the whites', launched a 'determined attack' on some white sailors from the *Constance*; a few local white civilians were also assaulted.[110] An armed party from the *Constance* was landed hurriedly to restore order and patrol the streets the rest of the night. The next morning the sailors were reinforced with guards from the WIR, who were stationed at different locations in Kingston and its suburbs. These measures were partly prompted by rumours that there was going to be another outbreak of violence during the peace celebrations to be held on the nineteenth. Although the strategy seem to have prevented any major disturbance during the celebrations in Kingston, a rowdy element, according to the *Gleaner*, committed some acts of lawlessness with impunity.[111] The festivities held at Morant Bay and Sav–la–Mar were also disrupted by unruly ex–servicemen.[112] Although the officials desired to expel Hercules from the island, they could not find sufficient cause in his speeches or telegrams to justify his expulsion.

Later, a group of seamen, and apparently some ex–servicemen, sent a lengthy petition to the governor explaining their grievances and concerns and seeking redress. Their arguments focused on the violation of what they termed their 'inalienable rights' as British subjects as a result of class and race oppression in England.[113] They made it known that they felt 'much aggrieved' and 'deeply dissatisfied and disappointed at the insidious attack and illegal outrage' perpetrated on their constitutional rights and privileges, although they had served as soldiers, sailors and merchant–marines and had been subjected to all sorts of dangers, while some whites bluntly refused to do likewise. For these reasons, they stated, the treatment they received in England was unjustifiable, un–British and 'against all the principles that sanctify humanity', and had shocked them 'terribly all around in every way'.[114] Clearly, their experiences overseas had forced them to question seriously their relationship with England and the empire. Yet, their willingness to use constitutional means to seek redress was perhaps some indication that beneath their expressions of anger was an enduring loyalty to England and the empire, and that they still regarded England as their 'Motherland'. Indeed, the stated aim of the petition was to ensure that they received justice, so that the honour and prestige of the empire might be upheld constitutionally, freed from class legislation, racial hatred and prejudice, and that harmony and peace would exist among the various races of the empire.

The authorities were willing to make some concessions but this apparently did not satisfy the men. The situation was made worse with the subsequent arrival in Jamaica of the seamen from the *Orca,* as this soon led to further disturbances in Kingston. On the afternoon of October 9, 1919, a large crowd led by seamen who, according to the police report, were in an 'ugly mood' began demonstrating outside the immigration office.[115] Attempts by the police to calm the protestors proved fruitless and when the police began clearing the crowd from the street, a riot ensued. The hostility of the crowd was directed against white people in general but white sailors were especially targeted and severely beaten. During the disturbance there were thousands of people on the streets and the town was 'in a state of high excitement'.[116] The police believed, perhaps mistakenly, that in general, the sympathy of the crowd lay with the authorities but there was a section which supported the seamen. Eventually the seamen were trapped and overwhelmed in the Queen's Hotel by a party of armed police.

On October 10, 15 of the rioters were tried in court and 11 convicted, two discharged and two remanded. Four were sentenced to 12 months hard labour each, five to six months and two received 60 days. More arrests were made subsequently. The deputy inspector-general, B. Toole, who had been responsible for organising the police attacks on the rioters, was highly commended by the governor, and Allen at the Colonial Office thought that if the police in Belize had been as vigilant as those in Jamaica, the numerous troubles there might have been 'nipped in the bud'.[117] An even more confident Darnley minuted on the report from Jamaica: 'After reading this we can feel more comfortable about Jamaica.'[118] The confidence of the officials was justified as there were no more major disturbances associated with the resettlement of the ex–servicemen and seamen. A land settlement scheme was established to assist the ex–servicemen but because the allocated land was in a remote area many could not take advantage of the scheme. The fact that approximately 4,036 of the ex–servicemen migrated to Cuba was probably a relief to the authorities and elites.[119] Although the planters were always fretful about any loss of labour from the colony, it is not likely that they would have raised any or much objection to the departure of the potentially dangerous ex–servicemen to Cuba.

Although the ex–servicemen did form an organisation which engaged in limited agitation, it was a far cry from the much feared Caribbean League. However, H.L. Brown, who had been involved in the formation of the Caribbean League at Taranto, did help to form a Jamaican off–spring of the UNIA called the Ethiopian Progressive and Cooperative Association.[120] The organisation planned to manufacture articles, conduct retail and wholesale business, cure and dispose of island produce and buy and sell properties. Other ex–servicemen seemed to have become involved in the UNIA, some because of their experiences overseas. For example, during a debate of the Lacovia Young Men Association on the usefulness of a branch of the UNIA in the area, ex–serviceman G. Chensus spoke in support of the UNIA in spite of fierce opposition.[121] He argued that the black race was kept down financially and educationally and that while he was serving with the BWIR he had often been told that the conflict was a white man's war and no blacks were wanted. He also felt that colour prejudice was rampant in the island generally and in institutions like the judiciary. For these reasons he felt that a branch of the UNIA in Lacovia would be 'a blessing to the island'.[122]

Trinidad

By July 1919 most of the ex–servicemen and many seamen had returned to Trinidad and they too were in an angry mood. Details of the suffering the blacks had suffered in England were carried by the *Argos,* which in one article, described the manner in which on one occasion a white mob had attacked a black man's funeral, cut off the head of the corpse and used it as a football.[123] Complaints were also made by the ex–servicemen about their treatment overseas and the local government's land settlement scheme. Cipriani too spoke of the 'contempt, humiliation, insults and suffering' heaped upon the BWIR while they were overseas.[124] In an attempt to pacify the ex–servicemen, the officials invited them to lead a parade at the Queen's Park Savannah on July 19, during the peace celebrations. However, only 132 joined the parade, while a large number in uniform and civilian dress merely looked on or booed those who were in the procession.

The reason for the poor turn–out, according to the inspector–general of police, was that the ex–servicemen were disappointed at not being armed for the occasion. He believed that they had planned to use the weapons to shoot down all the officers.[125] The hysteria surrounding the return of the ex–servicemen and the wave of worker unrest in that colony and the rest of the region, may have, however, led the authorities to overreact and exaggerate the intentions of the veterans. Conclusions arrived at about the ex–servicemen's motives were often based on speculation, rumour and the flimsiest evidence. In England too, disgruntled ex–servicemen were refusing to march in parades or participate in festivities to commemorate the armistice, as a way of expressing their grievances.[126]

However, during the peace celebrations a number of sailors from the H.M.S. *Dartmouth* and other local whites were severely assaulted by sections of the lower class and ex–servicemen, and 'very lewd and disparaging remarks were freely made about the white race and about their women folk' and a police inspector was stoned.[127] The *Port of Spain Gazette* severely condemned those who, it claimed, were spreading race hatred in the colony, and especially the ex–servicemen who it alleged had been wharf–idlers and criminals before enlisting.[128] Deeply concerned about the preservation of the British hegemony in the island and the disturbing influence of the Russian Revolution, the paper warned the authorities to take active steps to suppress violence and 'anything approaching Bolshevism in Trinidad'.[129] Not surprisingly, the officials blamed the *Argos* for inciting the blacks to violence. Influenced no doubt by the growing discontent in the colony, on July 24, a delegation, which included the mayor of Port–of–Spain and two black solicitors, successfully appealed to the acting governor to release the Trinidadians who were among a group of military prisoners on their way to Jamaica.[130] In justifying his decision to release them, the acting governor told the Colonial Office that 'a very strong feeling was at once aroused amongst the black section of the community and threats were openly made, not only by the usual idlers and loafers and irresponsible persons, but by black and coloured men of some standing and influence, that the whites should be killed'.[131]

As a result of the increased agitation in the colony, George Huggins and several other prominent whites petitioned the government for a permanent stationing of a white garrison in Trinidad and for the local whites to be armed.[132] They argued that while formerly indentured East Indian immigrants under white control could have been depended upon as a 'substantial counterpoise against troubles with negroes and vice–versa', with the abolition of indentureship this was no longer the case and the creole East Indian was now likely to 'either remain an interested spectator or join the mob'.[133] The petitioners also objected to the *Argos* being allowed to 'circulate all kinds of revolutionary, seditious and mischievous literature' with impunity. To reinforce their objections the whites withdrew their advertisements from the paper. The petitioners also warned that while the 1903 taxation riots in Trinidad had found men of all classes and colours on both sides, matters were now different and far more dangerous because a substantial section of the black population was openly proclaiming that it had no further use for the white man and meant to eliminate him.

While sharing the general anxiety of the local whites, the inspector–general of the constabulary nevertheless thought that the petition was too alarmist. He believed that if they would 'only cease cackling and spreading and enlarging on the wild rumours' the situation would soon be clear.[134] He shared their antipathy for the *Argos*, however, and wanted two gunboats stationed in Trinidad since their presence would be comforting to the community as a whole and have 'a very restraining influence on the lawless'.[135] A report from the commander–in–chief of the British naval forces in North America and the West Indies likewise felt that the presence of warships would exercise a 'moral effect on the agitators' in Trinidad.[136] As a result of these concerns, the HMS *Cambrian* was kept in Trinidad on the request of the acting governor and the subsequent approval of Lord Milner.

Meanwhile, the Discharged Soldiers' Central Authority, set up by the governor, was busy getting jobs for unemployed ex–servicemen and organising a land–settlement scheme, which allowed them each five acres of land which would be free if cultivated. By September 1919, the acting governor was praising the committee for helping to defuse the situation; he believed that there was no longer cause for alarm, but he failed to recognise the tide of worker discontent which had been mounting for some time. On December 1, 1919, the colony experienced a major social upheaval as black workers violently protested against conditions and especially the level of wages. The Trinidad Workingmen's Association, which had been revived under Captain Cipriani with the active participation of many ex–servicemen, played a major role in the events of December.[137] Cipriani's experiences overseas, where he frequently championed the rights of the soldiers, had made him popular among them and sharpened the leadership skills which were to help bring him to political prominence in Trinidad during the inter–war years. He seems to have been influenced by European socialism and even wore a red button on his lapel, while many of his followers wore red shirts to symbolise the Bolshevik revolution.[138] The disturbances prompted the authorities to call up the Merchants and Planters contingent to patrol the streets and 350 men of the Royal Sussex Regiment later arrived to maintain order. The presence of warships also had a calming effect on the protestors.

Grenada & The T.T.T. Gang

The arrival of Grenada's ex-servicemen also caused the authorities much anxiety as there were several incidents of misconduct and serious fights with the civilians.[139] To make matters worse, Marryshow and the other 'agitators' for political reform began encouraging the ex-servicemen to fight for the political, economic, social and moral progress of their people and country.[140] It is difficult to assess the extent to which Marryshow and his colleagues were able to influence the ex-servicemen but the veterans did sign a petition for representative government, which was forwarded to the Colonial Office. Marryshow was also among those who led deputations to the governor to express the grievances of the ex-servicemen. For his dedication, he was publicly thanked and cheered by a group of ex-servicemen under the leadership of ex-serviceman T.U. Buzz Butler, who later emerged as one of the most prominent figures in the 1930s disturbances in Trinidad.[141]

It was, however, the series of robberies and incendiary fires between late 1919 and early 1920 which severely damaged the properties of the merchants in the capital, St Georges, which most concerned and shocked the officials. These acts were carried out by a group which provocatively left typed warning notes at the scene of the crime indicating also that its name was the T.T.T. Gang, a label adopted from a scene in a movie shown at the Grenada Electric Theatre.[142] As a result, the merchants and authorities decided to implement several defensive measures. Sixty 'special constables' were enrolled from the staff of government departments and the major firms, and the leaders were given revolvers.[143] Electric lighting in the town was also significantly improved and extended, and a reward of £250 was offered for information about the gang. Despite calls for the cinema to be censored, the authorities merely warned the proprietors that any further complaint would result in their license being cancelled.[144]

Although fires and robberies had ceased by about February 1920, their perpetrators were never apprehended but the Grenada handbooks of the period indicate that the culprits were ex-servicemen. It was also believed by some individuals that the ex-servicemen were aided or influenced by Marryshow and the *West Indian*. A white who held 'a very important position' in Grenada, for instance, wrote to Sir Frederick Hall, a member of the British Parliament, informing him that they had all received warnings and that the gang wanted to 'clean up the whites and burn down government property' as a result of articles written in the *West Indian*.[145] This information was passed on to the Colonial Office but George Grindle felt that the trouble was due more to the increased cost of living rather than race conflict as Hall's correspondence had suggested.[146] The Colonial Office decided to leave the matter in the hands of the governor and local officials, who were believed to be 'fully alive to the situation', rather than to intervene from England.[147] A serious problem also developed with the arrival of the ex–servicemen in St. Lucia but the governor, as he admitted to the Colonial Office, was fortunately able to convince 60 of them to go to Cuba.[148]

By 1924, following a police strike in St. Lucia, more disturbances in British Honduras in 1920 and a riot in Jamaica in 1924, there was no more serious unrest in the region. At the same time, the imperial government moved to reinforce British hegemony with a visit by the Prince of Wales to the West Indies in September 1920, where he was enthusiastically received. The establishment of war memorials throughout the region and the emotional speeches made at these events, also served to evoke West Indian loyalty and further impress British ideals on the physical landscape of the region. Crucially, however, while the disturbances of the post–war period may have done little to resolve the many problems which characterised the West Indies, they signalled a developing collective consciousness of confidence and determination among blacks in their struggle for greater participation in society.

Postscript

The participation of West Indians in the Great War was clearly in many ways a great tragedy but as for the millions of other colonial peoples it also had positive results. It stimulated profound socio–economic, political and psychological change and greatly facilitated protest against the oppressive conditions in the colonies, and to some degree against colonial rule. Because all the effects of the war are not clearly discernible, its impact will continue to be debated. However, this study has attempted to show that in the context of the West Indies, the war was more important than previously thought, but that its significance lay not so much in the novelty of its impact as in the unprecedented way it exacerbated underlying tensions and contradictions implicit in West Indian society.

The war led to a contradiction between the rising cost of living and the stagnant or even, in some cases, declining level of wages. It also highlighted the increasing disparity in the quality of life enjoyed by the elites and that of the majority of the population, as well as between the stingy British imperial financial policy and the increasing welfare needs of the ex–slave population. Worsening socio–economic and political conditions greatly stimulated the growth of working–class consciousness and protest, which was reflected in the wave of violence, strikes and disturbances which characterised the region during and after the war, and laid the basis for the development and establishment of labour organisations such as the Trinidad Workingmen's Association and the British Guiana Labour Union. The conditions produced by the war also facilitated the growth of black consciousness and nationalism, which was being advocated by the radical section of the West Indian press, and political activists like Hercules and Garvey.

The direct participation of West Indians in the war as labourers and soldiers was critical in that it led to an important, if intangible, psychological transformation. This study has, however, attempted to show that while the political repercussion of the war on the black soldiers was certainly significant, the ex–servicemen acted more as accelerators and catalysts of changes already developing in West Indian society than as initiators of wholly new directions. In fact, as we have seen, when it suited them, they did not hesitate to abandon their association with the working–class in order to advance their own interests.

With the benefit of hindsight, it seems that the fears of the Colonial Office officials and local authorities about the ex–servicemen may have been exaggerated. Nevertheless, the turmoil brought British officials to realise that some measure of compromise was necessary in order to shore up British hegemony, not only in the West Indies but also throughout the empire. In the West Indies the expectations of black middle–class political activists that the war would result in major political and constitutional advance was clearly optimistic, even unrealistic. The passage of the Seditious Publications Ordinance in 1920 to suppress the influence of the radical press and 'dangerous foreign influences', made this painfully clear to the *West Indian*, which dejectedly observed:

> We had thought victory would have brought us peace and the fruits thereof, but we are in the same position as we were in 1913 and in some respects we are worse off. Sometimes we question ourselves asking: was it worth while for us, the *West Indian*, to have spent every ounce of our energies in working for the cause of the war, in leading the way in recruiting, in the press and on the platform, and in many untold ways offering sacrifices for the success of the Grenada contingent? Was it worth while? We still ask ourselves these questions today as we see ingratitude rear its ugly defenses against our legitimate aspirations as a people, and feel repression bearing down on us with sinister warning against thoughts of growth towards the ideal held up among us for our inspiration to service five years ago.[1]

The paper certainly had reason to lament, especially in the light of the granting in May 1919 of the franchise to about 3,000 mainly middle– and upper–class women in Jamaica in appreciation for their war services, as had happened in England in February 1918 on a broader scale.[2] However, all was not lost because as the movement for constitutional reform gained momentum throughout the region, the British government was forced to send a mission to the West Indies to assess the demands for reform.

The inquiry was carried out by the Honourable, Colonel E.F.L. Wood, M.P. , between December 1921 and February 1922.[3] Wood's recommendations laid the basis for a modified constitutional order in the form of limited elected representation in Grenada, Trinidad, Dominica, St. Lucia and St. Vincent from 1925 onwards and the Leewards from 1936.[4] Crucially, however, the Wood Report did little to resolve the social and economic crisis in the region and may in fact have compounded the problem. It advised, for instance, that unless assistance was forthcoming from private enterprise neither the imperial government nor the colonial government should embark upon any undertaking that were not absolutely essential.[5] The report also argued that it was imperative that the colonial governments should, if possible, balance their budget by reducing expenditure and that a conservative financial policy was 'dictated by necessity of the times'. [6]

The catastrophe which Marryshow and later W.M. Macmillan foresaw occurred in the 1930s, when most of the West Indian colonies were engulfed in a series of major disturbances. These heralded significant socio–economic and political changes in the region and led to a modification in British financial policy throughout the empire.[7] Importantly, the Moyne Commission which investigated the situation in the colonies concluded that the disturbances no longer represented a mere blind protest against a worsening of conditions, but a positive demand for the creation of new conditions that would render possible a better life.[8] Also significant was the observation of the 1937 Commission on Trinidad that the demand for change had come from a Trinidadian working–class opinion, increasingly affected by experiences of West Indian soldiers in World War One, industrial unrest in the United States and the spread of elementary education in the colony.[9] It may be reasonably argued, therefore, that the Great War had a direct and indirect influence on the main protests of the 1930s. Indeed, it is arguable that were it not for the events of the period between 1914 to 1920, the mass protests of 1930s and the changes they led to, may possibly have been delayed.

Appendix

Table B. I Official Financial Contributions to the War Effort

Colony	Revenue 1913-14 £	Maximum contribution to non-effective charges
British Guiana	608,633	F
Trinidad	970,789	£ 12,000 p. a.
Jamaica	1,267,543	(a):£ 6,000 p.a. for 40 years after war.
Barbados	214,865	£33,000 p. a.
		(£1,000 separation allowances.)
		(£2,000 non-effective charges)
		$10,000 p.a. (£ 2,083 6s 8d).
British Honduras	$590,982	(b) F except Antigua & St. Kitts
Leewards	174,456	£ 2,700 p. a
Grenada	91,258	£ 2, 000 p. a.
St Lucia	67,490	(c) £ 1,000 p.a.
St Vincent	34,373	F
Bahamas		

F = full liability.

The contributions were for the duration of the war except where stated and all colonies were expected to contribute to the initial expense of raising and transport. Contributions exceeded £6 per man in all cases except British Honduras, Antigua and St. Kitts.

(a) Jamaica owing to the hurricane of August 1915 and the uncertainty of the financial position of the colony, could not accept at that time the full liability and agreed to contribute this amount after the war for 40 years. The expenses for the first contingent were paid for locally by public subscription; other expenses were to be borne by imperial funds.
(b) Dominica and Montserrat accepted full liability for all non-effective charges. Antigua and St Kitts agreed to pay £200 and; £300 p.a. respectively until all charges were met, a special stamp being issued to provide funds.
(c) St Vincent could not accept this liability and was unable to pay any further military expenses which were then borne by imperial funds.

When further battalions were requested in October 1916 and January 1917, the Army Council accepted full responsibility for the entire cost of raising, maintaining, and transporting these units as well as for separation allowances and non-effective charges unprejudiced by any considerations of assistance which the colonies might be able to offer. With the exception of St. Vincent, all the territories agreed to bear, in respect of these further contingents, liability to the extent already accepted in respect of the earlier contingents.

Source: CO318/344- February 1917; Joseph, *The British West Indies Regiment*, 109.

Table B.2 Rates of Pay for B.W.I.R.

Major	16/–	a day
Captain	12/6	a day
Lieutenant	8/6	a day
2nd Lieutenant	7/6	a day
Company Sergeant Major	4/–	a day
Company Quarter-Master Sergeant	3/6	a day
Colour Sergeant Instructor in Musketry	3/3	a day
Sergeant	2/4	a day
Sergeant, Cook	2/10	a day
Corporal appointed, paid Lance Sergeant	2/–	a day
Corporal	1/8	a day
Private appointed, paid Lance Corporal	1/3	a day
Bugler	1/1	a day
Private	1/–	a day

In addition to the above rates of pay, men received proficiency pay at the rate of 3d. or 6d. per day according to qualifications after 2 years service with the colours.   Prior service in Colonial corps while under active service counted toward the 2 years

Source: C.O. 318/349/3108

Table B.3 Pensions Granted for Specific Injuries

Degree of Disablement	Specific injury	Proportion corresponding to degree of disablement	Disablement Pensions							
			If not entitled to a Service pension					Warrant of NC Officers entitled to Service Pensions	Private	
			Warrant Officer Case 1	Warrant Officer Case II	N.C. Officer Case II	N.C. Officer Case III	N.C. Officer Case IV			
		Percent	s. d.	s. d.	s. d.	s. d.	s. d.	s. d.	s. d.	
1	Loss of two or more limbs / Loss of an arm and an eye / Loss of a leg and an eye / Loss of both hands or of all fingers and thumbs / Loss of a hand and a foot / Total Loss of sight / Total paralysis / Lunacy / Wounds, injuries or disease resulting in disabled man being permanently bedridden / Wounds of or injuries to internal thorax or abdominal organs involving total permanent disabling effects. / Wounds of or injuries to head or brain involving total permanent disabling effects or Jacksonian epilepsy / Very severe facial disfigurement / Advanced cases of incurable disease	100	42 5	37 6	35 0	32 6	30 0	27 6	27 6	
2	Loss of both feet / Amputation of leg at hip or right arm at shoulder joint / Severe facial disfigurement / Total loss of speech	30	34 0	30 0	28 0	26 0	24 0	22 0	22 0	
3	Short thigh amputation of leg with pelvic band, or of left arm at shoulder joint or of right arm above or through elbow.	70	29 9	26 3	24 6	22 9	21 0	19 3	19 3	
4	Total loss of speech / Total Deafness / Amputation of leg above knee (other than 3), and through knee or of left arm above or through elbow or of right arm above or through elbow or of right arm below elbow	60	25 6	22 5	21 0	19 6	18 0	16 6	16 6	
5	Amputation of leg below knees (including Symes and Chopart's amputation), or of left arm below	50	21 3	18 9	17 6	16 3	15 0	13 9	13 9	
6	Loss of vision of one eye / Loss of thumbs or of four fingers of right hand	40	17 0	15 0	14 0	13 0	12 0	11 0	11 0	
7	Loss of thumb or of four fingers of left or of three fingers of right.	30	12 9	11 3	10 6	9 9	9 0	8 3	8 3	
8	Loss of two fingers of either hand	20	8 6	7 6	7 0	6 6	6 0	5 6	5 6	

Source: CO.318\349\31308

*B.W.I.R received similar pension rates to British Regiments

Table B.4 Contribution of Men to B.W.I.R. From Each Colony

Colony	Population	Officers	Men	Total %
Barbados	171,892	20	811	5.33
Bahamas	55,944	2	439	2.89
British Guiana	304,149	14	686	4.51
British Honduras	41,543	5	528	3.47
Jamaica	331,383	303	9,977	65.62
Trinidad & Tobago	333,552	40	1,438	9.46
Grenada	69,307	4	441	2.90
St. Lucia	48,637	5	354	2.33
St. Vincent	44,434	-	305	2.01
Leeward Islands	127,189	4	225	1.48
Total	2,028,030	397	15,204	100

Sources: C.O. 318/344, February 1917; *Report of the West Indian Contingent Committee*, September 30th 1917.'-

Table B.5   Instructions re. Separation Allowances

The Army Council have authorized the payment to the families of men who enlist for service with the Colours in the West Indian Contingent of the following rates of Separation Allowances. (which are those paid to soldiers of the West India

To wife of Regimental Sergeant-Major	2/3 a day
To wife of Quarter-Master Sergeant or Company Sergeant-Major	2/1 a day
To wife of Company Quarter-Master Sergeant or Company	1/4 a day
Sergeant, Corporal or Private	1/1 a day
To each child under 16 years of age	2d a day
If the soldier's wife is dead – for each motherless child	4d a day

The conditions on which the above rates of Separation Allowances will be issued are as follows:-

Married Soldiers

(a) The Allowance will commence from date of enlistment or of separation from family if later;

(b) In the case of soldiers who die while serving, separation allowances including the soldier's Army Orders 12.93 allotment will be continued for a period not exceeding 26 weeks from the date of notification of and 126 of 1915 death. The date of notification will mean the date on which a definite official notification of the death was first made to the payee. In all respects the payments of separation allowances after death for soldiers of the West Indian Contingent will be the same as in the case of British soldiers.

(c) No rations or quarters can be given to wives and families in addition to separation allowances.

Unmarried Soldiers

(a) The mother or other relative who has been wholly or partially dependent upon an unmarried soldier will receive separation allowance on the same conditions as in the case of a British soldier. The rates of separation allowance will not exceed the amount which the soldier used to pay for the support of his mother or other relative referred to above (i.e. not including anything which the soldier used to pay for his own maintenance) and in no case can the amount for one dependant exceed the rate of separation allowance and compulsory allotment for the wife of a married soldier.

(B) In the event of the death of the soldier payment will be continued as at (a) - (2) above. The soldier must in every case contribute his share of the allowance or no payment can be made. The contributions and rates of allowances in the case of unmarried soldiers are as follows:-

a. Corporals and Privates

	Weekly allowance to be paid.	Daily share to be paid by soldier
Not exceeding	3/-	1d
Over 3/- but not exceeding	5/-	2
5/- _	7/6	3
7/6 _	9/6	4
9/6 _	11/6	5

Exceeding 11/1 in cases which there are more persons than one dependent on the soldier (see par-48 - (d) Separation Allowance Regulations)   6

b. Warrant officers to Sergeants   Army Order 440 of 1914

	Weekly Allowance to be Paid.	Daily share to be paid by Soldier
Not exceeding	2/6	1d
Exceeding 2/6 but not exceeding	4/-	2
4/-	5/6	3
5/6	7/-	4
7/-	8/6	5
8/6	10/-	6
10/-	11/6	7
11/6	13/-	8
13/-	14/6	9
14/6	in cases in which there are more persons than one dependent on the soldier (see par. 48 Separation Allowance Regulations)	10

Source: C.O. 318/349/3108

*The above rates of allowances for dependents of unmarried soldiers were granted subject to payment of the contributions, after an investigation as far as circumstances permitted, on the lines laid down in paragraph 17 of Army orders No. 440 of 1914.

*The Paymaster in the West Indies was left to use his discretion in dealing with claims of families and dependents within the limits of the foregoing rates and regulations.

Notes

Introduction

1. For discussion on the concept of Total Warfare see, Ian F.W. Beckett, 'Total War', in Clive Emsley (et al.), *War, Peace and Social Change in Twentieth-Century Europe* (Milton Keynes and Philadelphia: Open University Press, 1989), pp. 26–44.

2. Patrick K. O'Brien, 'The Costs and Benefits of British Imperialism 1846 -1914', *Past and Present*, no. 120, August 1988, p. 163.

3. David Killingray, 'Repercussions of World War 1 in the Gold Coast', *Journal of African History*, vol.19, no.1, 1978, p. 39; Also, Eric J. Grove, 'The First Shots of the Great War: The Anglo-French Conquest of Togo, 1914', *Army Quarterly*, July, 1976.

4. Ibid.

5. O'Brien, *The Costs and Benefits*, p. 198.

6. For details on the African experience see, for example, D.C. Savage and J. Forbes Munro, 'Carrier Recruitment in the British East Africa Protectorate, 1914-1918', *Journal of African History*, vol. 7, no. 2, 1966; G.W.T. Hodges, 'African Manpower Statistics for the British Forces in East Africa, 1914–1918', *Journal of African History*, vol. 19, no.1, 1978; David Killingray and James Mathews, 'Beasts of Burden: British West African Carriers in the First World War', *Canadian Journal of African Studies*, vol. 13, nos. 1&2, 1979.

7. See, E.A. Benians (et al.), *The Cambridge History of the British Empire, 1870–1919* (Cambridge: Cambridge University Press, 1959), pp. 625 & 642.

8. C.L.R. James, *The Life of Captain Cipriani* (Nelson, Lancashire: Coulton, 1932), p. 27.

9. Neville Duncan, *Movements as Subculture: A Preliminary Examination of Social and Political Protests in the Anglophone Caribbean* (Barbados: UWI, Cave Hill, 1983), pp.1–3.

10. Richard Rathbone, 'World War 1 and Africa: Introduction', *Journal of African History*, vol.19, no.1, 1978, p. 1.

11. See, for example, The Barbados *Daily Nation* (12 November 1986), p. 7.

12. The Barbados *Daily Nation* (13 November 1989), p. 16.

Chapter 1 – Reactions to Outbreak of War

1. A.J. Christopher, *The British Empire at its Zenith* (London: Croom Helm, 1988), p. 1.

2. In many ways the notion of 'respectability' was a major factor differentiating West Indian society. Most whites, excluding groups like the 'Red Legs' of Barbados, were regarded as respectable but with non-white groups like the Blacks and Indians, the onus was on them to prove their respectability, which they tried to attain through education, occupation and style of life and displays of their acquisition of European culture. See, for example, Bridget Brereton, *Race Relations in Colonial Trinidad, 1870–1900* (London and New York: Cambridge University Press, 1979), p. 211.

3. Joyce M. Lumsden, 'Robert Love and Jamaican Politics', unpublished PhD thesis (Jamaica: UWI, 1987), p. 5.

4. Rupert Lewis, 'A Political Study of Garveyism in Jamaica and London, 1914-1940', unpublished MA thesis (Jamaica: UWI, 1971), p. 19.

5. Lumsden, 'Robert Love', p. 136.

6. Ibid.

7. The Grenada *West Indian* (11 October 1918), p. 5.

8. C.O.321\308\29007 Haddon-Smith to Milner, 11 May 1920.

9. The Antigua *Sun* (28 August 1914), p. 2; The Grenada *West Indian* (21 February, 1915), p. 4; The Barbados *Globe* (19 August, 1914), p. 3.

10. The Trinidad *Port of Spain Gazette* (22 June 1918), p. 5; Ibid., (25 June 1918).

11. The Barbados *Globe* (19 March 1917), p. 3 & (26 March 1917), p. 3.

12. The Trinidad *Port of Spain Gazette* (29 March 1918), p. 13.

13. The *West India Committee Circular* (3 November 1914), pp. 507-508.

14. C.O.137\705\41210 Marcus Garvey to Lewis Harcourt, 16 September 1914.

15. The Trinidad *Port of Spain Gazette* (17 February 1915); Errol Hill, 'Calypso and War', in *ISER/UWI–Calypso Research Project, vol. 1: Seminar on the Calypso* (Trinidad: UWI, 6-10 January 1986), pp. 9-10.

16. Full details of the West Indian war effort based on semi-official and official reports from the individual colonies may be found in, Sir Charles Lucas (ed.), *The Empire at War*, vol. 2 (London: Oxford University Press, 1923), pp. 325–437.

17. Brinsley Samaroo, 'The Trinidad Workingmen's Association and the Origins of Popular Protest in a Crown Colony', *Social and Economic Studies*, vol. 21, no. 2 June, 1972. p. 211.

18. The British Honduras *Clarion* (3 September 1914), p. 178.

19. See, for example, C.O.28\285\11213.

20. C.O.123\281\14418 Petition of the Unemployed of Belize enclosed in Governor Collet to Colonial Office, 5 March 1915.

21. Quoted in The Grenada *West Indian* (29 July 1916), p. 2; See also, The Grenada *West Indian* (12 October 1917), p. 7.

22. The Barbados *Weekly Illustrated* (3 August 1916). Extract reprinted in The Grenada *West Indian* (18 August 1916), p. 2.

23. The Bahamas *Tribune*, 3 October 1914, cited in Gail Saunders (et al.), *Sources of Bahamian History* (London and Basingstoke: Macmillan 1991), p. 161.

24. Under the Old Representative System of Government the full number of elected members could always command a majority in the legislature. Under pure Crown Colony government, however, there was an official majority in the legislature. Colonies with nominated unofficial majorities in the legislature were also regarded by the Colonial Office as Crown Colonies. The main feature of Crown Colony government was that power was concentrated in the hands of the Governor, subject to close scrutiny from London. The movement for Representative government in Grenada and other colonies was to a large extent a plea by the middle classes that because of their cultural, educational and economic achievements they be allowed active participation in government through the imperial conferment of political rights.

25. The Grenada *West Indian* (2 January 1915), p. 2.

26. Ibid.

27. The Grenada *West Indian* (20 June 1916), p. 2.

28. The Grenada *West Indian* (22 November 1916), p. 2.

29. Ibid.

30. The Grenada *Federalist* (4 October 1916), p. 2.

31. The Grenada *Federalist* (26 September 1914), p. 3.

32. See, for example, The Trinidad *Port of Spain Gazette*, 6 August 1914, p. 5; C.O.321\284\ 27921 War Diary of Officer Commanding the local forces at St. Lucia, 19 May 1915.

33. The British Honduras *Clarion* (18 February 1915), p. 182; The Trinidad *Port of Spain Gazette* (7 August 1914), p. 4; The Barbados *Standard* (12 September 1914), p. 5.

34. The Antigua *Sun* (28 August 1914), p. 3.

35. Lucas, *The Empire at War* pp. 321-328.

36. See, for example, The Trinidad *Port of Spain Gazette* (21 August 1914), p. 4; Ibid (11 August 1914), p. 9; The Barbados *Globe* (12 August 1914), p. 3.

37. The Grenada *Federalist* (18 August 1917), p. 2.

38. The Jamaica *Daily Chronicle* (5 June 1915), p. 4.

39. Ibid.

40. For the American situation see, Frank P. Zeidler, 'Hysteria in Wartime: Domestic Pressures on Ethnics and Aliens', in Winston A. Van Horne (ed.), *Ethnicity and War* (Milwaukee: University of Wisconsin, 1984), pp. 70-86; Stella Yarrow, 'The Impact of Hostility on Germans in Britain, 1914-1918', in Tony Kushner and Kenneth Lunn (eds.), *The Politics of Marginality: Race, the Radical Right and Minorities in Twentieth Century Britain* (London: Frank Cass, 1990), pp. 97-110.

41. See, for example, The *Trinidad and Tobago Year Book* 1919, p. 304; The Trinidad *Port of Spain Gazette* (9 July 1915), p. 10;

42. The British Honduras *Clarion* (27 July 1916), p. 12.

43. The Trinidad *Mirror* (2 May 1916), p. 6; Ibid (4 May 1916) & (6 May 1916).

44. C.O.295\505\26564 Enclosure no. 3 'Letter from Chamber of Commerce to W.M. Gordon, Acting Colonial Secretary', in W. Knaggs to Bonar Law 13 May 1916.

45. The Trinidad *Port of Spain Gazette* (7 May 1916), p. 6; C.O.295\505\26564 Enclosure no. 5, The Trinidad *Mirror* (12 May 1916), enclosed in W. Knaggs to Bonar Law, 13 May 1916.

46. C.O.295\505\21727 Bonar Law to Officer Administering Trinidad government, 10 May 1916.

47. C.O.295\505\21727 Minute of George Grindle dated 10 May 1916.

48. The Grenada *West Indian* (14 March 1919), p. 2.

49. The Jamaica *Gleaner* (11 August 1914), p. 17.

50. C.O.137\712\50114 Campbell to the President of the Board of Trade, 12 October 1915.

51. Ibid.

52. Ibid.

53. 'Germanizing Somewhere', The Barbados *Globe* (27 November 1914), p. 3; Ibid (30 November 1914), p. 3.

54. Ibid.

55. C.O.137\712\19661 Extract of letter by German Prisoner in Jamaica to the Red Cross, enclosed in, War Office to Colonial Office, 29 April 1915.

56. C.O.137\714\17259 Inquiry into shooting of Richard Hein by Private J. Thompson, enclosure 1, in Manning to Bonar Law, 25 March 1916.

57. C.O.295\505\30591 Enclosure 1, Acting governor (Trinidad), W. Knaggs to Bonar Law, 31 May 1916.

58. The *Trinidad and Tobago Yearbook*, 1918, p. 294.

59. The Grenada *West Indian* (15 January 1918), p. 6; See also, The *Trinidad and Tobago Year Book* 1919, pp. 291-300.

60. 'Echo of Uprising amongst interned Germans', The Trinidad *Port of Spain Gazette* (28 October 1916), p. 8.

61. James A. Beckford, *The Trumpet of Prophecy: a sociological study of Jehovah's Witnesses* (Oxford: Basil Blackwell, 1975), p. 10.

62. See, for the Jamaica experience, W.F. Elkins, *Street Preachers, Faith Healers and Herb Doctors in Jamaica 1890-1925* (New York: Revisionist Press, 1977); Philip Curtin, *Two Jamaicas: The Role of Ideas in a Tropical Colony 1830-1865* (Cambridge, Mass: Harvard University Press, 1955), pp. 168-177.

63. Ibid.

64. 'Mistaken Religious Belief', The Barbados *Globe* (16 October 1914), p. 3.

65. Ibid.

66. Elkins, *Street Preachers,* p. 62.
67. The Barbados *Sun* (22 May 1915), p. 3.
68. The St. Vincent *Times* (1 March 1917), p. 3 & (8 March 1917), p. 3 & (5 April 1917), p. 3.
69. Ibid.
70. See, for example, Richard D. Burton, 'Cricket, Carnival and Street Culture in the Caribbean' (University of London, ICS Postgraduate seminar: Caribbean Societies) 3 February 1986.
71. See, for example, The Trinidad *Port of Spain Gazette* (6 January 1917), p. 5 & (7 January 1917); The *Grenada Chronicle and Gazette* (19 January 1915), p. 2.
72. The Grenada *West Indian* (19 January 1917), p. 2.

Chapter 2 — Black Aspirations Expressed

1. 'Men who try to poison Recruiting', The *Jamaica Times*, (20 November 1915), p. 15.
2. The Grenada *Federalist* (27 October 1915), p. 2.
3. The *Jamaica Times* (20 November 1915), p. 15.
4. The Grenada *Federalist* (27 October 1915), p. 2.
5. This view was argued at length in a pamphlet written by Marryshow and appropriately entitled, 'Cycles of Civilization'. Over 500 copies were printed and distributed throughout the region and it was subsequently serialised in his newspaper. See for details, The Grenada *West Indian* (12 October, 1917), p. 7.
6. See, Patrick Bryan, *The Jamaica People, 1880–1902*, (London and Basingstoke: Macmillan, 1991), pp. 249-259.
7. In more recent times the theme of Africa's 'great past' has been strongly expressed in the works of various Caribbean and African nationalists, including: Walter Rodney, *How Europe Underdeveloped Africa* (Washington D.C.: Howard University Press, 1981); also, Basil Davidson, *Old Africa Rediscovered* (London: Victor Gollancz, 1959). A main issue in the debate is the question of whether slavery in Africa before the intrusion of the whites was parallel to the chattel slavery which developed in the New World. The debate is reviewed in Frederick Cooper, 'The Problem of Slavery in African Studies', *Journal of African History*, vol. 20, no. 1, 1979, pp. 103-125.
8. 'Reflections for Coloured Men who can but will not Fight', The Grenada *West Indian* (6 July 1917), p. 2.
9. The Grenada *West Indian* (6 July 1917), p. 2.
10. Ibid.
11. 'Africans, Germans and the British Empire: Is this a white man's war?', The Trinidad *Mirror* (3 September 1915), p. 4.
12. 'Members of the Contingent visit Negro Improvement Association', The Jamaica *Gleaner* (25 October 1915), p. 14.
13. The Grenada *West Indian* (20 February 1915), p. 2.
14. The Grenada *West Indian* (17 August 1917), p. 1.
15. Ronald Hyam, 'The Colonial Office Mind 1900-1914', in *Journal of Imperial and Commonwealth History*, vol. 8, no. 1, October 1979, p. 40.
16. See, Gad Heuman, *Between Black and White: Race, Politics, and the Free Coloreds in Jamaica, 1792-1865* (Oxford: Clio Press, 1981).
17. Philip Curtin, *Two Jamaicas: The Role of Ideas in a Tropical Colony 1830-1865* (Cambridge, Mass: Harvard University Press, 1985), p. 191.
18. C.O.318\315\309 January 10, 1906; Hyam, *The Colonial Office Mind*, pp. 43–44. The Cabinet decided on February 6, 1905 to withdraw troops from the West Indies and Bermuda and reduce the establishment in the Mediterranean. For more details on the process in the West Indies see, C.L. Joseph, 'The Strategic Importance of The British West Indies, 1882–1932', *Journal of Caribbean History*, vol. 7, November 1973.

19. The Grenada *Federalist* (20 June 1914), p. 2.

20. For details see, Patrick Emmanuel, *Crown Colony Politics in Grenada 1917-1951* (Barbados: ISER, 1978); Ann Spackman, (compiled by) *Constitutional Development of the West Indies 1922-1968* (Barbados: Caribbean Universities Press, 1975); H.A. Will, *Constitutional Change in the British West Indies 1880-1903* (Oxford: Clarendon Press, 1970).

21. G.K. Lewis, *The Growth of the Modern West Indies* (New York: Monthly Review Press, 1968), p. 170.

22. For the South African comparison see, Albert Grundlingh, *Fighting Their Own War: South African Blacks and the First World War* (Johannesburg: Ravan Press, 1987), pp. 50–51.

23. The Grenada *West Indian* (9 November 1917), p. 4.

24. Ibid.

25. Ibid., p. 2.

26. The Trinidad *Sunday Guardian* (13 March 1955), as cited in Emmanuel, *Crown Colony Politics*, p. 49.

27. 'The Fool's Adage', The Grenada *West Indian* (31 March 1915), p. 2.

28. 'Those Englishmen's letters', The Jamaica *Gleaner* (27 July 1915), p. 8; A.A. Cipriani, *Twenty–Five Years After: The British West Indies Regiment in the Great War 1914-1918*, reprint (London: Karia Press, 1993), p. 1.

29. 'The contingent criticized', The Jamaica *Daily Chronicle* (21 July 1915).

30. 'The contingent defended', The Jamaica *Daily Chronicle* (22 July 1915); The Jamaica *Gleaner* (27 July 1915), p. 8.

31. Herbert G. DeLisser, *Jamaica and the Great War* (Kingston, Jamaica: *Gleaner*, 1917), p. 25.

32. Elsa Goveia, *Slave Society in the British Leeward Islands at the end of the Eighteenth Century* (New Haven: Yale University Press, 1965), p. 148; See also, Roger N. Buckley, *Slaves in Red Coats: The British West India Regiments, 1795–1815* (London and New Haven: Yale University Press 1979), pp. 20-62.

33. Goveia, *Slave Society*, p. 329.

34. Post Emancipation disturbances, 1834-1914 are listed and related in Frank Cundall, *Political and Social Disturbances in the West Indies* (Jamaica: Institute of Jamaica, 1906).

35. See, Howard Johnson, 'Patterns of Policing in the Post–Emancipation British Caribbean, 1835-95', in David Anderson and David Killingray, *Policing The Empire: Government, Authority and Control 1830–1940* (Manchester and New York: Manchester University Press, 1991), pp. 71–91; Barry Higman, 'The First of August: Jamaica, 1838–1972' (Postgraduate Seminars, Mona, UWI/Dept. of History) May 1973.

36. See for example, 'Observe or Not?', The Jamaica *Gleaner* (14 August 1918), p. 8.

37. Higman, *The First of August*, p. 21

38. The Jamaica *Gleaner* (14 August 1918), p. 8.

39. 'Praise for our Men', The Jamaica *Gleaner* (2 February 1916), p. 8.

40. See, Grundlingh, *Fighting Their Own War,* pp. 37–54.

41. The Grenada *Federalist* (19 June 1915), p. 2.

42. The St Vincent *Times* (26 August 1915), p. 3.

43. The British Honduras *Clarion* (12 August 1915), p. 181.

44. 'Our boys in France: Will come back better men', The Trinidad *Port of Spain Gazette* (30 April 1918), p. 5.

45. 'Black Men and Germany', The Jamaica *Gleaner* (14 February 1916), p. 8.

46. The Jamaica *Gleaner*, (20 July 1915), p. 8; Ibid (14 February 1916), p. 8.

47. 'A Word to the Black Race', The Jamaica *Gleaner* (5 December 1902).

48. The Grenada *West Indian* (7 December 1917), p. 1.

49. The British Honduras *Clarion* (12 August 1915), p. 181.

50. The Jamaica *Gleaner* (12 July 1915), p. 13.

51. The Jamaica *Gleaner* (25 January 1916), p. 8.

52. The British Honduras *Clarion* (12 August 1915), p. 181.

53. 'Can we spare them?' The Jamaica *Gleaner* (25 January 1916), p. 8.

54. The British Honduras *Clarion* (12 August 1915), p. 181.

Chapter 3 – The Great Dilemma

1. C.O.137\709\25738 Manning to Harcourt, 2 June 1915.

2. See for example, C.O.551\81\48100 Enclosure 2, Captain C.G.S., 143rd Infantry Brigade to Major– General Callwell, Director of Military Operations, War Office, 11 November 1915.

3. David Killingray, 'The Idea of a British Imperial African Army', *Journal of African History*, vol. 20, no. 3, 1979, p. 422.

4. C.O.551\81\48100 Enclosure 1, War Office to Colonial Office, 16 November 1915.

5. *British Parliamentary Debates*, (House of Commons) vol. lxxxvi, no. 744, October 10– November 2, 1916, p. 117.

6. Ibid., vol. xciii, no. 751, April 30–May 25, 1917, p. 1126.

7. Killingray, *The Idea of a British Imperial African Army*, pp. 424– 425.

8. *British Parliamentary Debates*, vol. lxxxvi, no. 744, October 10–November 2, 1916, p. 875.

9. C.O.537\604\46680 Secret Memorandum by Bonar Law for the Cabinet on the Raising and Training of Native troops, 18 October 1915.

10. *British Parliamentary Debates*, vol. lxxxvi, no. 744, October 10–November 2, 1916, p. 116.

11. Ibid., pp. 116–117.

12. C.O.554\31\32699, Interdepartmental Conference 18 July 1916.

13. *British Parliamentary Debates*, vol. lxxxvi, No. 744, October 10–November 2, 1916, p. 117.

14. Ibid., vol. lxxv, no. 733, October 25–November 18, 1915, p. 1363.

15. C.O.318\333\46453 Dundonald to Harcourt, 23 November 1914.

16. C.O.318\333\50043 'West Indian Contingent', Minute of Grindle, 21 December 1914.

17. C.O.318\333\3355 Minute of official dated 7 September 1914.

18. C.O.28\284\44093 Governor L. Probyn to Harcourt, 27 October 1914. The Governor of Barbados during the war years was Sir Leslie Probyn who had previously been Governor of Sierra Leone. At the end of May 1918 Probyn replaced William Manning as Governor of Jamaica. His place at Barbados was taken by Lieut.– Colonel Charles O'Brien who had been Governor of the Seychelles.

19. See, for example, The British Honduras *Clarion* (15 July 1915), p. 70.

20. Details found in C.O.318\333 Harcourt to Kitchener at War Office, 22 April 1915.

21. C.O.318\333\33355 War Office to Colonial Office, 2 September 1914.

22. See, for example, Herbert G. DeLisser, *Jamaica and the Great War* (Jamaica: Gleaner, 1917), p. 33.

23. The *West India Committee Circular*, (Letter from Dr A.A. Myers, dated 7th November 1914), 15 December 1914, p. 598.

24. The Antigua *Sun* (28 August 1914), p. 3.

25. C.O.318\333 Harcourt to Kitchener at War Office, 22 April 1915.

26. C.O.318\333 War Office to Colonial Office, 14 December 1914.

27. See, C.O.318\333 Harcourt to Lord Stamfordham, 20 April 1915.

28. The Grenada *Federalist* (19 June 1915), p. 2.

29. Ibid; This probably referred to the battle of Isandlwana on 22 January 1879 where an army of over 20,000 Zulu warriors inflicted a humiliating and devastating defeat on several regiments of the British army and their black allies. For details see, Donald R. Morris, *The Washing of the Spears* (London: Sphere Books, 1973), pp. 355–390.

30. The Grenada *Federalist* (19 June 1915), p. 2.

31. The British Honduras *Clarion* (12 August 1915), p. 177.

32. Ibid.

33. C.O.318\333 Memorandum on proposed West Indian Contingent. Enclosure 1, in Dundonald to Harcourt, 23 November 1914.

34. Patrick Bryan, *The Jamaican People, 1880-1902* (London and Basingstoke: Macmillan, 1991), p. 70.
35. Paul Rich, 'Sydney Olivier, Jamaica and the Debate on British Colonial Policy in the West Indies', in Malcolm Cross and Gad Heuman (eds.), *Labour in the Caribbean* (London and Basingstoke: Macmillan, 1988), p. 226.
36. For a contemporary discussion on the issue of union with America or Canada see: H.G. DeLisser, *Twentieth Century Jamaica* (Jamaica: *Times*, 1913), pp. 1–32.
37. Philip Curtin, *Two Jamaicas: The Role of Ideas in a Tropical Colony 1830-1865*, (Cambridge, Mass: Harvard University Press, 1985) pp. 78–79.
38. James Morris, *Pax Britannica: The Climax of an Empire* (London: Faber and Faber, 1968), pp. 159–173.
39. Keith Williams, '"A Way Out of Our Troubles": The politics of Empire Settlement 1900–1922', in Stephen Constantine (ed.), *Emigrants and Empire: British Settlement in the Dominions between the Wars* (Manchester and New York: Manchester University Press, 1990), pp. 22–43.
40. C.O.318\333 Memorandum on proposed West Indian Contingent. Enclosure 1, in Dundonald to Harcourt, 23 November 1914.
41. C.O.318\333 Stamfordham to Harcourt, 17 April 1915.
42. C.O.318\333 Harcourt to Stamfordham, 20 April 1915.
43. See, Tim Travers, 'The Hidden Army: Structural Problems in the British Officer Corps, 1900– 1918', *Journal of Contemporary History*, vol. 17, no. 3, July 1982, p. 523.
44. C.O.318\333 Stamfordham to Harcourt, 22 April 1915.
45. C.O.318\333 Harcourt to Kitchener, 22 April 1915.
46. Ibid.
47. 'Jamaica contingent accepted', The *Jamaica Times* (29 May 1915), p. 16; The *Clarion* (12 August 1915), p. 181.
48. 'Britain's Myriad voices call', The Grenada *West Indian* (24 July 1915), p. 4.
49. The British Honduras *Clarion* (28 October 1915), pp. 484–485.
50. C.O.537\604\46680 Secret Memorandum by Bonar Law for the Cabinet on the Raising and Training of Native troops, 18 October 1915.
51. See, The *Reports of the West Indian Contingent Committee 1916-1919* I.C.S. Archives, University of London.
52. 'National Self-Respect', The Jamaica *Daily Chronicle* (21 July 1915), p. 4.
53. The *Jamaica Times* (7 August 1915), p. 14.
54. C.O.137\710\36649 Manning to Grindle 5 August 1915.
55. The Jamaica *Daily Chronicle* (1 July 1915), p. 4.
56. 'The Government and the People', The Trinidad *Port of Spain Gazette* (25 June 1915), p. 2.
57. The Grenada *Federalist* (14 July 1915), p. 3.
58. C.O.321\281\26449 Haddon– Smith to Harcourt, 7 June 1915.
59. C.O.137\710\33129 A. Aspinall to Grindle, 17 July 1915.
60. C.O.321\282\31385 Minute of Grindle dated 9 July 1915.
61. See appendix: Table B.1.
62. See appendix: Table B.2 & B.3.

Chapter 4 – Recruuitment Strategies

1. See appendix: Table B.4.
2. See, M.L Sanders and Philip Taylor, *British Propaganda during the First World War, 1914–18* (London and Basingstoke: Macmillan, 1982).
3. The Trinidad *Port of Spain Gazette* (20 June 1915), p. 6; Ibid (6 June 1915), p. 9.
4. The Grenada *Federalist* (28 June 1919), p. 2.

5. The British Honduras *Clarion* (28 October 1915), p. 490; For details on the reaction, attitude and role of the Church of England in the war see, Albert Marrin, *The Last Crusade: The Church of England in the First World War* (Durham, N.C.: Duke University Press, 1974); Also, Alan Wilkinson, *The Church of England and the First World War* (London: SPCK, 1978).
6. See, for example, 'The Pals', The Grenada *West Indian* (18 June 1916), p. 7.
7. See for details of the establishment, duties and membership of the Jamaica Central Recruiting Committee, J.C. Ford and F. Cundall, *The Handbook of Jamaica for 1919* (Jamaica: Government Printery, 1919), pp. 591–593.
8. For details on the notion of the 'martial races', see, Anthony H.M. Kirk–Greene, 'Damnosa Hereditas: Ethnic Ranking and the Martial Races Imperative in Africa', in *Ethnic and Racial Studies*, vol. 3, no. 4, October 1980, pp. 393–413; Stephen P. Cohen, *The Indian Army: Its Contribution to the Development of a Nation*, (Delhi: Oxford University Press, 1990), pp. 45–73.
9. The British Honduras *Clarion* (13 January 1916), p. 100; Ibid (27 January 1916), pp. 99–100; and (10 February 1916), p. 150.
10. The Jamaica *Gleaner* (2 November 1915), p. 8; Ibid (15 November 1915), p. 13; Ibid (19 November 1915), p. 13; The British Honduras *Clarion* (9 December 1915), p. 653. For details on the Maroons see, Mavis C. Campbell, *The Maroons of Jamaica, 1655–1796* (New Jersey: Africa World Press, 1990). Also, Richard Price, (ed.), *Maroon Societies: Rebel Slave Communities in the Americas* (Baltimore and London: Johns Hopkins University Press, 1979).
11. The Barbados *Standard* (29 January 1916), p. 5.
12. 'The Slacker', The *Jamaica Times* (9 March 1918), p. 4.
13. C.O. 321\297\15025 Minute of Darnley, 23 March 1917; Ibid 24 March 1917.
14. Ibid., Memorandum of Administrator R. P. Lobb to Governor Haddon–Smith, 12 February 1917.
15. C.O. 137\712\57687 India Office to Colonial Office, 14 December 1915; C.O. 137\711\52966.
16. C.O. 137\720\13244 Manning to Walter Long, 23 February 1917.
17. See for example, The British Honduras *Clarion* (14 October 1915), p. 434; Ibid (10 February 1916), p. 150.
18. The Trinidad *Port of Spain Gazette* (11 August 1917), p. 8.
19. Eric J. Leed, *No Man's Land: Combat and Identity in World War 1* (Cambridge: Cambridge University Press, 1979), p. 55; W.P. Livingstone, *Black Jamaica* (London: Sampson, Low & Marston 1900), pp. 262–263.
20. 'Recruits obtained in court', The Jamaica *Gleaner* (5 November 1915), p. 10.
21. 'Rogue or Recruit?', The British Guiana *Daily Argosy* (27 January 1916), p. 4.
22. 'Decamps after promising to enlist', The British Guiana *Daily Argosy* (6 May 1916), p. 4.
23. '"Bobo" Reece recalled', The Barbados *Globe* (31 May 1916), p. 3.
24. J.W. Fortescue, *A History of the British Army* vol. 1 (London: Macmillan, 1899), pp. 563–565.
25. The Jamaica *Gleaner* (28 January 1916), p. 8.
26. C.O.137\715\26475 Report of the Attorney-General, enclosed in Manning to Law, 19 May 1916; The Jamaica *Gleaner* (10 January 1916), p. 8; Similar incentives were offered to soldiers and their families in India and other countries of the empire. See for example, C. Ellinwood DeWitt, 'The Indian Army and Change, 1914–1918', in C. Ellinwood DeWitt and S. D. Pradhan (eds.), *India and World War 1* (New Delhi: Manohar Publications, 1978), pp. 197–198.
27. The Trinidad *Mirror* (16 February 1916), p. 7.
28. See for instance, The Barbados *Globe,* 'Stowaways on the Catalina', (6 October 1916), p. 3; See also C.O. 318\335\42513 Petition from British West Indians stranded in Brazil to Secretary of State, 4 August 1915, enclosed in Foreign Office, 15 September 1915.
29. 'A Review of Recruiting', The *Jamaica Times* (2 September 1916), p. 28

30. Patrick Bryan, *The Jamaican People, 1880–1902* (London and Basingstoke: Macmillan), 1991 p. 2.
31. The Jamaica *Gleaner* (12 October 1915), p. 13.
32. The British Honduras *Clarion* (9 March 1916), p. 261.
33. Ibid.
34. The Trinidad *Port of Spain Gazette* (15 August 1915), p. 3.
35. The Grenada *West Indian* (19 September 1915), p. 4.
36. The *Jamaica Times* (8 January 1916), p. 7.
37. The Antigua *Sun* (24 August 1915), p. 3; Herbert G. DeLisser, *Jamaica and the Great War* Jamaica: *Gleaner,* pp. 50–100; The band was also used with tremendous success in various African countries such as Nyasaland. See, for example, Melvin E. Page, 'The War of Thangata: Nyasaland and The East African Campaign, 1914–1918', *Journal of African History,* vol. 19, no. 1, 1978, p. 92.
38. See, for example, The Jamaica *Gleaner* (16 December 1915), p. 6.
39. See for a copy of the petition, The Grenada *Federalist* (21 September 1918), p. 2.
40. See, The Grenada *Federalist* (11 January 1919); C.O.318\358\22489.
41. Under the terms of the Military Services Convention Act of 1917, it was agreed with the United States government that if British subjects in America were excluded from conscription in the British forces then they could be taken into the United States Armed forces. See, David Killingray, All the King's Men?: Blacks in the British Army in the First World War 1914–1918', in Rainer Lotz and Ian Pegg (eds.), *Under the Imperial Carpet: Essays in Black History 1780–1950* (Crawley, Sussex: Rabbit, 1986), p. 178.
42. W.O.32\4765 'Enlistment of Coloured British subjects in U.S.A', General White to War Office, 5 September 1917.
43. Bahamas Archives Exhibition: 'The Bahamas During the World Wars, 1914–1918 and 1939–1945', Bahamas, Ministry of Education, 4–23 February, 1985, p. 12.
44. W.O.32\4765 'Enlistment of Coloured British subjects in the USA.', White to War Office, 5 September 1917.
45. Robin W. Winks, *The Blacks in Canada: A History* (New Haven and London: Yale University Press, 1971), pp. 314–315.
46. Ibid., p. 317.
47. Ibid.
48. Bridget Brereton, *Race Relations in Colonial Trinidad, 1870–1900* (London and New York: Cambridge University Press, 1979), p. 205.
49. The Trinidad *Mirror* (16 August 1915), p. 8; Ibid (17 September 1916), p. 4; The Bahamas *Tribune* (2 November 1915), p. 3; The Jamaica *Gleaner* (12 January 1916), p. 8.
50. C.L.R. James, *Beyond A Boundary* (London: Hutchinson, 1963), p. 40.
51. 'Public Officials and the Merchants' contingent', The Trinidad *Mirror* (22 October 1915), p. 4.
52. Sir George F. Huggins was head of one of the leading Trinidad firms – George F. Huggins and Company Limited. He went to Trinidad from St. Vincent in 1891 in search of a job but by the time of the First World War was president of the local Chamber of Commerce and perhaps the most influential person in the economic life of the colony. See, Michael Anthony, *Port-of-Spain in a World at War, 1939–1945* (Trinidad: Ministry of Sports, Culture and Youth Affairs, 1983) pp. 85–89.
53. C.O.295\503 Minute of G. Grindle, 15 November 1915 on Huggins to Law, 4 November 1915.
54. James, *Beyond A Boundary,* p. 40.
55. 'Letter to the Editor from H.H. Vernon', The British Honduras *Clarion* (11 November 1915), p. 547.
56. 'Trinidad's 'White' Private Contingent', The Grenada *West Indian* (23 November 1915), p. 2.

57. The Grenada *West Indian* (25 November 1915), p. 2.

58. 'A matter for serious inquiry', The Trinidad *Port of Spain Gazette* (17 May 1918), p. 11.

59. See, Captain H. Dow, *Record Service of members of the Trinidad Merchants' and Planters' Contingent 1915–1918* (Trinidad: Government Printery, 1925). There were 204 subscribers to the fund for the contingent and a total amount of $61,433.38 was raised.

60. C.O.137\726\42533 J. Challenor Lynch (Chairman of Barbados Recruiting Committee) to T.E. Fell (Colonial Secretary) 4 May 1918; Ibid T.E. Fell to Governor of Jamaica, 31 July 1918.

61. C.O.321\289\16100 Report of Administrator, Gideon Murray, 4 March 1916.

62. 'What are You doing?', The Jamaica *Gleaner* (22 April 1916), p. 8; The British Honduras *Clarion* (27 January 1916), p. 99.

63. Jeffrey P. Green, 'West Indian Doctors in London: John Alcindor (1873–1924) and James Jackson Brown (1882–1953)', *Journal of Caribbean History*, vol. 20, no. 1, 1986, p. 54.

64. C.O.321\282\40055 Governor Haddon–Smith to Bonar Law, 7 August 1915.

65. Ibid., War Office to W.S. Mitchell, 8 July 1915.

66. Ibid., Governor Haddon–Smith to Bonar Law, 7 August 1915.

67. Ibid.

68. Ibid., Minute of Darnley, 2 September 1915.

69. C.O.152\342 Minute of R.A. Wiseman on telegram by Officer Administering the Government of the Leeward Islands, 31 August 1914.

70. See, for example, Bryan, *The Jamaican People*, p. 250.

71. C.O.321\286\47950 War Office to Colonial Office, 16 October 1915.

72. Ibid., Minute of G. Grindle, 19 October 1915.

73. C.O.321\295\38029 Governor Haddon–Smith to Walter Long, 2 July 1917.

74. 'Of Pure European Descent', The Jamaica *Gleaner* (15 September 1917), p. 8.

75. A number of English women did try to get into the army as soldiers and in fact formed a regiment and were trained but the participation of women was confined to technical services. See, Lionel Tiger, *Men in Groups* (London: Nelson, 1971), p. 80.

76. The Grenada *Federalist* (7 November 1917), p. 3.

77. The Antigua *Sun* (25 August 1915), p. 3.

78. The *Jamaica Times* (20 November 1915), p. 17

79. The Jamaica *Gleaner* (16 October 1915), p. 8.

80. The Grenada *West Indian* (5 December 1916), p. 2; Ibid (6 July 1917), p. 1.

81. The British Honduras *Clarion* (28 October 1915), p. 489.

82. The British Honduras *Clarion* (11 November 1915), p. 543.

83. Virginia Woolf, *Three Guineas* (London: Hogarth Press, 1938), p. 320.

84. 'Been through about fifty hells', The Trinidad *Port of Spain Gazette* (2 September 1915), p. 9; 'The cowards here', The Jamaica *Gleaner* (13 September 1916), p. 13.

85. The British Honduras *Clarion* (11 November 1915), p. 543; Similar sentiments were expressed by the *Mirror* in order to discourage lower–class women from disrupting recruitment. See, The Trinidad *Mirror* (6 March 1916), p. 6.

86. Arthur Brittan and Mary Maynard, *Sexism, Racism and Oppression* (Oxford: Basil Blackwell, 1984), p. 131.

87. The Jamaica *Gleaner* (11 April 1916), p. 13.

88. The Grenada *Federalist* (28 September 1918), p. 3.

89. The British Honduras *Clarion* (21 October 1915), p. 461.

90. Ibid.

91. The literature on women and the family is vast but see, for example, Olive Senior, *Working Miracles: Women's Lives in the English–speaking Caribbean* (Barbados: ISER/UWI, 1991); Keith Hart, 'The Sexual Division of Labour', in Keith Hart (ed.), *Women and Sexual Division of Labour in the Caribbean* (Jamaica: Consortium Graduate School of Social Sciences, 1989); Judith Blake, *Family Structure in Jamaica: The Social Context of Reproduction* (New York: Free

Press of Glencoe, 1961); Patricia Mohammed and Catherine Shepherd (eds.), *Gender in Caribbean Development* (UWI, Jamaica: Women and Development Studies Project, 1988); Joycelin Massiah, *Women as Heads of Households in the Caribbean: Family Structure and Feminine Status* (Paris: UNESCO, 1983).

92. The rate of illegitimacy per hundred births for Trinidad in 1918 was 71 per cent, St Vincent 66.46 per cent, Grenada 54.6 per cent, British Guiana 56.3 per cent and in 1917 Antigua registered 75 per cent. In the case of Jamaica the rate steadily increased from an average of 62.4 per cent in 1910 to 70.07 per cent in 1919. See for details, Report of the Registrar General's Department for the period ending December 31, 1919, in *The Annual General Report of Jamaica (together with) The Department Reports 1919–1920*. I.C.S., Archives, pp. 17–22.

93. For details and regional variations, see for example, Senior, *Working Miracles*, p. 101; For comparative studies see, Margaret Lycette and William McGreevey, *Women and Poverty in the Third World* (Baltimore: Johns Hopkins University Press, 1983).

94. See, appendix: Table B.5.

95. The Jamaica *Gleaner* (16 January 1917), p. 8.

96. Ibid.; The Trinidad *Port of Spain Gazette* (31 July 1919), p. 13.

97. C.O.537\952\ Minute of Bonar Law on War Office correspondence, 8 September 1916.

98. The Trinidad *Port of Spain Gazette* (7 August 1915), p. 11; Ibid (19 August 1915), p. 11; The army's preference for single men was perhaps also influenced by society's commitment to the institution of marriage and by the belief that a man with less family attachments was likely to make a more efficient soldier.

99. C.O.321\282 Minutes of the Legislative Council, 3 September 1915, pp. 3–4.

100. For details on West Indian women's attitudes see, Senior, *Working Miracles*, pp. 36–37.

101. C.O.137\721\34825 Minute by L.S. Blackden, General Officer Commanding the Jamaica Troops 11 June 1917, enclosed in Manning to Long 15 June 1917.

102. The Grenada *Federalist* (1 December 1917), p. 3.

103. The *Jamaica Times* (19 May 1917), p. 6.

104. Ibid.

105. 'A nefarious practice', The Trinidad *Port of Spain Gazette* (19 August 1915), p. 11.

106. C.O.137\722\45927 Manning to Walter Long, 13 August 1917.

107. Ibid.; C.O.137\726\33929 Acting Governor to Long, 10 June 1918.

108. 'The trial of the mischief–making liar', The *Jamaica Times* (15 September 1917), p. 7.

109. Report of the Rio Cobre Home for Children of Men Who have served in the Jamaica War Contingent for the period ending March 31, 1920, in *The Annual General Report of Jamaica (together with) The Department Reports 1919–1920*. I.C.S., Archives, p. 59.

110. The Trinidad *Mirror* (7 December 1915), p. 7.

Chapter 5 – Miltary Selection and Civilian Health

1. The Grenada *West Indian* (19 September 1915), p. 4.

2. The *Jamaica Times* (5 June 1915), p. 18.

3. Ibid.

4. The Trinidad *Port of Spain Gazette* (25 August 1915), p. 11.

5. J.M. Winter, 'Some Aspects of the Demographic Consequences of the First World War in Britain', *Population Studies*, vol.30, no. 3 1976, p. 549.

6. C.O.318\344 Memorandum of H.T. Allen on Recruiting, February 1917.

7. The Jamaica *Gleaner* (8 March 1917), p. 3.

8. W.G. Macpherson (ed.), *Medical Services (General History)*, vol. 1, (London: H.M.S.O., 1921), p. 135.

9. Stephen Hill (compiled by), *Who's Who in Jamaica, 1919–1920* (Jamaica: *Gleaner* 1920), p. 241.

10. Ibid.
11. C.O.318\344\8314 War Office to Colonial Office, 14 February 1917.
12. Hill, *Who's Who in Jamaica, 1919–1920*, p. 241.
13. Hill, *Who's Who In Jamaica*, p. 247; For details on the termination of recruiting in Jamaica see, C.O.137\730\14951 War Diary of Local Forces.
14. J.H.W. Park, 'Note on the Causes for Rejections of Volunteers for the Jamaica War Contingents', in R.C. Earle and L. Oliver Crosswell (eds.), *The Jamaica Public Health Bulletin, 1917* (Jamaica: *Times* 1918), pp. 14–19.
15. Winter, *Demographic Consequences*, pp. 550–551.
16. Hill, *Who's Who in Jamaica, 1919–1920*, p. 246.
17. J.H.W. Park, 'Note on the Causes for Rejections of Volunteers for the Jamaica War Contingents', in Earle and Crosswell (eds.), *The Jamaica Public Health Bulletin, 1917*, p. 15.
18. Hill, *Who's Who in Jamaica, 1919–1920*, pp. 241–242.
19. W.P. Livingstone, *Black Jamaica* (London: Sampson, Low & Marston, 1990), pp. 176–177.
20. See, C.O.137\717 Six–Monthly Report on the Work carried out in the Government Bacteriological Laboratory March to September 1916. Enclosed in Jamaica despatch dated 11 November 1916.
21. Ibid.
22. H.D. Chambers, *Yaws* (London: J.A. Churchill, 1938), pp. 79–81.
23. Ibid., p. vii (preface)
24. J.M. Gurney, 'Malnutrition in Jamaica', seminar paper located at the (Caribbean Food and Nutrition Institute Library, Jamaica), 1973.
25. Park, *Note on the Causes for Rejections*, p. 16.
26. Ibid.
27. See for details on the confusion, H.D. Chambers, 'Further Light on the "Yaws–Syphilis" Problem', reprinted from *Transactions of the Royal Society of Tropical Medicine and Hygiene*, vol. 31, no. 2, July 1937, pp. 245–250; Megan Vaughn, *Curing Their Ills: Colonial Power and African Illness* (Cambridge: Polity, 1991).
28. 'The Difficulty in Recruiting', The Trinidad *Mirror* (3 March 1916), p. 4.
29. Ibid.
30. See for example, J.M. Winter, 'Military Fitness and Civilian Health in Britain During the First World War', in *Journal of Contemporary History*, vol.15, no. 2, 1980, pp. 209–244.
31. The Grenada *West Indian* (6 July 1917), p. 1.
32. The Grenada *Federalist* (11 July 1917), p. 3.
33. The Grenada *Federalist* (18 May 1918), p. 3.
34. Report on the sanitary condition of Kingston for 1916, in *The Jamaica Public Health Bulletin 1917*, p. 189.
35. The Jamaica *Gleaner* (22 October 1915), p. 8.
36. Ibid.; See also, The Jamaica *Gleaner* (24 July 1916), p. 8.
37. 'The Social Evil in Our Midst': Letter from R.E. Clarke, The Jamaica *Gleaner* (8 April 1916), p. 1. This letter may have been from the Rev. Edward Clarke described by Stephen Hill as 'a simple–minded, earnest, religious man of evangelical principles'. He died in 1917. For details see, Hill, *Who's Who in Jamaica*, pp. 369–370.
38. For a synopsis of the perspectives on the family see, Christine Barrow, 'Anthropology, The Family and Women in the Caribbean', in Patricia Mohammed and Catherine Shepherd (eds.), *Gender in Caribbean Development* (Jamaica: UWI/Women and Development Project, 1988), pp. 156–169; A more detailed and cross–cultural comparative discussion of the issues is provided in Sander L. Gilman, *Difference and Pathology: Stereotypes of Sexuality, Race, and Madness* (Ithaca and London: Cornell University Press, 1985).
39. Sydney Olivier, *Jamaica: The Blessed Island* (London: Faber and Faber, 1936), p. 372.
40. See, for example, The Grenada *West Indian* (13 September 1918), p. 1.
41. 'The Black Evil', Letter from G.E., The Jamaica *Gleaner* (14 April 1916), p. 14

42. Ibid.

43. One of earliest legal measures adopted to combat contagious diseases in Jamaica was the 1910 Yaws Notification Law. Under this law rural constables were employed to seek out and persuade affected people to undergo treatment in the out–patients' clinics. See, Gisela Eisner, *Jamaica, 1830–1930: A Study in Economic Growth* (London: University of Manchester Press, 1961), pp. 342–343.

44. For an authoritative treatment of these issues see, Sander L. Gilman, *Disease and Representation: Images of Illness from Madness to AIDS* (Ithaca and London: Cornell University Press, 1988).

45. The Jamaica *Gleaner* (20 January 1917), p. 14.

46. W.G. Macpherson (ed.), *Medical Services: Diseases of the War*, vol. 2 (London: H.M.S.O., 1923), pp. 118–119.

47. C.O.318\344\44010 War Office to Colonial Office on 3 September 1917.

48. Macpherson, *Medical Services (General History)* vol. 2, 1923, p. 146.

49. C.O.318\340\56610 War Office to Colonial Office, 25 November 1916.

50. See, M.S. Stone, 'The Victorian Army: Health, Hospitals and Social Conditions as encountered by British Troops during the South African War, 1899–1902', PhD thesis, I.C.S. University of London, 1992, p. 230.

51. 'More stringent measures', The Jamaica *Gleaner* (25 July 1916), p. 8.

52. Ibid.

53. Macpherson, *Medical Services (General History)* vol. 2, 1923, pp. 145–146.

54. C.O.321\295\48584 Haddon–Smith to Walter Long, 5 September 1917; Ibid., enclosures, 'Minutes of the Legislative Council', 29 June 1917 to 24 August 1917.

55. C.O.321\300\1170 'Report of colonial surgeon on working of the V.D. ordinance', enclosed in Haddon–Smith to Walter Long, 9 December 1918.

56. Macpherson, *Medical Services: Diseases of the War*, vol.2, 1923, p. 140.

57. C.O.321300\1170 'Report of colonial surgeon on working of the V.D. ordinance', enclosed in Haddon–Smith to Walter Long 9 December 1918.

58. The *Federalist*, 11 October 1919, p. 3.

59. C.O.137\725\20299 Manning to Long, 30 March 1918.

60. C.O.137\725\20299 Extracts from the Annual Reports of the Medical Department and the Central Board of Health, 1916–1917, enclosed in Governor Manning to Walter Long, 30 March 1918.

61. Report of the Island Medical Department for the period ending March 1919, in *The Annual General Report of Jamaica (together with) The Department Reports 1918–1919*. I.C.S., Archives, p. 143.

62. Ibid.

63. C.O.137\722\38886 Manning to Long, 17 July 1917.

64. J.C. Ford and F. Cundall, *Handbook of Jamaica, 1919* (Jamaica: Government Printery, 1919), p. 536.

65. See for details on the development of penicillin and its impact on the treatment of diseases, Claude Quetel, *History of Syphilis* (Cambridge: Polity in association with Blackwell, 1990), pp. 248–272; For the initial use of penicillin in Jamaica, see G.B. Colonial Office: *Jamaica Colonial Report for 1946*, pp. 43–44. During the Second World War the question of venereal diseases again became a major issue in the region. For the Trinidad case see, Michael Anthony, *Port-of-Spain in a World at War, 1939–1945* (Trinidad: Ministry of Sports, Culture and Youth Affairs, 1983), pp. 193–197.

66. The Trinidad *Port of Spain Gazette* (25 August 1915), p. 11.

67. The Grenada *West Indian* (18 September 1915), p. 5.

68. 'A hardship on Recruiting', The Trinidad *Mirror* (1 December 1915), p. 4.

69. The *Jamaica Times* (26 May 1917), p. 6.

70. The Grenada *West Indian* (6 July 1917), p. 1.

71. See for example, 'Between the Scissors', The Grenada *West Indian* (25 June 1916), p. 5

72. The Grenada *West Indian* (27 September 1918), p. 4.

73. The Grenada *Federalist* (6 October 1915), p. 2; The Grenada *West Indian* (4 October 1915), p. 2.

Chapter 6 – Resistance to Recruitment

1. The Antigua *Sun* (25 August 1915), p. 3.

2. The Antigua *Sun* (27 September 1915), p. 3.

3. The Bahamas *Tribune* (14 August 1915), p. 2.

4. The Trinidad *Port of Spain Gazette* (15 August 1915), p. 3.

5. The British Honduras *Clarion* (28 October 1915), p. 490.

6. 'A Serious Protest', The Grenada *West Indian* (18 September 1915), p. 8

7. The Jamaica *Gleaner* (27 November 1915), p. 8.

8. Stephen A. Hill (compiled by), *Who's Who in Jamaica, 1919–1920* (Jamaica: *Gleaner,* 1920), pp. 240–241.

9. C.O.137\716\43238 'Report of Attorney-General, E. St. John Branch' enclosed in Manning to Law, 26 August 1916.

10. The Grenada *Federalist* (25 August 1915), p. 2.

11. The British Honduras *Clarion* (28 October 1915), p. 487; Ibid (21 October 1915), p. 464

12. Ibid.

13. The Trinidad *Port of Spain Gazette* (14 August 1917), p. 3.

14. Ibid.

15. The *Jamaica Times* (5 February 1916), p. 8.

16. The Trinidad *Mirror* (6 March 1916), p. 6.

17. 'A Pernicious Song', The Trinidad *Mirror* (16 March 1916), p. 4; Details and music to the song are located at the British Library (Official Publications), Reference No. H.3995.EE, Piantadosi Songs, no. 20.

18. The Trinidad *Federalist* (28 March 1917), p. 2.

19. The Grenada *West Indian* (17 January 1919), p. 2.

20. The Grenada *West Indian* (9 June 1917), p. 5.

21. The Trinidad *Port of Spain Gazette* (14 January 1917), p. 13; The British Honduras *Clarion* (15 July 1915), p. 70; Extract from 'The *Voice* of Dominica' (24 January 1917), cited in The Antigua *Sun* (15 March 1917), p. 3.

22. See, David Trotman, *Crime in Trinidad: Conflict and Control in a Plantation Society, 1838–1900* (Knoxville: University of Tennessee Press, 1986), pp. 183–212; Patrick Bryan, *The Jamaican People, 1880–1902,* (London and Basingstoke: Macmillan, 1991) pp. 28–30; See also the various articles in, Malcolm Cross and Gad Heuman (eds.), *Labour in the Caribbean* (London and Basingstoke: Macmillan, 1988).

23. See, Trotman, *Crime in Trinidad,* p. 210.

24. 'Only a White Man's war', The Trinidad *Mirror* (6 September 1915), p. 4; The British Honduras *Clarion* (23 March 1916), p. 322.

25. The British Honduras *Clarion* (21 October 1915), p. 461.

26. The Barbados *Standard* (29 January 1916), p. 5.

27. The British Honduras *Clarion* (21 October 1915), p. 461.

28. 'Letter to the Editor from "A Creole"', The British Honduras *Clarion* (4 November 1915), p. 520.

29. The Trinidad *Port of Spain Gazette* (2 May 1917), p. 11.

30. 'Cowardly Slackers', The Trinidad *Port of Spain Gazette* (4 September 1915), p. 9.

31. Ibid (3 October 1917), p. 11.

32. The Trinidad *Port of Spain Gazette* (10 September 1915), p. 11.

33. 'Two Shirkers on Trial', The Trinidad *Port of Spain Gazette* (11 September 1915), p. 9.

34. The Grenada *West Indian* (29 May 1918), p. 6.

35. See, 'A disloyal Trinidadian: Imbued with deep pro–German sentiment', The Trinidad *Port of Spain Gazette* (28 April 1917), p. 5; The Trinidad *Port of Spain Gazette* (29 January 1918), p. 11.

36. 'Teasing B.G. recruits', The British Guiana *Daily Argosy* (4 May 1916), p. 4.

37. Ibid.

38. The British Honduras *Clarion* (12 April 1917), p. 352.

39. The British Honduras *Clarion* (21 October 1915), p. 461.

40. 'Fined for Disloyalty', The Barbados *Globe* (24 November 1915), p. 3.

41. 'The West Indian Contingent', The Barbados *Globe* (17 September 1915), p. 3.

42. 'Disloyal Talk', The Jamaica *Gleaner* (18 April 1918), p. 10.

43. 'Case of Discharged Men', The *Jamaica Times* (16 September 1916), p. 12.

44. The Jamaica *Gleaner* (3 August 1916), p. 8.

45. 'Our unemployed would–be soldiers', The Trinidad *Mirror* (12 September 1916), p. 4.

46. 'Reginald Stanford's case', The Trinidad *Port of Spain Gazette* (13 February 1917), p. 3.

47. The Jamaica *Gleaner* (3 August 1916), p. 8.

48. 'Seven shillings a week', The Jamaica *Gleaner* (6 March 1917), p. 8.

49. The Jamaica *Gleaner* (29 November 1916), p. 8.

50. The Trinidad *Port of Spain Gazette* (19 June 1918), p. 3

51. 'Letter to the Editor from "A Young Man"', The Grenada *West Indian* (6 July 1917), p. 1.

52. 'Another call to arms', The Grenada *West Indian* (5 December 1916), p. 2.

53. The British Honduras *Clarion* (10 February 1916), p. 153.

54. 'Some mischievous reports', The *Jamaica Times* (29 May 1915), p. 14.

55. The Jamaica *Gleaner* (23 October 1915), p. 8.

56. 'The present situation in the Great War', The *Jamaica Times* (21 August 1915), p. 14.

57. The Trinidad *Port of Spain Gazette* (17 March 1918), p. 2.

58. The Grenada *West Indian* (26 August 1916), p. 2; Ibid., (21 June 1918), p. 2.

59. 'Returned Heroes', The St. Vincent *Times* (29 November 1917), p. 3; The Grenada *West Indian* (19 July 1918), p. 6.

60. 'A Misfortune', The Jamaica *Gleaner* (5 April 1916), p. 8.

6. For a copy of medical report on the condition of the men at Halifax see, The Jamaica *Gleaner* (8 June 1916), p. 2.

62. 'Misfortune to Volunteers: Authentic details', The Jamaica *Gleaner* (8 April 1916), p. 3.

63. The Grenada *West Indian* (20 June 1916), p. 2; The Jamaica *Gleaner* (22 May 1916), p. 8

64. 'Are Imperial Troops', The Jamaica *Gleaner* (10 June 1916), p. 13.

65. For reference to the socio–political impact of the *Mendi* disaster see, Albert Grundlingh, *Fighting Their Own War: South African Blacks and the First World War* (Johannesburg: Ravan Press, 1978), p. 139; Norman Clothier, *Black Valour: The South African Native Labour Contingent, 1916–1918 and the sinking of the "Mendi"*, (Pietermaritzburg: University of Natal Press, 1987), pp. 48–100; The Jamaica *Gleaner* 'Loss of Mendi' (21 August 1917), p. 13.

66. The Jamaica *Gleaner* 'Pneumonia Outbreak' (2 March 1917), p. 9; 'Report on the Sanitary Condition of the City and Parish of Kingston for 1916', in Edw..R.C. Earle and Oliver L. Crosswell (eds.), *The Jamaica Public Health Bulletin, 1917* (Jamaica: Times 1918), p. 189. Crosswell was the Medical Officer of health for Kingston and Earle was the Health Officer for Port Royal.

67. 'With White Hearts', The Jamaica *Gleaner* (14 April 1916), p. 8.

68. 'The Return of our Wounded', The *Jamaica Times* (3 June 1916), p. 22.

69. The Jamaica *Gleaner* (2 June 1916), p. 13; Ibid (7 June 1916), p. 13.

70. 'The Situation Today', The Jamaica *Gleaner* (27 May 1916), p. 8.

71. The Jamaica *Gleaner* (8 June 1916), p. 8.

72. Herbert G. DeLisser, *Jamaica and the Great War* (Jamaica: *Gleaner*, 1917), p. 135; For further details on recruitment in Panama see, The Grenada *West Indian* (20 July 1917), p. 3.

and (12 October 1917), p. 8; Also, Stephen A. Hill (compiled by), *Who's Who in Jamaica, 1919–1920* (Jamaica: *Gleane,r* 1920), pp. 242–243.

73. C.O.321\294\24920 Report on the third Grenada Contingent by Major G.W. Smith, 3 April 1917.

74. Ibid.

75. Hill, *Who's Who in Jamaica, 1919–1920*, p. 240.

76. The Grenada *Federalist* (8 July 1916), p. 2.

77. C.O.321\294\24920 Report on the third Grenada Contingent by Major G.W. Smith, 3 April 1917.

78. 'Warning to Deserters', The Barbados *Globe* (31 May 1916).

79. 'Notice to Recruits', The Trinidad *Port of Spain Gazette* (3 April 1917), p. 13.

80. C.O.318\344 Minute of George Grindle, 28 February 1917.

81. The British Honduras *Clarion* (10 February 1916), p. 148.

82. Ibid.

83. The British Honduras *Clarion* (2 March 1916), p. 233. In some areas of British Guiana the arrival of the recruiting sergeant produced panic and desertion among the men. In New Amsterdam for instance, the rumour that compulsion would be resorted to in order to get recruits resulted in 'bus loads' of men leaving the town until they thought the danger was over. See 'The Recruiting Campaign', The British Guiana *Daily Argosy* (12 January 1917), p. 4.

84. The British Honduras *Clarion* (9 March 1916), p. 260.

85. Ibid.

86. See, Gordon K. Lewis, *The Growth of the Modern West Indies* (New York: Monthly Review Press), pp. 289–307.

87. The British Honduras *Clarion* (30 March 1916), p. 429.

88. The British Honduras *Clarion* (2 March 1916), p. 233.

89. 'Recruits in Trouble', The British Guiana *Daily Argosy* (5 October 1916), p. 4.

90. See, for instance, 'Recruits in a Brawl', The Barbados *Standard* (5 February 1916), p. 5.

91. 'Last Saturday's Soldier–Police Affray: An Eyewitness version', The Trinidad *Port of Spain Gazette* (12 December 1916), p. 11; For slightly different version of the incident see, 'The Demerara Troops in Trinidad', The British Guiana *Daily Argosy* (4 January 1917).

92. 'Police and Military', The Trinidad *Port of Spain Gazette* (13 December 1916), p. 13.

93. 'The Police and Recruits', The Trinidad *Mirror* (6 September 1915), p. 4.

94. 'A dastardly attack', The Trinidad *Port of Spain Gazette* (30 June 1917), p. 3.

95. W.O.95\5446 Diary of General Officer commanding Troops in Jamaica July 1914 to December 1919: Entry of 25 December 1915.

96. C.O.137\716\36244 War Diary of the Staff Officer of the local forces for the period 1 November 1915 to 30 June 1916.

97. The Jamaica *Gleaner* (12 October 1916), p. 8.

98. 'Men confined to barracks', The Jamaica *Gleaner* (8 June 1916), p. 13.

99. 'Continuation of the Enquiry at Camp into recent disturbances: attitude of people', The Jamaica *Gleaner* (6 February 1917), p. 4; Ibid (3 February 1917), p. 6.

100. C.O.137\711\290 War Diary of the Staff Officer of the local forces.

101. See for details on the prostitutes, Bryan, *The Jamaica People*, p. 28.

102. 'The Contingent Riot', The Jamaica *Gleaner* (12 July 1917), p. 8.

103. 'This will never do', The Jamaica *Gleaner* (18 July 1917), p. 8.

104. Ibid.

105. W.O.95\5446 Diary of General Officer Commanding Troops in Jamaica, July 1914 to December 1919: Entry of 16 May 1917.

106. See for instance, David Trotman, *Crime in Trinidad*, pp. 134–182; Bryan, *The Jamaican People*, pp. 266–282.

107. 134 In the context of West Africa it was thought that conscription could not easily or equitably be imposed on societies composed predominantly of non–literate peoples who not only lived in widely scattered communities but moreover, had a variety of systems of traditional rule. There was also concern over adopting a policy which resembled the system of forced labour which the French had enforced and which produced widespread resistance. The fear of similar disturbances was an important reason for the Colonial Office's emphasis on caution to the imposition of conscription in the British territories. For details of British attitude to conscription in West Africa see, David Killingray, 'The Colonial Army in the Gold Coast: Official Policy and Local Response, 1890–1947', PhD thesis, S.O.A.S., University of London, 1982, pp. 275–276.

108. DeLisser, *Jamaica and the Great War*, p. 117.

109. Ibid., p. 125

110. C.O.318\344\10160 Long to Manning, 28 February 1917

111. 'The King Assents', The Jamaica *Gleaner* (7 July 1917), p. 6.

112. 'The Legislature Favours Conscription', The Jamaica *Gleaner* (8 March 1917), p. 3.

113. 'Letter from "OnLooker"', The Jamaica *Gleaner* (19 March 1917), p. 4.

114. For some discussion on the Eugenicists' views on the effects of the war see, J.M. Winter, 'Britain's "Lost Generation" of the First World War', *Population Studies*, vol. 31, no. 3, 1977, pp. 449–466.

115. 'Letter from James L. Sawers', The Jamaica *Gleaner* (19 March 1917), p. 4.

116. The Jamaica *Gleaner* (19 March 1917), p. 4.

117. 'Letter from A.B. Lowe', The Jamaica *Gleaner* (16 March 1917), p. 10.

118. 'Done nothing For Jamaica?', The Jamaica *Gleaner* (21 March 1917), p. 8.

119. Ibid.

120. 'Registration for Military Service', The *Jamaica Times* (2 June 1917), p. 9.

121. See, Hill, *Who's Who in Jamaica*, p. 360.

122. C.O.137\721\34825 Resolution on the Military Service Bill, enclosed in Manning to Long, 15 June 1917; See also, The Jamaica *Gleaner* (3 April 1917), p. 11.

123. Ibid., Minute of J.H.W. Park, 5 June 1917. It is worth noting that there were at the time a number of West Indian women serving as Red Cross nurses in Syria, France, England, America and other places where they tended troops of every nationality. This aspect of West Indian contribution to the war needs to be explored in detail. For some information see, J.C. Cundall and F. Ford, *The Handbook of Jamaica for 1919*, (Jamaica: Government Printing Office, 1919), pp. 672–673.

124 The *Jamaica Times* (31 March 1917), p. 22.

125. C.O. 137\723\1554 Report on Registration Under the Military Service Law, no.16, 1917; C.O.137\724\2986 memorandum from Brig.-General Blackden to War Office, 19 April 1917.

Chapter 7 – Service and Working Conditions Overseas

1. C.0.318\336 War Office to Colonial Office, 30 October 1915.

2. Ibid., 25 October 1915.

3. Ibid., 16 August 1915.

4. Lt.–Colonel C. Woodhill, *A Few Notes on the History of the British West Indies Regiment* (Jamaica: [unpublished] West India Reference Library, 1919), p. 2.

5. Ibid.

6. Frank Cundall, *Jamaica's Part in the Great War 1914–1918* (London: Institute of Jamaica, 1925), p. 29.

7. Stephen A. Hill, *Who's Who in Jamaica, 1919-1920* (Jamaica: *Gleaner*, 1920), p. 240.

8. C.O.318\341\40033 A. Aspinall to the Medical Officer at Withnoe Camp, 22 August 1916.

9. For the enlistment of West Indians living in England see for example, C.O.318\339\28543; C.O.318\340\46561. Lord Derby was the Director General of recruiting. Under his scheme men were required to be attested, thereby undertaking to serve when and if called upon to do so, but a system of tribunals was also established whereby men with good personal or national reasons could be exempted. Single men was also liable to be called up for service before married men.

10. 'Letter from a Trinidadian at Seaford', The Trinidad *Port of Spain Gazette* (11 January 1916), p. 10.

11. 'Letter from Colonel Barchard to the Governor, British Guiana, dated 10 December 1915', The Trinidad *Mirror* (25 January 1916), p. 4.

12. 'Recalcitrant Recruit Returned to Colony', The British Guiana *Daily Argosy* (6 November 1915), p. 5.

13. C.O.318\339\2946 Colonel Barchard to Colonial Office, 4 January 1916.

14. Ibid.

15. C.O.318\336\49175 Barchard to Colonial Office, 24 October 1915; Also C.O.318\336\48246.

16. The British Guiana *Daily Chronicle* (10 November 1915).

17. The British Guiana *Daily Argosy* (6 November 1915), p. 5.

18. Ibid.

19. Lawrence James, *Mutiny* (London: Buchan and Enright, 1987).

20. Ian Beckett, 'The Nation in Arms, 1914–18', in F.W. Beckett and Keith Simpson (eds.), *A Nation in Arms: A Social Study of the British Army in the First World War* (Manchester: Manchester University Press, 1985), pp. 22–23.

21. W.O.95\4732 Woodhill to War Office, 17 June 1917; The Grenada *West Indian* (12 October 1917), p. 5.

22. In January 1915 Djemal Pasha, the Turkish Minister of Marine, personally led a force of 22,000 men secretly across the Sinai Peninsula from Beerseba and attacked the Canal. The assault was unsuccessful and Djemal had 2,000 casualties. Although there were no further Turkish attacks against the Canal the threat was ever present. See, R.E. Dupuy and T.N. Dupuy, *The Encyclopedia of Military History* (London and Sydney: Jane's Publishing, 1970), p. 957.

23. This group was composed of 7 officers and 300 other ranks from the 1st BWIR; 3 officers and 100 other ranks from the 2nd and 3 officers and 100 other ranks from the 3rd. For a listing of the individuals in this group see, C.O.318\340\42980 & C.O.318\340\44456. The campaign in East Africa was waged against the German forces led by General von Lettow Vorbeck who through a variety of guerrilla tactics was able prolong the conflict in that region until the armistice was signed in Europe in November 1918.

24. Akinjide Osuntokun, *Nigeria in the First World War* (London: Longman, 1979), p. 240.

25. C.O.318\339\31100 Chief of Imperial Staff to General Commanding Officer (Secret), 28 June 1916.

26. Ibid Murray to Chief of Imperial Staff, 29 June 1916.

27. C.O.318\347\18005 G.O.C. Mesopotamia Expeditionary Force to War Office, 23 June 1917.

28. W.O.95\4732 Woodhill to War Office, 'Report of the BWIR in Egypt', 17 June 1917.

29. Woodhill, *A Few Notes*, p. 3.

30. C.O.318\340\46494 War Office to Colonial Office, 28 September 1916.

31. Robin Kilson, 'Calling Up The Empire: The British Military Use of Non-White Labour in France, 1916–1920' (Unpublished Ph.D Thesis Harvard University, November 1990), p. 132.

32. Ibid pp. 108–109.

33. C.O.537\952\42950 Minute of Bonar Law on War Office correspondence, 8 September 1916.

34. See Kilson, *Calling Up the Empire*, pp. 2–132.

35. Beckett, *The Nation in Arms*, pp. 13–14.

36. C.O.318\340 Law to Governors of Jamaica, Trinidad, Barbados, Bermuda and Windwards, 2 October 1916.

37. W.O.32\5145 L. Probyn to Bonar Law, 4 October 1916.

38. Ibid., Manning to Law, 4 October 1916.

39. Ibid., Haddon–Smith to Law, 4 October 1916.

40. For details of this conference see, *Diary of 1st BWIR*, hand written bounded original copy (I.C.S), pp. 32–34.

41. Some of these letters were subsequently published in the press, see for instance, The Grenadian *West Indian* (28 September 1917), p. 8; Ibid (4 March 1918), p. 8.

42. *Diary of 1st BWIR* (I.C.S), p. 33.

43. Ibid p. 34.

44. Woodhill, *A Few Notes*, p. 4.

45. The British Guiana *Daily Argosy* (6 November 1915), p. 5.

46. The Grenada *West Indian* (28 September 1917), p. 8.

47. Woodhill, *A Few Notes*, p. 4; C.L. Joseph, The British West Indies Regiment, 1914–1918, *Journal of Caribbean History*, vol. 7, November 1973, p. 108.

48. Joseph, *The British West Indies Regiment*, p. 105.

49. For details on the locations and movements of the various battalions on the Western front see, Cundall, *Jamaica's Part*, pp. 58–70.

50. BWIR. HONOURS AND DISTINCTIONS

Distinguished Service Order	5
Military Cross	9
Military Cross with Bar	1
Membership of the Order of the Br.Empire	2
Distinguished Conduct Medal	8
Military Medal	37
Military Medal with Bar	1
Meritorious Service Medal	13
Royal Humane Society's Medal	4
Medaille d' Honneur	1
Mentioned in Despatches	49

51. See, for example, C.O.318\344\35242 W.J. Murray to War Office, 24 June 1917; The *West India Committee Circular* (6 March 1919).

52. C.O.318\344\55651 War Office to Colonial Office, 8 November 1917.

53. During the Arras offensive 9 April to 6 June 1917, six were killed and 16 wounded; In the Messines offensive, 7 June to 30 July 1917, 16 were killed and 60 wounded; In the period of the third battle of Ypres, 31 July to 19 September 1917, 13 were killed and 131 wounded, while in the period 20 September to 31 December of the same battle, 44 were killed and 246 wounded. No figures are available for the Somme offensive but see for further details, The War Office: *Statistics of the Military Effort of the British Empire during the Great War, 1914–1920* (London, 1922), pp. 324–327.

54. C.O.318\344\48562 Minute of H.T. Allen, 19 July 1917; See also, C.O.318\344\55651 Minute of Grindle, 24 November 1917 & Minute of Darnley, 20 November 1917. For publication of the reports in local papers see for example, The Grenada *West Indian* (30 March 1918), p. 8; Ibid (7 June 1918), pp. 1–2.

55. The Grenada *West Indian* (7 June 1918), p. 1.

56. A.E. Horner, *From the Islands of the Sea: Glimpses of a West Indian Battalion in France* (Nassau, Bahamas: Guardian, 1919), p. 8.

57. For details on the diet of the various troops and the various experiments the army carried out in order to combat deficiency diseases see, Macpherson (ed.), *Medical Services (Hygiene of*

the War), vol. 2 (London: H.M.S.O., 1923), pp. 1–132. It should be noted however that unlike in the case of the BWIR., scales of rations for members of the WIR, like the African soldiers, were usually calculated differently from European troops. Their diet was inferior in quality, variety and quantity to that of the Europeans. See for details, C.O.318\354\27950 Petition of West India Regiment to the King, enclosed in Probyn to Milner, 20 May 1920.

58. Macpherson, *Medical Services (Hygiene of the War)*, vol. 2, 1923, p. 63.

59. Macpherson, *Medical Services (General History)*, vol. 2, 1923, p. 142.

60. Macpherson, *Medical Services (Hygiene of the War)*, vol. 2, 1923, pp. 63.

61. Profiteering was not confined to Mesopotamia. It was very prevalent in the British Army. See for instance, J.G. Fuller, *Troop Morale and Popular Culture in the British and Dominion Armies 1914–1918* (Oxford: Claredon Press, 1991), p. 60.

62. C.O.123\296 *Report of the Commission appointed by the Governor to enquire into the Origin of the Riot in the Town of Belize which began on the night of the 22 July 1919*, 10 October 1919, evidence of S.A. Haynes (hereafter *Report of the Belize Commission*).

63. Ibid.

64. *Report of the West Indian Contingent Committee*, 30 September, 1919, p. 4.

65. See, Albert Grundlingh, *Fighting Their Own War: South African Blacks and the First World War* (Johannesburg: Ravan Press, 1978) pp. 88–89; David Killingray and James Mathews, 'Beasts of Burden: British West African Carriers in the First World War', *Canadian Journal of African Studies*, vol. 13, no. 1, 1979, p. 10.

66. J.M. Winter, 'Britain's "Lost Generation" of the First World War', *Population Studies*, vol. 31, no. 3, 1977, pp. 450–451.

67. Hill, *Who's Who in Jamaica*, p. 249.

68. C.O.123\296 *Report of the Belize Commission*, evidence of D.N. McKoy.

69. Ibid., evidence of G.W. Hulse.

70. Horner, *From the Islands of the Sea*, p. 19

71. Ibid.

72. See, for example, The Grenada *West Indian* (21 December 1917), p. 2.

73. Macpherson, *Medical Services (General History)*, vol. 2, p. 146.

74. Ibid., p. 143.

75. C.O.318\345\61094 Harry Brown to Algernon Aspinall, 5 December 1917.

76. Ibid. Emphases in the original text.

77. Ibid., Minute of H.T. Allen, 20 December 1917.

78. C.O.318\347\2244 H. Creedy (War Office) to H.F. Batterbee (Colonial Office), 8 January 1918.

79. C.O.318\347\12090 Creedy to Batterbee 8 March 1918.

80. For a monthly break down of the casualties see, C.O.318\345\61094

81. Ibid., Minute of H.T. Allen, 20 December 1917; C.O.318\345\52334 Memorandum of Governor Manning, 23 October 1917.

82. C.O.318\347\12090 Creedy to Batterbee, 8 March 1918.

83. Ibid., Minute of George Grindle, 15 March 1918.

84. See, Cundall, *Jamaica's Part*, pp. 78–79.

85. The Grenada *West Indian* (5 July 1918), p. 7.

86. For the various correspondences relating to the BWIR/ WIR conflict, see, A. A. Cipriani,[reprint] *Twenty-Five Years After: The British West Indies Regiment in the Great War (1914–1918)*, London: Karia Press, 1993), pp. 54–59.

87. C.O.318\347\17779 (Secret) G.O.C. (East Africa) to War Office, 9 April 1918.

88. C.O.318\347\19021 (Secret) War Office to G.O.C., 11 April 1918.

89. In June Major Porter was relieved by Major R. Leader who took over in August. In the interim Captain R.S. Martinez of the West India Regiment served as the senior officer.

90. Cipriani, *Twenty-Five Years After*, p. 57; Sir Etienne Dupuch, *A Salute to Friend and Foe* (Nassau, Bahamas: Tribune, 1986), pp. 66–67.

91. The experience of the West Indians was not unique. Many West African troops and carriers for instance, collapsed from starvation and lack of water and many more survived by chewing roots and bark from trees. See, David Killingray, 'The Colonial Army in the Gold Coast: Official Policy and Local Response, 1890–1947', PhD thesis, S.O.A.S., University of London, 1982, p. 323.

92. E. Knight (compiled by), The *Grenada Handbook and Directory 1946* (Barbados: Advocate, 1946), p. 347.

93. Cipriani, *Twenty-Five Years After*, p. 45.

94. The Trinidad *Port of Spain Gazette* (4 October 1917), p. 11.

95. Ibid.

96. *Diary of 1st BWIR.* (I.C.S), p. 85.

97. Ibid pp. 87–95.

98. *Diary of 1st BWIR* (I.C.S), pp. 129–130.

99. Ibid p. 154; W.O.95\4732 *Diary of 2nd BWIR* entry of 3 July 1918.

100. See for details, W.O.95\4732 Commander-in-Chief of Egyptian Expeditionary Force to War Office, 17 December 1918.

101. *Diary of 1st BWIR*, (ICS), p. 191.

102. See an account of the events by Captain A.A. Cipriani, in Gerard Besson and Bridget Brereton (eds.), *The Book of Trinidad* (Trinidad: Paria Publishing, 1992), pp. 418–419.

103. *Diary of 1st BWIR* (ICS), pp. 197–198.

104. See, for instance, The Grenada *Federalist* (7 December 1918), p. 3; The British Honduras *Clarion* (20 March 1919), p. 322.

105. C.O.123\296 *Report of Belize Commission*, evidence of S.A. Haynes.

106. Ibid., evidence of D.N. McKoy.

107. *Report of Mesopotamia Commission*: Appointed by Act of Parliament to enquire into the Operations of War in Mesopotamia 1915–1916. Together with a separate report by Commander J. Wedgwood (London, 1917).

108. See for example, Macpherson,(ed.), *Medical Services (General History)*, vol. 1, 1921.

109. C.O.123\296 *Report of the Belize Commission*, evidence of S.A. Haynes.

110. Ibid.

111. Ibid.

112. Ibid., evidence of Sergeant Tennyson.

113. Dupuch, *A Salute to Friend and Foe*, p. 45.

114. C.O.318\347 minute of Fiddian on enclosed note of Everard im Thurn, 8 October 1918.

115. Horner, *From the Islands of the Sea*, p. 62.

116. 'How Aubrey Williams Got to England', The Trinidad *Port of Spain Gazette* (9 July 1915), p. 6.

117. A base depot for the BWIR was originally at Withnoe Camp, England but it was subsequently transferred to Egypt. There was however, a smaller one established at Le Havre for the troops in France.

118. C.O.321\307\27753 F.F. Middleweek to Sir William Donovan, 22 February 1919.

119. See paragraph 133 of *The King's Regulations and Orders for the Army, 1912*, Reprinted with Amendments published in Army Orders up to 1 August 1914 (London: HMSO, 1914), pp. 25–26.

120. Ibid., J. McDowall to A.E. Aspinall, 18 April 1919.

121. Ibid., Aspinall to Secretary of State, 7 May 1919.

Chapter 8 —Miltary Relations

1. Erving Goffman, *Asylums* (Harmondsworth: Penguin Books 1961), p. 11.

2. See for example, Douglas Haig, *Extracts From General Routine Orders*, Issued to the British Armies in France (London: H.M.S.O., 1918) p. 80.

3. A.E. Horner, *From the Islands of the Sea: Glimpses of a West Indian Battalion in France* (Nassau, Bahamas: Guardian 1919), p. 7.

4. The *Manchester Guardian* (16 May 1918), in *Great Britain Army: Album of 1st B.W.I.R.*, Press cuttings taken from British and Commonwealth newspapers, 9 September 1915–12 February 1919 (Institute of Commonwealth Studies, University of London, Archives).

5. The Trinidad *Port of Spain Gazette* (9 July 1915), p. 9.

6. Charles B. Handy, *Understanding Organizations* (Harmondsworth: Penguin Books, 1976), p. 134.

7. C. Enloe, *Does Khaki Become You?: The Militarization of Women's Lives* (London: Pluto, 1983), p. 14

8. Sir Etienne Dupuch, *A Salute to Friend and Foe* (Nassau, Bahamas: Tribune, 1982) p. 44.

9. As quoted in, J.G. Fuller, *Troop Morale and Popular Culture in the British and Dominion Armies 1914–1918*, (Oxford: Clarendon Press, 1990), p. 24.

10. Jacklyn Cock, *Women and War in South Africa* (London: Open Letters, 1992), p. 58; See also, Enloe, *Does Khaki Become You?*, pp. 13–14.

11. For various examples see, Helen Michalowski, 'The Army Will Make a 'Man' Out of You', in Pam McAllister (ed.), *Reweaving the Web of Life: Feminism and Nonviolence* (Philadelphia: New Society Publishers, 1982), pp. 326–335; Cock, *Women and War*, p. 59; Enloe, *Does Khaki Become You?*, p. 14.

12. Goffman, *Asylums*, pp. 23–24.

13. S. Macdonald, 'Drawing the Lines – Gender, Peace and War: An Introduction', in S. Macdonald (et al.), *Images of Women in Peace and War: Cross–Cultural and Historical Perspectives* (Basingstoke: Macmillan in association with Oxford Women's Studies Committee, 1987), p. 16. Emphasis in original.

14. See, Michel Foucault, *The History of Sexuality: An Introduction* (Translated from French by Robert Hurley), (Harmondsworth: Penguin Books, 1981).

15. Michel Foucault, *Discipline and Punish: The Birth of The Prison* (Harmondsworth: Penguin Books, 1975). For the core points of Foucault's concept of power see also, pp. 26–31 & 186–194.

16. Ibid., pp. 202–203.

17. Ibid., p. 202.

18. Ibid., p. 5.

19. Fuller, *Troop Morale*, p. 23.

20. The Barbados *Globe* (3 May 1916), p. 3.

21. See, Fuller, *Troop Morale*, pp. 21–23.

22. Dupuch, *A Salute to Friend and Foe*, p. 54.

23. Ibid., pp. 54–66.

24. Ibid., p. 54.

25. Ibid., p. 55

26. See, Etienne Dupuch, *Tribune Story* (London: Ernest Benn, 1967).

27. C.O.123\296 *Report of the Belize Commission*, evidence of Sergeant Tennyson.

28. C.O.123\296 *Report of the Belize Commission*, evidence of S.A. Haynes.

29. The Grenada *West Indian* (28 February 1919), p. 1.

30. The Grenada *West Indian* (29 February 1919), p. 1.

31. C.O.28\294 A.W. Stoute to W.H. Stoker, 31 July 1918; Ibid Stoute to Stoker, 1 August 1918; Ibid Stoker to Darnley, 5 August 1918.

32. The Grenada *West Indian* (28 February 1919), p. 1.

33. Ibid.

34. Ibid.

35. C.O.123\296 *Report of the Belize Commission*, evidence of G.W. Hulse.

36. Horner, *From the Islands of the Sea*, p. 48.

37. *The West Indian Contingent Committee Report*, 30 June 1918, p. 2.

38. C.O.123\296 *Report of the Belize Commission*, evidence of G.W. Hulse.
39. C.O.123\296 *Report of the Belize Commission*, evidence of D.N. McKoy.
40. Michael Argyle, 'Non–Verbal Communication in Human Social Interaction', in Robert A. Hinde (ed.), *Non–Verbal Communication* (London: Cambridge University Press, 1972), p. 243.
41. Personal Interview: with Charles Rice, 15 July 1991.
42. Goffman, *Asylums*, pp. 159–280.
43. The Grenada *West Indian* (18 January 1917), p. 2.
44. The Grenada *West Indian* (4 July 1919), p. 3.
45. James Walvin, *Black and White: The Negro and English Society, 1555–1945* (Harmondsworth: Penguin Books, 1973), p. 174; James Walvin, 'Black Caricature: the Roots of Racialism', in Charles Husband (ed.), *'Race' in Britain: Continuity and Change* (London: Hutchinson, 1982), pp. 59–72
46. Jonathan Rutherford, 'Who's That Man?', in Rowena Chapman and Jonathan Rutherford (eds.), *Male Order: Unwrapping Masculinity* (London: Lawrence and Wishart, 1988), p. 29.
47. The Grenada *West Indian* (18 July 1919), p. 1.
48. Guida West and Rhoda Lois Blumberg, 'Reconstructing Social Protest from a Feminist Perspective', in West and Blumberg (eds.), *Women and Social Protest* (New York: Oxford University Press, 1990) p. 17.
49. Horner, *From The Islands of the Sea*, pp. 48–49.
50. Norman Manley, 'The Autobiography of Norman Washington Manley', *Jamaica Journal*, vol. 7, no. 1, March–June, 1973, p. 6.
5. Horner, *From The Islands of the Sea*, p. 49.
52. The Grenada *West Indian* (18 January 1917), p. 2.
53. The Grenada *West Indian* (28 February 1919), p. 1.
54. The Grenada *West Indian* (18 July 1919), p. 1.
55. C.O.123\295\48750, Eyre Hutson to Milner, 31 July 1919.
56. Ibid., Minute of Darnley on Hutson to Milner.
57. Avner Offer, *The First World War: An Agrarian Interpretation* (New York: Oxford University Press, 1989), pp. 198–214.
58. A.A. Cipriani, *Twenty-Five Years After: The British West Indies Regiment in the Great War 1914–1918* (London: Karia Press, 1993) p. 70.
59. For discussion on the Egyptian Revolution of 1919 see, Selma Botman, *Egypt From Independence to Revolution, 1919–1952* (New York: Syracuse University Press, 1991), pp. 25–72.
60. 'Account of Sergeant Percival Vasquez', The British Honduras *Clarion* (22 April 1920), p. 469.
61. Ibid.
62. The Grenada *West Indian* (7 April 1917), p. 3.
63. Melvin E. Page, *Introduction: Black Men in a White Men's War* (London: Macmillan, 1987), p. 8.
64. B.P. Willan, 'The South African Native Labour Contingent, 1916–1918', *Journal of African History*, vol. 19, no. 1, 1978, p. 73.
65. Manley, *Norman Washington Manley*, p. 12.
66. Horner, *From the Islands of the Sea*, p. 35.
67. C.O.123\296 *Report of the Belize Commission*, evidence of S.A. Haynes.
68. Anthony Trollope, *The West Indies and the Spanish Main* (London: Chapman and Hall, 1859), p. 56. For some indication of the persistence of this legacy of colonialism see, George Lamming, *The Emigrants* (London and New York: Allison and Busby, 1954), pp. 128–129.
69. Horner, *From the Islands of the Sea*, p. 51.
70. C.O.123\296 *Report of the Belize Commission*, evidence of G.W. Hulse.
71. Horner, *From the Islands of the Sea*, p. 51.
72. Manley, *Norman Washington Manley*, p. 7.

73. Edward Spiers, *The Army and Society 1815–1914* (London and New York: Longman, 1980), p. 1.
74. Ibid.
75. The British authorities likewise felt that without white officers from the 'proper class' Indian troops were useless. See for details, Jeffrey Greenhut, 'The Imperial Reserve: The Indian Corps on the Western Front, 1914–1915', *Journal of Imperial and Commonwealth History*, vol. 12, no. 1, October 1983, p. 61.
76. James, *The Life of Captain Cipriani*, p. 27.
77. Horner, *From the Islands of the Sea*, p. 47.
78. C.L.R. James, *The Life of Captain Cipriani*, (Nelson, Lancashire: Coulton, 1932), p. 30.
79. Dupuch, *A Salute to Friend and Foe*, p. 57.
80. The Grenada *West Indian* (5 July 1918), p. 6.
81. Personal Interview: with Charles Rice, 15 July 1991.
82. Lt. Colonel C. Woodhill, *A Few Notes on the History of the British West Indies Regiment* (Jamaica: [unpublished] West India Reference Library, 1919) p. 5.
83. Ibid.
84. J.M. Winter, 'Britain's "Lost Generation" of the First World War', in *Population Studies*, vol. 31, 1977, pp. 456–460
85. See, Keith Simpson, 'The Officers', in Beckett and Simpson (eds.), *A Nation in Arms*, pp. 64–93.
86. J.C. Ford and F. Cundall, *The Handbook of Jamaica for 1919*, (Jamaica: Government Printery, 1919), pp. 588–591.
87. C.O.137\725\10162 letter from officer of 2nd B.W.I.R., Egypt, intended for the Legislature and the Governor, 12 June 1917.
88. C.O.318\337\54116 Minute of G. Grindle, 26 November 1915.
89. War Office. *Manual of Military Law* (London: Harrison and sons [under the authority of His Majesty's Stationery Office], 1914), p. 471. Sections 94–95; Also, Killingray, *All the King's Men?*, p. 168. For a detailed discussion of the issues see, Killingray, 'Race and Rank in the British Army in the Twentieth Century', *Ethnic and Racial Studies*, vol. 10, no. 3, July 1987, pp. 276–290.
90. C.O.28\294\56561 J.C. Hope to J.C. Lynch, 2 August 1918.
91. C.O.137\725\10162 Letter from officer of 2nd BWIR, Egypt, intended for the Legislature and the Governor, 12 June 1917.
92. The Grenada *West Indian* (28 February 1919), p. 1.
93. Horner, *From the Islands of the Sea*, p. 50.
94. The *Palestine News* (30 May 1918), p. 4; Horner, *From the Islands of the Sea*, p. 50.
95. C.O.28\294\56561 Minute of Fiddian, 18 December 1918.
96. Killingray, *All the King's Men*, p. 306, no. 28.
97. Dupuch, *A Salute to Friend and Foe*, pp. 64–65.
98. Killingray, *All the King's Men*, p. 174.
99. The Grenada *West Indian* (23 November 1917), p. 6.
100. Ibid.
101. Dupuch, *A Salute to Friend and Foe*, pp. 63–64.
102. The British Honduras *Clarion* (1 February 1917), p. 110.
103. The British Honduras *Clarion* (9 March 1916), p. 260.
104. Personal Interview: with Charles Rice, 15 July 1991.
105. The Grenada *West Indian* (13 August 1916), p. 5; Ibid 23 November 1917, p. 6.
106. 'West Indian Jealousies', The Barbados *Globe* (23 April 1917), p. 3.
107. The Trinidad *Port of Spain Gazette* (9 January 1916), p. 9.
108. Horner, *From the Islands of the Sea*, pp. 33–34.
109. Personal Interview: with Charles Rice, 15 July 1991.
110. C.O.123\295\48750 Eyre Hutson to Milner, 31 July 1919.

111. Education in the Army: *Second Interim Report of the Adult Education Committee* (London: H.M.S.O., 1918), p. 353.

112. Personal Interview: with Charles Rice, 15 July 1991.

113. Education in the Army: *Second Interim Report*, p. 353.

114. Norman Dixon, *On The Psychology of Military Incompetence* (London: Jonathan Cape, 1976), p. 286; Tim Travers, *The Killing Ground: The British Army, the Western Front and the Emergence of Modern Warfare 1900-1918* (London: Allen and Unwin, 1987), pp. 39–42.

115. J. Bayo Adekson, 'Ethnicity and Army Recruitment in Colonial Plural Societies', in *Ethnic and Racial Studies*, vol. 2, no. 2, April 1979, p. 156.

116. Travers, *The Killing Ground*, pp. 39–42.

Chapter 9 – Civilian Relations and Recreation

1. C.O.137\720\12455 Minute of General Officer commanding Troops, Jamaica, 9 February 1917.

2. A.E. Horner, *From the Islands of the Sea: Glimpses of a West Indian Battalion in France* (Nassau, Bahamas: Guardian, 1919), p. 12; 'Letters From Our Soldiers', The *Jamaica Times* (1 January 1916), p. 17.

3. The Grenada *West Indian* (11 October 1918), p. 3.

4. 'English fond of the Dark Chaps', The *Jamaica Times* (8 January 1916), p. 7

5. G.B. Army. *Album of 1st BWIR*, cutting from 'Weekly Despatch', (14 November 1915).

6. James Walvin, *Black and White: The negro and English Society, 1555-1945* (Harmondsworth: Penguin Books, 1973), pp. 189–215.

7. 'Letter from Sergeant of 8th BWIR', The Trinidad *Port of Spain Gazette* (11 February 1919), p. 10.

8. Ibid.

9. G.B. Army. *Album of 1st BWIR*, 'The Daily Telegraph', quoted in The *Daily Mirror* (8 November 1915).

10. G.B. Army. *Album of 1st BWIR*, 'The Daily News and Leader', quoted in The *Daily Mirror* (8 November 1915).

11. G.B. Army. *Album of 1st BWIR*, cutting from 'Natal Witness' (25 January 1916).

12. G.B. Army. *Album of 1st BWIR*, cutting from *Daily News* (12 October 1915).

13. Frantz Fanon, *Black Skin White Masks* (London: MacGibbon and Kee, 1968), p. 36.

14. Horner, *From the Islands of the Sea*, p. 49.

15. 'A British Honduras Boy writes from India', The British Honduras *Clarion* (11 October 1917), p. 7.

16. The Trinidad *Port of Spain Gazette* (11 February 1919), p. 10; See also, The British Honduras *Clarion* (8 November 1917), p. 6.

17. Kenneth Little, *Negroes in Britain: A study of Racial Relations in English Society* (London: Routledge and Kegan Paul, 1972), p. 281.

18. Anthony Richmond, *Colour Prejudice in Britain* (London: Routledge and Kegan Paul, 1954) p. 59.

19. The Trinidad *Mirror* (11 November 1915), p. 9 (13 December 1915).

20. C.O.318\352\68867.

21. The Trinidad *West Indian*, Extract from 'The Glasgow Weekly Record' (12 October 1917), p. 1.

22. Kobena Mercer and Isaac Julien, 'Race, Sexual Politics and Black Masculinity: A Dossier', in Rowena Chapman and Jonathan Rutherford (eds.), *Male Order: Unwrapping Masculinity* (London: Lawrence and Wishart, 1988), pp. 106–107; See also, Winthrop Jordan, 'First Impressions: Initial English confrontations with Africans', in Charles Husbands (ed.), *"Race" in Britain: Continuity and Change* (London: Hutchinson, 1982), pp. 53–56.

23. Personal Interview: with Ernest Marke, 17 December 1991.

24. Fanon, *Black Skin White Masks*, p. 63.
25. Ibid., p. 72.
26. The British Honduras *Clarion* (1 June 1916), p. 599.
27. 'Letter from Private G. J. Dadd', The *Jamaica Times* (1 January 1916), p. 17.
28. 'Diary of H.S.V.G.', The Jamaica *Gleaner* (4 March 1916), p. 4.
29. Personal Interview: with Ernest Marke, 17 December 1991.
30. Michael Banton, *White and Coloured: The Behaviour of British People towards Coloured Immigrants* (London: Cape, 1959), p. 131.
31. 'Letter from Private Norris Roach', The Grenada *West Indian* (15 March 1918), p. 3.
32. Horner, *From the Islands of the Sea*, p. 40.
33. Ibid., p. 56.
34. Sir Etienne Dupuch, *A Salute to Friend and Foe* (Nassau,Bahamas: Tribune, 1982) p. 60.
35. See, Peter Stanley, 'A Horn To Put Your Powder In: Interpreting artefacts of British soldiers in colonial Australia', *Journal of Australian War Memorial*, 13 October 1988, p. 11.
36. John Costello, *Love, Sex and War: Changing Values 1939–45*, (London: Pan Books, 1986), p. 289.
37. See, Edward Spiers, *The Army and Society 1815-1914*, (London: Longman, 1980), pp. 60–63; Myna Trustram, *Women of the Regiment: Marriage and the Victorian Army* (Cambridge: Cambridge University Press, 1984), pp. 116–229.
38. Frances Finnegan, *Poverty and Prostitution* (Cambridge: Cambridge University Press, 1979), p. 9.
39. Lucy Bland, 'In the name of Protection: the policing of women in the First World War', in Julia Brophy and Carol Smart (eds.), *Women–In–Law: Explorations in Law, Family and Sexuality* (London and Boston: Routledge and Kegan Paul, 1985), pp. 23–49.
40. See for example, Allan Brandt, *No Magic Bullet: A Social History of Venereal Disease in the United States since 1880* (New York and Oxford: Oxford University Press, 1985), pp. 109–117.
41. Although many women had internalised and therefore shared the dominant male opinion, there were those (feminists) who fiercely insisted on male responsibility and viewed prostitution as a form of women's oppression by men. See, Sheila Jeffreys, *The Sexuality Debates* (New York and London: Routledge and Kegan Paul, 1987).
42. 'What is to be done?', The Jamaica *Gleaner* (24 July 1916), p. 8.
43. The *Palestine News* (5 September 1918), p. 1.
44. Ibid.
45. Ibid.
46. W.G. Macpherson (ed.), *Medical Services (Diseases of the War)* vol. 2 (London: H.M.S.O., 1923), pp. 123–124.
47. Ibid., pp. 124–136.
48. Douglas Haig, *Extracts from General Routine Orders* (London: H.M.S.O., 1918), p. 71.
49. Personal Interview: with Charles Rice, 15 July 1991.
50. Norman Clothier, Black Valour: The South African Native Labour Contingent, 1916–1918, and the sinking of the "Mendi", (Pietermaritzburg: University of Natal Press, 1987), p. 126.
51. The *Voice*, 28 June 1919, p. 4.
52. Macpherson, *Medical Services: (Diseases of the War)* vol. 2, 1923, p. 125.
53. Ibid.
54. Allan Brandt, *No Magic Bullet: A Social History of Venereal Disease in the United States since 1880*, (New York and Oxford: Oxford University Press, 1985), p. 116.
55. Ibid.
56. The Jamaica *Gleaner* (24 July 1916), p. 8.
57. 'More Stringent Measures', The Jamaica *Gleaner* (25 July 1916), p. 8.
58. Dupuch, *A Salute to Friend and Foe*, p. 60.

59. Personal Interview: with Charles Rice, 15 July 1991.
60. Colin J. Williams and Martin S. Weinberg, *Homosexuals and the Military: A Study of less than Honourable Discharge* (New York: Harper and Row, 1971), p. 56; See also, Costello, *Love, Sex and War*, pp. 155–156.
61. Costello, *Love Sex and War*, p. 156.
62. See for example, T. Dunbar Moodie (with Vivienne Ndatshe and British Sibuyi), 'Migrancy and Male Sexuality on the South African Gold Mines', *Journal of Southern African Studies*, vol. 14, no. 2, January 1988, pp. 228–256.
63. 'The assassination of gunner Lang', The Trinidad *Port of Spain Gazette* (24 July 1919), p. 8; Ibid (23 July 1919), p. 4.
64. The Grenada *West Indian* (11 April 1919), p. 4.
65. The *West India Committee Circular* (22 February 1917), p. 74; The Grenada *West Indian* (12 May 1917), p. 3 & Ibid (12 April 1918), p. 2; *The West Indian Contingent Committee Report*, 30 June 1918, p. 2.
66. Letter from private James Clement, The Trinidad *Mirror* (8 May 1916), p. 5.
67. G.B. Army. *Album of 1st BIWR*, cutting from 'Weekly Despatch' (14 November 1915).
68. The Grenadian *West Indian* (13 August 1916), p. 5.
69. Ibid; Also (4 July 1919), p. 2.
70. 'How Aubrey Williams Got to England', The Trinidad *Port of Spain Gazette* (9 July 1915), p. 9.
71. See, John Terraine, *Impacts of War 1914–1918* (London: Hutchinson, 1970), pp. 114–115; J.M. Winter, 'Britain's "Lost Generation" of the First World War', *Population Studies*, vol. 31, no. 3, 1977, p. 456.
72. The Trinidad *Port of Spain Gazette* (9 July 1915), p. 6.
73. The *Palestine News*, (25 April 1918), p. 9; The Grenada *West Indian* (16 August 1918), p. 2.
74. Horner, *From The Islands of the Sea*, p. 57.
75. The Grenada *West Indian* (13 August 1916), p. 5; Ibid (4 July 1919), p. 3.
76. The Grenada *West Indian* (29 August 1916), p. 2; Ibid (4 July 1919), p. 3.
77. The Grenada *West Indian* (25 October 1918), p. 4.
78. The *West Indian Contingent Committee Report 1918*, p. 2; See also, The Grenada West *Indian* (3 March 1917), p. 2.
79. The British Honduras *Clarion* (8 August 1918), pp. 153–154.
80. The Grenada *West Indian* (18 January 1917), p. 2.
81. The Grenada *West Indian* (14 December 1916), p. 2.
82. The Grenada *West Indian* (30 August 1918), p. 1.
83. See, 'BWI Cricketers in Egypt', The Jamaica *Gleaner* (26 November, 1918), p. 11.
84. The *Palestine News* (18 April 1918), p. 8; Ibid (25 April 1918), p. 9.
85. C.L.R James, *Beyond A Boundary* (London: Hutchinson, 1963); See also, The *West Indian* (11 March 1915), p. 2.
86. C.O.123\296 *Report of the Belize Commission*, evidence of Sergeant Grant.
87. The British Honduras *Clarion* (6 February 1919), p. 151.
88. The Grenada *West Indian* (13 August 1916), p. 5.
89. The Grenada *West Indian* (4 July 1919), p. 3.
90. The Grenada *West Indian* (6 June 1919), p. 4.
91. Personal Interview: with Charles Rice, 15 July 1991.
92. 'The Die–Hards Triumph', The British Honduras *Clarion* (12 April 1917), p. 360.
93. For similar attitudes among the British soldiers see, Eric J. Leed, *No Man's Land: Combat and Identity in World War 1* (London: Cambridge University Press, 1979), pp. 192–213.

Chapter 10 – Declining Morale and Revolt at Tarino

1. The Grenada *West Indian* (31 August 1917), p. 8.
2. C.O.318\345 Memorandum of H.T. Allen dated 20 August 1917.
3. WO 93\49 Records of Soldiers Shot by Sentence of Court Martial 1914–1918.
4. See for example, 'Trinidad Soldier Executed in Italy: Murdered a Barbadian Comrade: Ably defended by Jamaican', *The Voice*, (28 June 1919), p. 4.
5. Ibid.
6. Douglas Haig, *Extracts From General Routine Orders* (London: H.M.S.O, 1918), p. 58; See also, A. Babington, *For The Sake Of Example* (London: Leo Cooper and Warburg, 1983), p. 3.
7. J. Ramson, *Carry On: Or Pages from the life of a West Indian Padre in the Field* (Jamaica: The Educational Supply Co., 1918), p. 18; See also W.O.93\49 Records of Soldiers Shot by Sentence of Court Martial 1914–1918.
8. Ibid., p. 19.
9. For a full discussion on the procedures and purpose of 'Execution at Dawn' see, Babington, *For The Sake of Example*, pp. 44–53.
10. David Cannadine, 'War and Death, Grief and Mourning in Modern Britain', in Joachim Whaley (ed.), *Mirrors of Mortality: Studies in the Social History of Death* (London: Europa Publications, 1981), p. 206.
11. Ibid., p. 209.
12. Eric J. Leed, *No Man's Land: Combat and Identity in World War 1* (London: Cambridge University Press, 1979), p. 126; See also Marc Ferro, *The Great War 1914–1918* [Translated by Nicole Stone] (London: Routledge and Kegan Paul, 1973), p. 47.
13. 'Letter from C.H. Jenkins', The British Honduras *Clarion* (5 September 1918), p. 270.
14. Elaine Showalter, *The Female Malady: Women, Madness and English Culture 1839-1980* (London: Virago, 1987), p. 168.
15. Showalter, *The Female Malady*, p. 168.
16. The relationship between madness and the emasculation of men produced by passivity has been examined in, Pat Barker, *Regeneration* (Harmondsworth: Penguin, 1992), pp. 107–108.
17. Sir Etienne Dupuch, *A Salute to Friend and Foe* (Nassau, Bahamas: Tribune), p. 72; Ibid., pp. 58–59.
18. See for example, Leed, *No Man's Land*, pp. 163–192.
19. Dupuch, *A Salute to Friend and Foe*, p. 81.
20. C.O.137\735\71769 War Office to Colonial Office 17 October, 1919.
21. C.O.137\735\35271 War Office to Colonial Office, 13 June, 1919.
22. C.O.137\735\68802 Report of the Assistant Superintendent of Rampton Lunatic Asylum, 17 November 1919.
23. See, 'Reports of the Lunatic Asylum', in *The Annual General Reports of Jamaica (together with) The Department Reports 1918-1920.* I.C.S., Archives.
24. Dupuch, *A Salute to Friend and Foe*, pp. 78–79.
25. The Grenada *West Indian* (7 November 1919), p. 1.
26. C.O.318\353\12341 Haddon–Smith to Colonial Office, 1 March 1920.
27. See for details of problems of psychiatry in the region, Frederick Hickling, 'Psychiatry in the Commonwealth Caribbean: a brief historical overview', extract from the *Bulletin of the Royal College of Psychiatry*, vol. 12, (copy located at UWI, medical library, Jamaica), pp. 434–436; Also, 'Reports of the Lunatic Asylum', in *Annual General Reports of Jamaica, 1917-1927*, ICS, Archives.
28. *Report of the Jamaica Lunatic Asylum for year ended 31 March 1918.*
29. See, W.O.95\4732 *Diary of 2nd BWIR.*
30. Letter from Private A.J. Lawson, The Grenada *West Indian* (23 May 1919), p. 6; Stephen R. Ward, 'Intelligence Surveillance of British Ex-Servicemen, 1918–1920', *The Historical Journal*, vol. 16, no. 1, 1973, p. 183.

31. The British Honduras *Clarion* (22 April 1920), p. 469.
32. A.A. Cipriani, [reprint] *Twenty-Five Years After: The British West Indies Regiment in the Great War 1914-1918*, (London: Karia Press, 1993), p. 35.
33. W.G. Macpherson (ed.), *Medical Services (General History)* vol. 2 , (London: H.M.S.O., 1923), p. 144.
34. C.O.123\296 *Report of the Belize Commission*, evidence of F.H.E. McDonald.
35. W.O.95\4732 *Diary of 2nd BWIR*.
36. C.O.318\348\20991 Soldiers Petition enclosed in Haddon–Smith to Milner, 22 February 1919.
37. George Lamming, *The Pleasures of Exile* (London: Allison and Busby, 1984), p. 214.
38. C.O.28\294 M. Murphy to Secretary of State for the Colonies, 6 December 1918.
39. C.O.28\294\56561 J.C. Hope to J.C. Lynch, 2 August 1918.
40. C.O.28\294\56561 O'Brien to Long, 14 October 1918.
41. C.O.318\347\51686 Roland Green, 25 October 1918, enclosing letter from Sergeant BWIR, Egypt, 27 July 1918. The full text of the letter can be found in Peter Fraser, *Some Effects of the First World War on the British West Indies*, (Collected Seminar Papers, Caribbean Societies, vol.1, I.C.S., University of London, 1982), pp. 26–27.
42. *Diary of 1st BWIR*, (I.C.S.), enclosed letter of West Indian Contingent Committee to Walter Long, 30 December, 1918; See also , C.O.318\347\63228.
43. *Diary of 1st BWIR*, (I.C.S.), enclosed letter of West Indian Contingent Committee to Milner, 15 January 1919.
44. C.O.318\351\7242 Minute of Grindle dated 3 January 1919.
45. Ibid.
46. Ibid., Minute of Lord Milner dated 3 February 1919.
47. Ibid., Draft Memorandum on Pay of British West Indies Regiment and Other Coloured Colonial Units, 3 February 1919.
48. Ibid., Minute of Milner dated 4 February 1919.
49. *Diary of 1st BWIR*, (ICS), enclosed letter of Grindle to West Indian Contingent Committee, 1 March 1919; *Report of the West Indian Contingent Committee*, December 1918, p. 2; W.O.95\4732 *Diary of 2nd BWIR*
50. The armistice was on 11 November 1918 but formal peace was marked by the Treaty of Versailles which was concluded on 28 June 1919.
51. C.O.28\294\56561.
52. C.O.318\347 Base Commandant, Taranto to War Office, 9 December 1918.
53. Cipriani, *Twenty-Five Years After*, p. 65.
54. See, W.F. Elkins, 'A Source of Black Nationalism in the caribbean: The Revolt of the British West Indies Regiment at Taranto, Italy', *Science and Society*, vol. 33, no. 2, Spring 1970, p. 102.
55. C.O.318\350\2590 Major Maxwell Smith to G.O.C. Taranto, 27 December 1918.
56. Ibid.
57. C.O.318\350\2590, (Secret) Thuiller to General Head Quarters, Italy, 29 December 1918.
58. C.O.318\353\6843 Report on complaints of BWIR enclosed in Governor Chancellor to Milner, 8 January 1920.
59. Ibid enclosure No.2, Copy of Base Routine Orders, Taranto, 17 July 1919.
60. Lt.–Colonel C. Woodhill, *A Few Notes on the History of the British West Indies Regiment*, (Jamaica: [unpublished] West India Reference Library, 1919), p. 11.
61. The Grenada *West Indian* (23 May 1919), p. 1.
62. See, Cipriani, *Twenty-Five Years After*, p. 62.
63. C.O.318\353\17262 Letter from Captain C.L. Roper to Major J.B. Thursfield enclosed in Governor Probyn to Milner, 19 March 1920.
64. Cipriani, *Twenty-Five Years After*, pp. 66–67.
65. C.O.318\350\2590 Minute of G. Grindle, 17 January 1920.

66. Ibid., Minute of E.R. Darnley, 16 January 1920.

67. Ibid., Minute of Grindle, 17 January 1920.

68. Norman Manley, 'The Autobiography of Norman Washington Manley', *Jamaica Journal*, vol. 7, no. 1, March–June, 1973), p. 14.

69. Harry Haywood, *Black Bolshevik: Autobiography of an Afro–American Communist* (Chicago: Liberator Press, 1978), pp. 1–35; Robin Winks, *The Blacks in Canada: A History* (New Haven and London: Yale University Press, 1971), p. 319.

70. Peter Fryer, *Staying Power* (London: Pluto Press, 1984), p. 297.

71. Ibid.

72. C.O.318\347\46353 Extract from the *Times* (26 September 1918).

73. Ibid.

74. Fryer, *Staying Power*, p. 297.

75. C.O.318\347 Enclosed note of Everard im Thurn to Colonial Office, 8 October 1918.

76. See, Jacqueline Jenkinson, 'The 1919 Race Riots in Britain: A Survey', in R. Lotz and I. Pegg (eds.), *Under the Imperial Carpet: Essays in Black History 1780–1950* (Crawley, Sussex: Rabbit Press, 1986), pp. 182–309; Also, C.O.318\352\66887.

77. Fryer, *Staying Power*, p. 300.

78. Ibid.

79. Ibid., p. 302.

80. C.O.318\352\62494 Chief Constable Williams to Director of Intelligence, Scotland Yard, 9 October 1919.

81. Ibid.

82. C.O.318\352\70187 Report of Chief Constable Morley, 25 November 1919.

83. Ibid.

84. Ibid.

85. C.O.323\814\282–3 Repatriation of Coloured Men, 24 June 1919.

86. The Grenada *Federalist* (27 September 1919), p. 2.

87. The Grenada *West Indian* (4 July 1919), p. 1.

88. C.O.318\349\65927.

89. C.O.318\351\68553 A. Aspinall to H.T. Allen, 1 December 1919.

90. Ibid.

91. Ibid Lt.-Colonel S. Keating to War Office, 5 December 1919.

92. Patrick Bryan, *The Jamaican People, 1880–1902* (London and Basingstoke: Macmillan, 1991), pp. 94–95.

93. C.O.318\349\68867 Bryan to Milner, 15 November 1919.

94. C.O.318\349\71715 Haddon–Smith to Colonial Office, 17 December 1919.

95. C.O.318\353\13743 Haddon–Smith to Milner, 16 February 1920.

Chapter 11 —The Climax

1. C.O.318\349 Statement regarding conditions of Labour in Jamaica.

2. C.O.318\355\45125 Haddon–Smith to Milner, 13 August 1920.

3. The Grenada *Federalist* (25 May 1918), p. 2.

4. C.O.318\355\46334 Report of the Commissioners appointed to enquire into the causes and results of the increased cost of the necessaries of life in British Guiana, 1920.

5. See, C.O.321\308\28943; C.O.318\356\47298; C.O.318\356\49858.

6. A.W.H. Hall, *Report on Economic and Financial Conditions in the British West Indies* (London: H.M.S.O., 1921), pp. 16–17.

7. Ibid.

8. See for example, C.O.321\309\39187; C.O.137\726\39484.

9. See for English comparison, J.S. Boswell and B.R. Johns, 'Patriots or Profiteers?: British Businessmen and the First World War', *Journal of European Economic History*, vol. 2, no. 2, Fall 1982.

10. C.O.318\355\46334 Report of the Commissioners.

11. C.O.318\355\45125 Haddon–Smith to Milner, 13 August 1920

12. See, Brinsley Samaroo, 'The Trinidad Workingmen's Association and the Origins of Popular Protest in a Crown Colony', *Social and Economic Studies*, vol.21, no.2, June 1972, p. 212.

13. See, for example, The Trinidad *Port of Spain Gazette* (6 August 1914), p. 2.

14. The Antigua *Sun* (25 June 1917), p. 3.

15. E. Knight (compiled by), The *Grenada Handbook and Directory, 1946* (Barbados: Advocate, 1946), p. 76.

16. Ibid.

17. Ibid.

18. C.O. 123\296\66222, Eyre Hutson to the Secretary of State, 30 October 1919.

19. See, W.K. Marshall, '19th Century Crises in the Barbadian Sugar Industry', in W.K. Marshall (ed.), *Emancipation 2*, Barbados: NCF\UWI, 1987, pp. 85–101.

20. See, Otis, Starkey, [reprint] *The Economic Geography of Barbados* (Westport, Connecticut, 1971), pp. 132–133; Hall, *Report on Economic and Financial Conditions*, p. 6.

21. Fritz Baptiste, 'The United States and West Indian Unrest 1914–1939', Working Paper no. 18, ISER, UWI 1978, p. 5.

22. The Grenada *Federalist* (30 May 1917), p. 3.

23. The Jamaica *Gleaner* (18 August 1917), p. 8.

24. C.O.318\355\45125; The British Honduras *Clarion* (18 July 1918).

25. See W.M.M.S: *Reports of the Wesleyan Methodist Missionary Society, 1914–1919*.

26. See, for instance, The Grenada *Federalist* (14 February 1920), p. 2

27. The Antigua *Sun* (19 March 1915), p. 3.

28. The Grenada *West Indian* (30 January 1920), p. 5.

29. Jamaica *Blue Book* (Criminal Statistics) 1913–1920.

30. See, for details, C.O.137\722\47735; C.O.137\726\39484; C.O.137\727\51991.

31. The Grenada *Federalist* (25 August 1917), p. 3; See also, The Trinidad *Port of Spain Gazette* (9 January 1915).

32. Ibid.

33. The Barbados *Globe* (18 August 1916).

34. See for comparisons, J.M. Winter, 'Aspects of the Impact of the First World War on Infant Mortality in Britain', *Journal of European Economic History*, vol. 11, 1982; J.M. Winter, 'The Impact of the First World War on Civilian Health in Britain', *Economic History Review*, vol. 30, 1977; Richard A. Lobdell, 'Economic Determinants of Jamaican Mortality, 1881–1935', paper presented to the 13th Conference of Caribbean Historians Guadeloupe, April, 1981.

35. Baptiste, *The United States and West Indian Unrest*, p. 18.

36. C.O.318\355\41697 Governor, Leeward Islands to Colonial Office, 30 July 1920.

37. The Grenada *West Indian* (9 May 1919), p. 2; The Grenada *Federalist* (11 May 1918), p. 2.

38. C.O.318\355\45125 Haddon–Smith to Milner, 13 August 1920.

39. See Bonham Richardson, *Panama Money in Barbados, 1900–1920*, (Knoxville: University of Tennessee Press, 1985); Velma Newton, *The Silver Men: West Indian Labour Migration to Panama 1850-1914* (Jamaica: ISER/UWI, 1984).

40. See Peter Fraser, 'Some Effects of the First World War on the British West Indies'. Collected Seminar Papers, *Caribbean Societies* vol. 1, ICS, University of London, 1982, pp. 29–32.

41. Joan French and Honor Ford–Smith, *Women, Work and Organization in Jamaica 1900–1944* (Jamaica: Sistren Research, 1986), pp. 260–272.

42. The Barbados *Globe* (26 February 1917).

43. Ibid., pp. 30–31.

44. The Jamaica *Gleaner* (21 September 1915), p. 6.

45. See for Barbados, The Barbados *Globe* (3 January 1919); (15 & 22 January 1919).

46. The British Honduras *Clarion* (22 August 1918), p. 209–243.

47. C.O.123\292 Acting Governor Walter to Long, 29 August 1918.

48. The Grenada *West Indian* (9 May 1919), p. 1.

49. Ibid., p. 4.

50. Gordon K. Lewis, *The Growth of the Modern West Indies*, New York: Monthly Review Press, 1968, pp. 158 & 247.

51. Ibid.

52. C.O.318\348\18293 Governor O'Brien to Milner, 4 March 1919.

53. Ibid.

54. For details see, Lord Hankey, *The Supreme Command 1914–1918* vol. 1 (London: Allen and Unwin, 1961), pp. 4–9.

55. C.O.318\350\10550 Homfray to Hankey, 14 January 1919.

56. C.O.318\350\10550 Minute of E.R. Darnley, 18 February 1919.

57. Ibid.Telegram from Milner to the Governors, 20 February 1919.

58. C.O.137\731\34400 Governor Probyn to Milner, 22 May 1919.

59. Ibid.

60. Ibid. Memorandum by Brig.–General A.R. Gilbert, Commanding Forces in Jamaica, enclosed in Probyn to Milner.

61. C.O.137\730\19216 Probyn to Milner, 28 March 1919.

62. C.O.318\348\38685 Governor Probyn to Milner, 9 June 1919.

63. C.O. 137\730\22666 Probyn to Milner, 29 March 1919.

64. C.O.123\296 *Report of the Belize Commission*, evidence of H. Melhado; C.O.123\295\48750 Hutson to Milner, 31 July 1919.

65. C.O.123\296 *Report of the Belize Commission*, evidence of Robert Wyatt.

66. Ibid. evidence of E.A. Baber.

67. Ibid. evidence of W.H. Hoar; See also appendix P, 'Offences Committed'

68. Ibid. evidence of J.A. Gardiner.

69. Ibid. evidence of J. Blades.

70. Ibid. evidence of I.F. Staine.

71. Ibid.

72. C.O.123\295\48750 Hutson to Milner, 31 July 1919.

73. Hutson to Milner, 21 October 1919 enclosed in, C.O.123\296 *Report of the Belize Commission.*

74. C.O.123\296 *Report of the Belize Commission*, evidence of J. Clark.

75. Ibid. evidence of J. Blades.

76. C.O.123\295\48749 Hutson to Milner, 30 July 1919.

77. Ibid.

78. C.O.123\296\65701 Eyre Hutson to Milner, 23 October 1919.

79. C.O.123\295\48749 Hutson to Milner, 30 July 1919.

80. Baptiste, *The United States and West Indian Unrest*, p. 11.

81. Keith Jeffrey, 'Sir Henry Wilson and the Defence of the British Empire, 1918–22', *Journal of Imperial and Commonwealth History*, vol. 5, no. 3, May 1977, pp. 270–273.

82. Ibid., p. 276.

83. See C.O.318\350\64424; C.O.318\350\70980; C.O.318\350\10550.

84. The British Honduras *Clarion* (31 July 1919).

85. C.O.123\296 *Report of the Belize Commission*, appendix N, 'Extract from the *Independent*, 13 August 1919'.

86. The *Clarion*, 22 August 1918.

87. Peter Ashdown, 'Marcus Garvey, The UNIA and the Black Cause in British Honduras, 1914–1949', *Journal of Caribbean History* vol. 15, 1981, pp. 45–46.

88. Ibid.

89. C.O.123\296\66222 Hutson to Colonial Office, 30 October 1919.

90. C.O.318\349\60455 Acting Governor H. Bryan to Milner, 3 October 1919; Also, C.O.318\349\59570.

91. Ibid.

92. C.O.318\349\60449 Bryan to Milner, 21 October 1919; Also, C.O.318\349\60450.

93. C.O.318\349\46818 O'Brien to Milner, 18 July 1919.

94. C.O.318\355\31424 Minute of official dated, 29 June 1920.

95. C.O.318\356\2746 'Report of the Returned Soldiers Committee', enclosed in O'Brien to Milner, 9 December 1920.

96. Ibid.

97. See, Robin W. Winks, *The Blacks in Canada: A History* (New Haven and London: Yale University Press, 1971), pp. 288–314.

98. C.O.318\356\2746; Also, Basil, Maughan, 'Some Aspects of Barbadian Emigration to Cuba 1919–1935', *Journal of the Barbados Museum and Historical Society*, vol. 37, no. 3, 1985, pp. 239–247.

99. David Browne, 'The Era of Working Class Political Organizations in Early 20th Century Barbados: UNIA AND WMA.', Cave Hill, UWI, History Dept., Seminar Paper no. 6, 22 June 1989, p. 18a.

100. F.A. Hoyos, *Barbados: A History from the Amerindians to Independence*, (London and Basingstoke: Macmillan, 1978), pp. 195–197.

101. F.A. Hoyos, *Builders of Barbados* (London and Basingstoke: Macmillan, 1972), pp. 117–125.

102. The *Jamaica Times* (17 May 1919), p. 10.

103. Ibid.

104. A total of £292,311 was paid out to the ex-servicemen by the authorities and the men also deposited savings amounting to £3,477 in the local bank. C.O.318\355\45808, Probyn to Milner, 26 August 1920.

105. Ibid.

106. Ibid., Minute of T.H.P., 7 June 1919.

107. Ibid., Minute of H.T. Allen, 16 June 1919.

108. C.O.137\733\50990 Acting Governor R. Johnstone to Milner, 14 August 1919.

109. C.O.137\733\50990 Johnstone to Milner, 14 August 1919.

110. Ibid.

111. The Jamaica *Gleaner* (22 July 1919).

112. The *Jamaica Times* (9 August 1919), p. 16.

113. C.O.318\349\60449 Petition of Seamen to Acting Governor H. Bryan, enclosed in Bryan to Milner, 21 October 1919; Also C.O.318\349\60450.

114. Ibid.

115. C.O.318\349\67533 Minute of Deputy Inspector–General, enclosed in Bryan to Milner, 7 November 1919.

116. Ibid.

117. Ibid., Minute of H.T. Allen, 28 November 1919.

118. Ibid., Minute of E.R. Darnley, 28 November 1919.

119. Frank Cundall, *Jamaica's Part in the Great War 1914–1918,* (London: Institute of Jamaica, 1925), p. 84.

120. W. F. Elkins, *Street Preachers, Faith Healers and Herb Doctors in Jamaica 1890–1925* (New York: Revisionist Press, 1977). p. 68.

121. The Jamaica *Gleaner* (1 October 1920), p. 4

122. Ibid.

123. This section on Trinidad is constructed mainly from the official sources and Tony Martin, 'Revolutionary Upheaval in Trinidad, 1919: Views From British and American Sources', in Tony Martin, *The Pan-African Connection* (Massachusetts: The Majority Press, 1983), pp. 47–58; Samaroo, *The Trinidad Workingmen's Association*, pp. 205–222.

124. See, The *Trinidad Guardian* (22 August 1919).

125. C.O.295\521 G.H. May, Inspector General of Constabulary to the Colonial Secretary, 29 July 1919.

126. Stephen R. Ward, 'Intelligence Surveillance of British Ex–Servicemen, 1918–1920', *The Historical Journal*, vol. 16, no. 1, 1973, p. 187.

127. See, Martin, *Revolutionary Upheaval*, p. 318.

128. The Thinking *Port of Spain Gazette* (25 July 1919), p. 11.

129. Ibid.

130. C.O.295\521 Acting Governor of Trinidad, W.M. Gordon to Milner, 29 July 1919.

131. Ibid.

132. C.O.295\522 G.F. Huggins, et al., to Colonial Secretary, 30 July 1919 enclosed in O.A.G. (Best) to Milner, 7 August 1919.

133. Ibid.

134. C.O.295\522 May to Colonial Secretary, 5 August 1919.

135. Ibid.

136. C.O.318\350\64201.

137. Samaroo, *The Trinidad Workingmen's Association*, pp. 212–219.

138. Ibid.

139. The Grenada *West Indian* (18 July 1919), p. 1; The Grenada *Federalist* (9 August 1919), p. 3.

140. The Grenada *West Indian* (6 June 1919), p. 6.

141. The Grenada *West Indian* (12 September 1919), p. 3; For details on Butler, see Richard W. Jacobs, *Butler Versus the King* (Trinidad: Key Caribbean Publications, 1976).

142. The Grenada *Federalist* (22 November 1919), p. 3.

143. C.O.321\308\8256 Minute of Grenada's administrator enclosed in Haddon–Smith to Milner, 22 January 1920.

144. Ibid.

145. C.O.321\308\8256 Letter from Sir Frederick Hall to Colonial Office, 17 February 1920.

146. Ibid. Minute of George Grindle, 19 February 1920.

147. Ibid. Minute of E.R. Darnley, 19 February 1920.

148. C.O.321\310\17064 Haddon–Smith to Milner, 6 March 1920.

Postscript

1. The Grenada *West Indian* (8 October 1920), p. 2.

2. See, Linnette Vassell, 'The Movement for the vote for women 1918–1919', in *The Jamaican Historical Review*, vol. XV11, 1993, pp. 40–54.

3. *Report of the Visit of the Hon. E.F.L. Wood, M.P. to the West Indies and British Guiana, 1921–1922* (London: H.M.S.O., 1922).

4. See, Patrick Emmanuel, *Crown Colony Politics in Grenada 1917–1951*, Barbados: ISER (Occasional papers no. 7), 1978, pp. 36–72.

5. *Wood Report*, p. 44.

6. Ibid.

7. See, W.M. Macmillan, *Warning From the West Indies* (London: Faber and Faber, 1935). For some detail on the 1930s riots see, Ken, Post, *Arise Ye Starvelings: The Jamaican Labour Rebellion of 1938 and its Aftermath* (The Hague: Martinus Nijhoff, 1978).

8. *Report of the West India Royal Commission, 1938–1939*, Chairman Lord Moyne (London: H.M.S.O., 1945), p. 8.

9. *Trinidad and Tobago Disturbances, 1937, Report of the Commission* (London: H.M.S.O., 938), p. 79.

Bibliography

Libraries and Archives

Institute of Commonwealth Studies Library and Archives
School of Oriental and African Studies Library and WMMS Archives
Institute of Education Library
Birbeck Library
London School of Economics Library
Imperial War Museum Library
Royal Commonwealth Society Library
British Library (Bloomsbury) & Newspaper section (Colindale)
Wellcome Institute (London)
Rhodes House Library (Oxford)
Black Cultural Archives (Brixton)
Barbados Museum
Barbados Archives
UWI Cavehill Library
UWI Mona Library (Special Collection)
Institute of Jamaica Library
Montserrat Public Library (Archival Collection)

Public Records Office (Official Correspondences and Reports)

CO 321–Windward Islands
CO 137–Jamaica
CO 295 Trinidad
CO 318 West Indies (general)
CO 28 Barbados
CO 152 Leeward Islands
CO 123 British Honduras
CO 537 South Africa
WO 32 Miscellaneous Reports and Letters
WO 95\5446 Diary of GOC Troops Jamaica, July 1914–December 1919.
WO 93\49 Records of Soldiers Shot by Sentence of Court Martial 1914–1918.
WO 95\4732 Diary of 2nd BWIR

Newspapers

West Indian

Argos (Trinidad)
Clarion (British Honduras)
Daily Argosy (British Guiana)
Daily Chronicle (British Guiana)
Daily Nation (Barbados)
Daily Chronicle (Jamaica)
Federalist (Grenada)
Gleaner (Jamaica)
Globe (Barbados)
Grenada Chronicle and Gazette
Herald (Barbados)
Independent (British Honduras)
Jamaica Official Gazette
Mirror (Trinidad)
Port of Spain Gazette (Trinidad)
Standard (Barbados)
Sun (Antigua)
Times (Jamaica)
Times (St. Vincent)
Tribune (Bahamas)
Trinidad Guardian
Weekly Illustrated (Barbados)
West Indian (Grenada)

Other

African Telegraph (London–based)
Daily Mirror (British)
Daily News and Leader (British)
Daily Telegraph (British)
Daily News (British)
Glasgow Weekly Record (British)
London Times (British)
Natal Witness (South African)
Palestine News (Palestine)
Weekly Despatch (British)
West India Committee Circular (London–based)

Semi–official and Official Documents

Reports and Miscellaneous Documents

Annual General Reports of Jamaica (together with) The Departmental Reports, 1910–1920,
   Kingston, Jamaica: Government Printing Office, 1920.
Bahamas Archives Exhibition: The Bahamas During the World Wars, 1914–1918 and
   1939–1945. Bahamas: Ministry of Education, 4–23 February 1985.

British Parliamentary Debates (House of Commons) 1916–1919.

G.B. Colonial Office: *Colonial Reports (Jamaica) 1910–1920 & 1946.*

G.B. Colonial Office: *Colonial Reports (Barbados) 1910–1920.*

G.B. Colonial Office: *Colonial Reports (British Honduras) 1910–1920.*

G.B. Colonial Office: *Colonial Reports (Trinidad) 1910–1920.*

G.B. Colonial Office: *Colonial Reports (Grenada) 1910–1920.*

Earle, EDw.R.C. and Crosswell, Oliver L., (eds), *The Jamaica Public Health Bulletin, 1917,* Jamaica: *Times,* 1918.

Education in the Army: *Second Interim Report of the Adult Education Committee,* London: H.M.S.O., 1918.

Ford, J.C., and Cundall, F., *The Handbook of Jamaica for 1919.* Jamaica: Government Printing Office, 1919.

G.B. Army: Album of the 1st BWIR

Haig, Douglas, *Extracts From General Routine Orders,* London: H.M.S.O., 1918.

Hall, A.W.H., *Report on Economic and Financial Conditions in the British West Indies,* London: H.M.S.O., 1921.

Jamaica Blue Book, 1913–1920.

Knight, E. (compiled by), *The Grenada Handbook and Directory, 1946,* Barbados: *Advocate,* 1946.

R.C.I.: *Proceedings of the Royal Colonial Institute,* London, 1907.

Report of Commission on Trinidad and Tobago Disturbances, 1937, London: H.M.S.O., 1938. Cmd.5641.

Report of the Commission appointed by the Governor to enquire into the Origin of the Riot in the town of Belize which began on the night of the 22 July 1919. C.O.123\296.

Report of the Commissioners appointed to Enquire into the Causes and Results of the Increased Cost of the Necessaries of Life in British Guiana, 1920. C.O.318\355\46334.

Report of the Visit of the Hon. E.F.L. Wood, M.P., to the West Indies and British Guiana, 1921–1922, London: H.M.S.O., 1922. Cmd.1679.

Report on the British Honduras Census 1911 & 1921.

Report on the Grenada Census, 1911 & 1921.

Report on the Jamaica Census, 1911 & 1921.

Report of the West India Royal Commission, 1938–1939 (Chairman Lord Moyne), London: H.M.S.O., 1945. Cmd.6607.

Reports of the West Indian Contingent Committee, 1916–1919.

W.M.M.S.: *Reports of the Wesleyan Methodist Missionary Society, 1914–1919.*

War Office: *Field Service Pocket Book,* London: H.M.S.O., 1926.

War Office: *Manual of Military Law,* London: Harrison and Sons, 1914.

War Office: *Report of the Mesopotamia Commission: Appointed by Act of Parliament to enquire into the operations of War in Mesopotamia, 1915–1916. (Together with a separate report by Commander J. Wedgwood),* London: H.M.S.O., 1917.

War Office: *Statistics of the Military Effort of the British Empire during the Great War, 1914–1920.* London: H.M.S.O. 1922.

War Office: *The King's Regulations and Orders for the Army, 1912. (Reprinted with amendments published in Army Orders up to 1st August 1914),* London: H.M.S.O., 1914.

Interviews

Charles Rice, 15 July 1991 (Barbados)
Ernest Marke, 17 December 1991 (London)

Unpublished Theses

Ashdown, Peter, 'Race, Class and the Unofficial Majority in British Honduras 1890–1949', PhD thesis, University of Sussex, 1979

Killingray, David, 'The Colonial Army in the Gold Coast: Official Policy and Local Response, 1890–1947', PhD thesis, S.O.A.S., University of London, 1982.

Kilson, Robin, 'Calling Up the Empire: The British Use of Non–White Labour in France 1916–1920', PhD thesis, Harvard University 1990.

Lewis, Rupert, 'Political Study of Garveyism in Jamaica and London, 1914–1940', MA thesis, UWI, Mona, 1971.

Lumsden, Joyce M., 'Robert Love and Jamaica Politics', PhD thesis, UWI, Mona, 1987.

Stone, M.S., 'The Victorian Army: Health, Hospitals and Social Conditions as encountered by British Troops during the South African War, 1899-1902', PhD thesis, I.C.S., University of London, 1992.

Stone, M.S., 'The Victorian Army: Health, Hospitals and Social Conditions as encountered by British Troops during the South African War, 1899-1902', PhD thesis, I.C.S., University of London, 1992.

Secondary Works

Books

Anderson, David and Killingray, David, *Policing the Empire: Government, Authority and Control 1830–1940*, Manchester and New York: Manchester University Press, 1991.

Anthony, Michael, *Port-of-Spain in a World at War, 1939–1945*, Trinidad: Ministry of Sports, Culture and Youth Affairs, 1983.

Babington, A., *For the Sake of Example*, London: Leo Cooper and Warburg, 1983.

Banton, Michael, *White and Coloured: The Behaviour of British People towards Coloured Immigrants*, London: Cape, 1959.

Barker, Pat, *Regeneration*, Harmondsworth: Penguin, 1992.

Beckett, Ian. F.W. and Simpsom, Keith, *A Nation in Arms: A Social Study of the British Army in the First World War*, Manchester: Manchester University Press, 1985.

Beckford, James A., *The Trumpet of Prophecy: A Sociological study of Jehovah's Witnesses*, Oxford: Basil Blackwell, 1975.

Beckford, George L., *Persistent Poverty*, Jamaica: Maroon Publishing House, 1972.

Beckles, Hilary. *Black Rebellion in Barbados: The Struggle Against Slavery, 1627-1838*, Bridgetown: Carib, 1984.

Benians, E.A. (et al.), *The Cambridge History of the British Empire, 1870-1919*, Cambridge: Cambridge University Press, 1959.

Benn, Denis, *The Growth and Development of Political Ideas in the Caribbean, 1774–1983*, Jamaica: ISER\UWI, 1987.

Berkin, Carol R. and Lovett, Clara M., *Women, War and Revolution*, New York and London: Holmes and Meier, 1980.

Besson, Gerard and Brereton, Bridget (eds.), *The Book of Trinidad*, Trinidad: Paria Publishing, 1992.

Blake, Judith, *Family Structure in Jamaica: The Social Context of Reproduction*, New York: Free Press of Glencoe, 1961.

Botman, Selman, *Egypt from Independence to Revolution, 1919-1952*, New York: Syracuse University Press, 1991.

Bousquet, Ben and Douglas, Colin, *West Indian Women at War: British Racism in World War 11*, London: Lawrence and Wishart, 1991.

Brandt, Allan, *No Magic Bullet: A Social History of Venereal Disease in the United States since 1880*, New York and Oxford: Oxford University Press, 1985.

Brereton, Bridget, *Race Relations in Colonial Trinidad, 1870-1900*, London and New York: Cambridge University Press, 1979.

Brittan, Arthur and Maynard, Mary, *Sexism, Racism and Oppression*, Oxford: Basil Blackwell, 1984.

Brophy, Julia and Smart, Carol (eds.), *Women in Law: Explorations in Law, Family and Sexuality*, London and Boston: Routledge and Kegan Paul, 1985.

Brownmiller, S., *Against Our Will: Men, Women and Rape*, London: Secker and Warburg, 1975.

Bryan, Patrick, *The Jamaica People*, 1880-1902, London and Basingstoke: Macmillan, 1991.

Buckley, Roger N., *Slaves in Red Coats: The British West India Regiments, 1795-1815*, London and New Haven: Yale University Press, 1979.

Campbell, Mavis C., *The Maroons of Jamaica, 1655-1796*, New Jersey: Africa World Press, 1990.

Carnegie, James, *Some Aspects of Jamaica Politics, 1918-1938*, Jamaica: Institute of Jamaica, 1973.

Chambers, H.D., *Yaws* London: J.A. Churchill, 1938.

Chapman, Rowena and Rutherford, Jonathan, *Male Order: Unwrapping Masculinity*, London: Lawrence and Wishart, 1988.

Christopher, A.J., *The British Empire at its Zenith*, London: Croom Helm, 1988.

Cipriani, A.A., [reprint], *Twenty-Five Years After: The British West Indies Regiment in the Great War 1914-1918*, London: Karia Press, 1993.

Clark, Alan, [reprint] *The Donkeys*, London: Pimlico, 1993.

Clayton, Anthony, *France, Soldiers and Africa*, London: Brassey's, 1988.

Clothier, Norman, *Black Valour: The South African Native Labour Contingent, 1916-1918 and the sinking of the "Mendi"*, Pietermaritzburg: University of Natal Press, 1987.

Cobley, Alan G., *Class and Consciousness: The Black Petty Bourgeoisie in South Africa, 1924-1950*, New York: Greenwood Press, 1990.

Cobley, Alan G., and Thompson Alvin (eds.), *The African-Caribbean Connection: Historical and Cultural Perspectives*, Bridgetown: Dept. of History, UWI & the NCF, 1990.

Cock, Jacklyn, *Women and War in South Africa*, London: Open Letters, 1992.

Cohen, Stephen P., *The Indian Army: Its Contribution to the Development of a Nation*, Delhi: Oxford University Press, 1990.

Constantine, Stephen (ed.), *Emigrants and Empire: British Settlement in the Dominions between the Wars*, Manchester and New York: Manchester University Press, 1990.

Costello, John, *Love, Sex and War: Changing Values 1939–45*, London: Pan Books, 1986.

Cross, Malcolm and Heuman, Gad (eds.), *Labour in the Caribbean*, London and Basingstoke: Macmillan, 1988.

Cundall, Frank, *Political and Social Disturbances in the West Indies: A Brief Account and Bibliography*, Kingston, Jamaica: Institute of Jamaica, 1906.

Cundall, Frank, *Jamaica's Part in the Great War 1914–1918*, London: Institute of Jamaica, 1925.

Curtin, Philip, *Two Jamaicas: The Role of Ideas in a Tropical Colony 1830–1865*, Cambridge, Mass: Harvard University Press, 1985.

Davidson, Basil, *Old Africa Rediscovered*, London: Victor Gollancz, 1959.

DeLisser, Herbert G., *Twentieth Century Jamaica*, Jamaica: *Times*, 1913.

DeLisser, Herbert G., *Jamaica and the Great War*, Jamaica: *Gleaner*, 1917.

DeWitt, C. Ellinwood and S.D. Pradhan (eds.), *India and World War 1*, New Delhi: Manohar Publications, 1978.

Dixon, Norman, *On the Psychology of Military Incompetence*, London: Jonathan Cape, 1976.

Dow, Captain H., *Record Service of members of the Trinidad Merchants' and Planters' Contingent, 1915–1918*, Trinidad: Government Printery, 1925.

Dupuch, Sir Etienne, *Tribune Story*, London: Ernest Benn, 1967.

Dupuch, Sir Etienne, *A Salute to Friend and Foe*, Nassau, Bahamas: Tribune, 1982.

Dupuy, R.E. and Dupuy, T.N., *The Encyclopedia of Military History*, London and Sydney: Jane's Publishing, 1970.

Eisner, Gisela, *Jamaica, 1830–1930: A Study in Economic Growth*, London: University of Manchester Press, 1961.

Elkins, W.F. *Street Preachers, Faith Healers and Herb Doctors in Jamaica 1890–1925*, New York: Revisionist Press, 1977.

Elshtain, J., *Women and War*, New York: Basic Books; Brighton: Harvester Press, 1987.

Emmanuel, Patrick, *Crown Colony Politics in Grenada 1917–1951*, Barbados: ISER (Occasional papers no. 7.), 1978.

Emsley, Clive (et al.), *War, Peace and Social Change in Twentieth Century Europe*, Milton Keynes and Philadelphia: Open University Press, 1989.

Enloe, C., *Does Khaki Become You? The Militarization of Women's Lives*, London: Pluto, 1983.

Fanon, Frantz, *The Wretched of the Earth*, Harmondsworth: Penguin Books, 1967.

Fanon, Frantz, *Black Skin White Masks*, London: MacGibbon and Kee, 1968.

Ferro, Marc, *The Great War 1914–1918*, London: Routledge and Kegan Paul, 1973.

Finnegan, Frances, *Poverty and Prostitution*, Cambridge: Cambridge University Press, 1979.

Floud, Roderick (et al.), *Height, Health and History: Nutritional Status in the United Kingdom, 1750–1980*, Cambridge: Cambridge University Press, 1990.

Ford, Amos A., *Telling the Truth: The Life and Times of the British Honduran Forestry Unit in Scotland, 1940–44*, London: Karia Press, 1984.

Ford, J.C. and Cundall, F., *The Handbook of Jamaica, 1919*, Jamaica: Government Printery, 1919.

Fortescue, J.W., *A History of the British Army*, vol. 1, London: Macmillan, 1899.

Foucault, Michel, *Discipline and Punish: The Birth of the Prison*, Harmondsworth: Penguin Books, 1975.

Foucault, Michel, *The History of Sexuality: An Introduction*, Harmondsworth: Penguin Books, 1981.

French, Joan and Ford–Smith, Honor, *Women, Work and Organization in Jamaica 1900–1944*, Jamaica: Sistren Research, 1986.

Fryer, Peter, *Staying Power*, London: Pluto Press, 1984.

Fuller, J.G., *Troop Morale and Popular Culture in the British and Dominion Armies 1914–1918*, Oxford: Clarendon Press, 1990.

Gill, Douglas and Dallas, Gloden, *The Unknown Army*, London: Verso, 1985.

Gilman, Sander L., *Difference and Pathology: Stereotypes of Sexuality, Race, and Madness*, Ithaca and London: Cornell University Press, 1985.

Gilman, Sander L., *Disease and Representation: Images of Illness from Madness to Aids*, Ithaca and London: Cornell University Press, 1988.

Gilroy, Paul, *There Ain't No Black in the Union Jack*, London: Hutchinson, 1987.

Goffman, Erving, *Asylums*, Harmondsworth: Penguin Books, 1961.

Gordon, Shirley, *A Century of West Indian Education: A Source Book*, London: Longman, 1963.

Goveia, Elsa, *Slave Society in the British Leeward Islands at the end of the Eighteenth Century*, New Haven: Yale University Press, 1965.

Gramsci, Antonio, *Prison Notebooks*, (Edited and translated by Quintin Hoare and Geoffrey N. Smith) London: Lawrence and Wishart, 1971.

Grundlingh, Albert, *Fighting their Own War: South African Blacks and the First World War*, Johannesburg: Ravan Press, 1978.

Hall, Douglas, *Five of the Leewards, 1834–1870*, Newcastle upon Tyne: Athenaeum Press, 1971.

Halperin, Vladimir, *Lord Milner and the Empire: The Evolution of British Imperialism*, London: Odhams Press, 1952.

Hanagan, M. and Stephenson, Ch.(eds.), *Confrontation, Class Consciousness and the Labour Process: Studies in Proletarian Class Formation*, New York: Greenwood Press, 1986.

Handy, Charles B., *Understanding Organizations*, Harmondsworth: Penguin Books, 1976.

Hankey, Lord, *The Supreme Command 1914–1918*, London: Allen and Unwin, 1961.

Hart, Keith (ed.), *Women and Sexual Division of Labour in the Caribbean*, Jamaica: Consortium Graduate School of Social Sciences, 1989.

Haywood, Harry, *Black Bolshevik: Autobiography of an Afro–American Communist*, Chicago: Liberator Press, 1978.

Heuman, Gad, *Between Black and White: Race, Politics, and the Free Coloreds in Jamaica, 1792–1865*, Oxford: Clio Press, 1981.

Higman, B.W. (ed.), *Trade, Government and Society in Caribbean History: Essays Presented to Douglas Hall*, Kingston, Jamaica: Caribbean Universities Press, 1983.

Hill, Stephen, A. (compiled by), *Who's Who in Jamaica 1919–1920*, Jamaica: *Gleaner*, 1920.

Hinde, Robert A. (ed.), *Non–Verbal Communication*, London: Cambridge University Press, 1972.

Horner, A.E., *From the Islands of the Sea: Glimpses of a West Indian Battalion in France*, Nassau, Bahamas: *Guardian*, 1919.

Hoyos, F.A., *Builders of Barbados*, London and Basingstoke: Macmillan, 1972.

Hoyos, F.A., *Barbados: A History From the Amerindians to Independence*, London and Basingstoke: Macmillan, 1978.

Husband, Charles (ed.), *"Race" in Britain: Continuity and Change*, London: Hutchinson, 1982.

Jacobs, W. Richard, *Butler Versus the King*, Trinidad: Key Caribbean Publications, 1976.

James, C.L.R., *The Life of Captain Cipriani*, Nelson, Lancashire: Coulton, 1932.

James, C.L.R., *Beyond a Boundary*, London: Hutchinson, 1963.

James, C.L.R., *Black Jacobins*, New York: Vintage Books, 1963.

James, Lawrence, *Mutiny*, London: Buchan and Enright, 1987.

Jeffreys, Sheila, *The Sexuality Debates*, New York and London: Routledge and Kegan Paul, 1987.

Johnston, Harry H., *The Black Man's Part in the War*, London: Simpkin, Marshall & Kent, 1917.

Kushner, Tony and Lunn, Kenneth (eds.), *The Politics of Marginality: Race, the Radical Right and Minorities in Twentieth Century Britain*, London: Frank Cass, 1990.

Lamming, George, *The Emigrants*, London and New York: Allison and Busby, 1954.

Lamming, George, *The Pleasures of Exile*, London: Allison and Busby, 1984.

Leed, Eric J., *No Man's Land: Combat and Identity in World War 1*, London: Cambridge University Press, 1979.

Lewis, Arthur, *Labour in the West Indies*, London: New Beacon Books, 1938.

Lewis, G.K., *The Growth of the Modern West Indies*, New York: Monthly Review Press, 1968.

Lewis, G.K., *Main Currents in Caribbean Thought*, Jamaica: Heinemann, 1983.

Lindsay, Louis (ed.), *Methodology and Change*, Mona, Jamaica: ISER/UWI, 1978.

Little, Kenneth, *Negroes in Britain: A Study of Racial Relations in English Society*, London: Routledge and Kegan Paul, 1972.

Livingstone, W.P., *Black Jamaica*, London: Sampson, Low & Marston, 1900.

Lotz, Rainer and Pegg, Ian (eds.), *Under the Imperial Carpet: Essays in Black History 1780-1950*, Crawley, Sussex: Rabbit Press, 1986.

Lucas, Sir Charles (ed.), *The Empire at War*, vol. 2, London: Oxford University Press, 1923.

Lycette, Margaret and McGreevey William, *Women and Poverty in the Third World*, Baltimore: Johns Hopkins University Press, 1983.

Macdonald, S., (et al.), *Images of Women in Peace and War: Cross-Cultural and Historical Perspectives*, Basingstoke: Macmillan in association with Oxford Women's Studies Committee, 1987.

MacMillan, W.M., *Warning From the West Indies*, London: Faber and Faber, 1935.

Macpherson, W.G.(ed.), *Medical Services (General History)*, vol. 1, London: H.M.S.O., 1921.

Macpherson, W.G., (ed.), *Medical Services (Diseases of the War)*, vol. 2, London: H.M.S.O., 1923.

Macpherson, W.G.(ed.), *Medical Services (General History)* vol.2, London: H.M.S.O, 1923.

Macpherson, W.G. (ed.), *Medical Services (Hygiene of the War)*, vol. 2, London: H.M.S.O., 1923.

Marke, Ernest, *In Troubled Waters: Memoirs of Seventy Years in England*, London: Karia Press, 1975.

Marks, Shula and Engels, Dagmar (eds.), *Contesting Colonial Hegemony: Gramsci and Imperialism*, London: British Academic Press, 1993.

Marlowe, John, *Milner: Apostle of Empire*, London: Hamish Hamilton, 1976.

Marrin, Albert, *The Last Crusade: The Church of England in the First World War*, Durham, N.C: Duke University Press, 1974.

Marshall, Woodville (ed.), *Emancipation 2*, Barbados: UWI\NCF, 1987.

Martin, R.M., *History of the West Indies*, vol.1. London: Whittaker, 1836.

Martin, Tony, *The Pan-African Connection*, Massachusetts: The Majority Press, 1983.

Marwick, Arthur, *The Deluge: British Society and the First World War*, Harmondsworth: Penguin Books, 1967.

Marwick, Arthur, *War and Social Change in the Twentieth Century: A Comparative Study of Britain, France, Germany, Russia and the United States*, London: Macmillan, 1974.

Massiah, Joycelin, *Women as Heads of Households in the Caribbean: Family Structure and Feminine Status*, Paris: U.N.E.S.C.O., 1983.

McAllister, Pam (ed.), *Reweaving the Web of Life: Feminism and Non-Violence*, Philadelphia: New Society Publishers, 1982.

Millette, James, *The Genesis of Crown Colony Government, Trinidad 1783-1810*, Trinidad: Moko Enterprises, 1970.

Mohammed, Patricia and Shepherd, Catherine (eds.), *Gender in Caribbean Development*, UWI, Jamaica, Women and Development Project, 1988.

Morris, Donald R. *The Washing of the Spears*, London: Sphere Books, 1973.

Morris, James, *Pax Britannia: The Climax of an Empire*, London: Faber and Faber, 1968.

Newton, Velma, *The Silver Men: West Indian Labour Migration to Panama 1850-1914*, Kingston, Jamaica: ISER\UWI 1984.

Offer, Avner, *The First World War: An Agrarian Interpretation*, New York: Oxford University Press, 1989.

Olivier, Sydney, *Jamaica: The Blessed Island*, London: Faber and Faber, 1936.

Osuntokun, Akinjide, *Nigeria in the First World War*, London: Longman, 1979.

Page, Melvin E., *Africa and the First World War*, London: Macmillan, 1987.

Perry, F.W., *The Commonwealth Armies: Manpower and Organization in Two World Wars*, Manchester: Manchester University Press, 1988.

Post, Ken, *Arise Ye Starvelings: The Jamaican Labour Rebellion of 1938 and its Aftermath*, The Hague: Martinus Nijhoff, 1978.

Price, Richard (ed.), *Maroon Societies: Rebel Slave Communities in the Americas*, Baltimore and London: Johns Hopkins University Press, 1979.

Quetel, Claude, *History of Syphilis*, Cambridge: Polity in association with Blackwell, 1990.

Ramson, J., *Carry On: Or pages from the life of a West Indian Padre in the Field*, Jamaica: The Educational Supply Co., 1918.

Richardson, C. Bonham, *Panama Money in Barbados, 1900-1920*, Knoxville: University of Tennessee Press, 1985.

Richardson, David (ed.), *Abolition and its Aftermath: The Historical Context 1790–1916,* London: Frank Cass, 1985.

Richmond, Anthony, *Colour Prejudice in Britain,* London: Routledge and Kegan Paul, 1954.

Rodney, Walter, *The Groundings With My Brothers,* London: Villiers Publications, 1969.

Rodney, Walter, *History of the Guyanese Working People 1881–1905,* London: Johns Hopkins University Press, 1981.

Rodney, Walter, *How Europe Underdeveloped Africa,* Washington D.C.: Howard University Press, 1981.

Ryan, Selwyn, *Race and Nationalism in Trinidad and Tobago,* Toronto: University of Toronto Press, 1972.

Sanders, M.L. and Taylor, Philips, *British Propaganda during the First World War, 1914–18,* London and Basingstoke: Macmillan, 1982.

Saunders, Gail (et al.), *Sources of Bahamian History,* London and Basingstoke: Macmillan, 1991.

Scobie, Edward, *Black Britannia,* Chicago: Johnson Publishers, 1972.

Senior, Olive, *Working Miracles: Women's Lives in the English–Speaking Caribbean,* Barbados: ISER\UWI, 1991.

Sertima, Ivan Van (ed.), *African Presence in Early Europe,* New Brunswick and Oxford: Transaction Publishers, 1988.

Sheridan, Richard, *Doctors and Slaves: A Medical and Demographic History of Slavery in the British West Indies,* Cambridge: Cambridge University Press, 1985.

Sherlock, Philip, *Norman Manley: A Biography,* London: Macmillan, 1980.

Showalter, Elaine, *The Female Malady: Women, Madness and English Culture 1839–1980,* London: Virago, 1987.

Skelley, Alan. R., *The Victorian Army at Home,* London: Croom Helm, 1977.

Smith, M.G., *The Plural Society in the British West Indies,* Berkeley: University of California Press, 1965.

Smith, M.G., *Culture, Race and Class in the Commonwealth Caribbean,* UWI, Mona, Jamaica: Department of Extra–Mural Studies, 1984.

Solomos, John, *Race and Racism in Contemporary Britain,* London: Macmillan, 1989.

Spackman, Ann (compiled by), *Constitutional Development of the West Indies 1922–1968,* Barbados: Caribbean Universities Press, 1975.

Spiers, Edward, *The Army and Society 1815–1914,* London: Longman, 1980.

Summers, Anne, *Angels and Citizens: British Women as Military Nurses, 1854–1914,* London: Routledge and Kegan Paul, 1988.

Taylor, Sir Henry, *My Political Memoirs,* Nassau, Bahamas: Private Publication, 1987.

Terraine, John, *Impacts of War 1914–1918,* London: Hutchinson, 1970.

Thompson, Alvin (ed.), *Emancipation 1,* Barbados: UWI\NCF, 1984.

Thompson, Alvin, *Colonialism and Underdevelopment in Guyana, 1580–1803,* Bridgetown: Carib, 1987.

Thompson, Paul, *The Voice of the Past,* Oxford and New York: Oxford University Press, 1978.

Tiger, Lionel, *Men in Groups,* London: Nelson, 1971.

Travers, Tim, *The Killing Ground: The British Army, the Western Front and the Emergence of Modern Warfare 1900–1918,* London: Allen and Unwin, 1987.

Trollope, Anthony, *The West Indies and the Spanish Main*, London: Chapman and Hall, 1859.

Trotman, David, *Crime in Trinidad: Conflict and Control in a Plantation Society, 1838-1900*, Knoxville: University of Tennessee Press, 1986.

Trustram, Myna, *Women of the Regiment: Marriage and the Victorian Army*, Cambridge: Cambridge University Press, 1984.

Van Horne, Winston A. (ed.), *Ethnicity and War*, Milwaukee: University of Wisconsin, 1984.

Vaughan, Megan, *Curing their Ills: Colonial Power and African illness*, Cambridge: Polity, 1991.

Walvin, James, *Black and White: The Negro and English Society, 1555–1945*, Harmondsworth: Penguin Books, 1973.

West, Guida and Blumberg, Rhoda Lois (eds.), *Women and Social Protest*, New York: Oxford University Press, 1990.

Whaley, Joachim (ed.), *Mirrors of Mortality: Studies in the Social History of Death*, London: Europa Publications, 1981.

Wilkinson, Alan, *The Church of England and the First World War*, London: S.P.C.K., 1978.

Will, H.A., *Constitutional Change in the British West Indies 1880–1903*, Oxford: Clarendon Press, 1970.

Williams, Colin J., and Weinberg, Martin S., *Homosexuals and the Military: A Study of less than Honourable Discharge*, New York: Harper and Row, 1971.

Williams, Eric, *The Negro in the Caribbean*, Westport, Connecticut: Negro Universities Press, 1942.

Williams, Eric, *British Historians and the West Indies*, London: Andre Deutsch, 1966.

Williams, Eric, *Capitalism and Slavery*, London: Andre Deutsch, 1967.

Winks, W. Robin, *The Blacks in Canada: A History*, New Haven and London: Yale University Press, 1971.

Woodhill, Lt.–Colonel C., *A Few Notes on the History of the British West Indies Regiment*, Jamaica: (unpublished) West India Reference Library, 1919.

Woolf, Virginia, *Three Guineas*, London: Hogarth Press, 1938.

Unpublished Seminar Papers

Bacchus, M.K., 'The Political Dimensions of the Development of Education in the Caribbean', I.C.S., University of London, postgraduate seminar, Caribbean Societies, 27 May 1985.

Browne, David, 'The Era of Working Class Political Organization in Early 20th Century Barbados: U.N.I.A. AND W.M.A.', Cavehill, UWI, History Dept., Seminar Paper No. 6, 22 June 1989.

Burton, Richard D., 'Cricket, Carnival and Street Culture in the Caribbean', ICS, University of London, postgraduate seminar, Caribbean Societies, 3 February 1986.

Duncan, Neville, 'Movements as Subculture: A Preliminary Examination of Social and Political Protests in the Anglophone Caribbean', Barbados: UWI, Cavehill, November, 1983.

Fraser, Peter D., 'Education and the Retreat of Capitalism in the British West

Indies, 1834–1939: Notes', I.C.S., University of London, postgraduate seminar, Caribbean Societies, 24 January 1982.

Gurney, J.M., 'Malnutrition in Jamaica', Seminar paper (Caribbean Food and Nutrition Institute Library), Jamaica, 1973.

Higman, Barry, 'The First of August: Jamaica 1838–1972', postgraduate seminar, Mona, UWI, History Dept., May 1973.

Samaroo, Brinsley, 'The Mirror of War: Trinidad Newspaper Coverage of the First World War, 1914–1918', paper presented at Tenth Conference of Caribbean Historians, 26 March–1 April, 1978.

Wilmot, Swithin, 'Emancipation in Action: Workers and Wage Conflicts in Jamaica 1838–1848', paper presented at 16th Annual Conference of Caribbean Historians, Barbados, 1984.

Published Articles and Pamphlets

Adekson, J. Bayo, 'Ethnicity and Army Recruitment in Colonial Plural Societies', *Ethnic and Racial Studies*, vol. 2, no. 2, April 1979.

Andrew, C.M., and Kanya–Forstner, A.S., 'France, Africa and the First World War', *Journal of African History*, vol. 19, no. 1, 1978.

Argyle, Michael, 'Non–verbal Communication in Human Social Interaction', in A. Hinde (ed.), *Non–verbal Communication*, London: Cambridge University Press, 1972.

Ashdown, Peter, 'Marcus Garvey , the UNIA and the Black cause in British Honduras, 1914–1949', *Journal of Caribbean History*, vol. 15, 1981.

Asiwaju, A.I., 'Migration as Revolt: The Example of the Ivory Coast and the Upper Volta before 1945', *Journal of African History*, vol. 17, no. 4, 1976.

Banton, Michael, 'Analytical and Folk Concepts of Race and Ethnicity', *Ethnic and Racial Studies*, vol. 2, no. 2, April 1979.

Baptiste, Fritz, *The United States and West Indian Unrest 1914–1939*, Working Paper No.18, ISER, UWI, 1978.

Bland, Lucy, 'In the Name of Protection: The Policing of Women in the First World War', Julia, Brophy and Carol, Smart (eds.), *Women in Law: Explorations in Law, Family and Sexuality*, London and Boston: Routledge and Kegan Paul, 1985.

Boswell, J.S. and Johns, B.R., 'Patriots or Profiteers? British Businessmen and the First World War', *Journal of European Economic History*, vol. 2, no. 2, 1982.

Brereton, Bridget, 'Post Emancipation Protest in the Caribbean: The "Belmana Riots" in Tobago, 1876', *Caribbean Quarterly*, vol. 30, 1984.

Cannadine, David, 'War and Death, Grief and Mourning in Modern Britain', in Joachim Whaley (ed.), *Mirrors of Mortality: Studies in the Social History of Death*, London: Europa, 1981.

Chambers, H.D., 'Further Light on the "Yaws–Syphilis" Problem', reprinted from *Transactions of The Royal Society of Tropical Medicine and Hygiene*, vol. 31, no. 2, July 1937.

Cooper, Frederick, 'The Problem of Slavery in African Studies', *Journal of African History*, vol. 20, no. 1, 1979.

Craton, Michael, 'Continuity Not Change: The Incidence of Unrest among ex–slaves in the British West Indies 1838–1876', *Slavery and Abolition*, vol. 9, no. 2, September, 1988.

Creveld, Martin Van, 'Thoughts on Military History', *Journal of Contemporary History*, vol. 18, no. 4, October 1983.

Crowder, Michael, 'The 1914–1918 European War and West Africa', in J.F.A. Ajayi and Michael Crowder (eds.), *History of West Africa*, vol. 2, London: Longman, 1974.

Dewey, P.E., 'Military Recruiting and the British Labour Force during the First World War', *The Historical Journal*, vol. 27, no. 1, 1984.

Dunn, Richard S., 'The Crisis of Subsistence in the British West Indies during and after the American Revolution', *William and Mary Quarterly*, 33 October 1976.

Echenberg, Myron J., 'Paying the Blood Tax: Military Conscription in French West Africa 1914–1929', *Canadian Journal of African Studies*, vol. 9, 1975.

Elkins, W.F., 'A Source of Black Nationalism in the Caribbean: The Revolt of the British West Indies Regiment at Taranto, Italy', *Science and Society*, vol. 33, no. 2, Spring 1970.

Ellinwood, DeWitt C., 'The Indian Army and Change 1914–1918', in DeWitt C. Ellinwood and S.D. Pradhan (eds.), *India and World War 1*, New Delhi: Manohar Publications, 1978.

Fraser, Peter, 'Some Effects of the First World War on the British West Indies', Collected Seminar Papers, *Caribbean Societies* vol. 1, ICS, University of London, 1982.

Green, Jeffrey P., 'West Indian Doctors in London: John Alcindor (1873–1924) and James Jackson Brown (1882–1953)', *Journal of Caribbean History*, vol. 20, no. 1, 1986.

Green, W.A., 'Was Emancipation a Success?: The Abolitionist Perspective', in David, Richardson (ed.), *Abolition and its Aftermath*, London: Frank Cass, 1985.

Greene, Eddie, 'Caribbean Research: Some Comments and Conclusions', in Louis Lindsay (ed.), *Methodology and Change*, Mona, Jamaica: ISER\ UWI, 1978.

Greenhut, Jeffrey, 'The Imperial Reserve: The Indian Corps on the Western Front 1914–1915', *Journal of Imperial and Commonwealth History*, vol. 12, no. 12, October 1983.

Grove, Eric J., 'The First Shots of the Great War: The Anglo–French Conquest of Togo, 1914', *Army Quarterly*, July 1976.

Grundlingh, Albert, 'The Impact of the First World War on South African Blacks', in Page (ed.), *Africa and the First World War*, N.Y.: St Martin's Press, 1987.

Hall, Stuart, 'Race, Articulation and Societies Structured in Dominance', in *Sociological Theories: Race and Colonialism*, U.N.E.S.C.O., 1980.

Hart, Keith, 'The Sexual Division of Labour', in Keith Hart (ed.), *Women and Sexual Division of Labour in the Caribbean*, Jamaica: Consortium Graduate School of Social Sciences, 1989.

Hickling, Frederick, 'Psychiatry in the Commonwealth Caribbean: A Brief Historical Overview', extract from the *Bulletin of the Royal College of Psychiatry*, vol. 12, copy located at UWI, medical library, Jamaica.

Higman, B.W., 'Theory, Method and Technique in Caribbean Social History', *Journal of Caribbean History*, vol. 20, no. 1, 1985.

Hill, Errol, 'Calypso and War', in *ISER/ UWI, Calypso Research Project, vol. 1, Seminar on the Calypso*, Trinidad: UWI, 6–10 January, 1986.

Hodges, G.W.T., 'African Manpower Statistics for the British Forces in East Africa, 1914–1918', *Journal of African History*, vol. 19, no. 1, 1978.

Hyam, Ronald, 'The Colonial Office Mind 1900–1914', *Journal of Imperial and Commonwealth History*, vol. 8, no. 1, October 1979.

Jenkinson, Jacqueline, 'The 1919 Race Riots in Britain: A Survey', in R. Lotz and I. Pegg (eds.), *Under the Imperial Carpet*, Sussex: Rabbit Press, 1986.

Johnson, Howard, 'Patterns of Policing in the Post–Emancipation British Caribbean 1835–95', in David, Anderson and David, Killingray, *Policing the Empire: Government, Authority and Control 1830–1940*, Manchester and New York: Manchester University Press 1991.

Jordan, Winthrop, 'First Impressions: Initial English Confrontations with Africans', in Charles Husbands (ed.), *"Race" in Britain: Continuity and Change*, London: Hutchinson, 1982.

Joseph, C.L., 'The British West Indies Regiment 1914–1918', *Journal of Caribbean History*, vol. 12, May 1971.

Joseph, C.L., 'The Strategic Importance of the British West Indies 1882–1932', *Journal of Caribbean History*, vol. 7, November 1973.

Killingray, David, 'Repercussions of World War 1 in the Gold Coast', *Journal of African History*, vol. 19, no. 1, 1978.

Killingray, David and Mathews, James, 'Beasts of Burden: British West African Carriers in the First World War', *Canadian Journal of African Studies*, vol. 13, no. 1 1979.

Killingray, David, 'The Idea of a British Imperial African Army', *Journal of African History*, vol. 20, no. 3, 1979.

Killingray, David, 'All the King's Men ?: Blacks in the British army in the First World War 1914–1918', in Rainer Lotz and Ian Pegg (eds.), *Under the Imperial Carpet: Essays in Black History 1780–1950*, Crawley, Sussex: Rabbit 1986.

Killingray, David, 'Race and Rank in the British Army in the Twentieth Century', *Ethnic and Racial Studies*, vol. 10, no. 3, 1987.

Killingray, David, 'Soldiers, Ex–Servicemen and Politics in the Gold Coast, 1939–1950', *Journal of Modern African Studies*, vol. 21, no. 3, 1988.

Kirk–Greene, Anthony H.M., 'Damnosa Hereditas: Ethnic Ranking and the Martial Races Imperative in Africa', *Ethnic and Racial Studies*, vol. 3, no. 4, October 1980.

Luedtke, Alf, 'Cash, Coffee–Breaks, Horseplay: Eigensinn and Politics among Factory Workers in Germany, cira 1900', in M. Hanagan and Ch. Stephenson (eds.), *Confrontation, Class Consciousness and the Labour Process: Studies in Proletarian Class Formation*, New York: Greenwood Press, 1986.

Macdonald, S., 'Drawing the Lines – Gender, Peace and War: An Introduction', in S. Macdonald (et al.), *Images of Women in Peace and War: Cross–Cultural and Historical Perspectives*, Basingstoke: Macmillan in association with Oxford Women's Studies Committee, 1987.

Manley, Norman, 'The Autobiography of Norman Washington Manley', *Jamaica Journal*, vol. 7, no. 1, March–June, 1973.

Manyoni, Joseph, 'Legitimacy and illegitimacy: Misplaced Polarization in Caribbean Family Studies', *Canadian Review of Sociology and Anthropology*, vol. 14, no. 4, 1977.

Marshall, W.K., '"Vox Populi": The St Vincent Riots and Disturbances of 1862', in B.W. Higman (ed.), *Trade, Government and Society in Caribbean History: Essays presented to Douglas Hall*, Kingston: Caribbean Universities Press, 1983.

Marshall, W.K., 'Amelioration and Emancipation in Barbados', in Alvin Thompson (ed.), *Emancipation 1*, Barbados: UWI\NCF, 1984.

Mathews, James K., *'Reluctant Allies: Nigerian Responses to Military Recruitment, 1914–1918'*, in Page (ed.), Africa and the First World War, N.Y.: St Martin's Press, 1987.

Maughan, Basil, 'Some Aspects of Barbadian Emigration to Cuba 1919–1935', *Journal of the Barbados Museum and Historical Society*, vol. 37, no. 3, 1985.

Mercer, Kobena and Julien, Isaac, 'Race, Sexual Politics and Black Masculinity: A Dossier', in Rowena Chapman and Jonathan Rutherford (eds.), *Male Order: Unwrapping Masculinity*, London: Lawrence and Wishart, 1988.

Michalowski, Helen, 'The Army Will Make a "Man" Out of You', in Pam McAllister (ed.), *Reweaving the Web of Life: Feminism and Nonviolence*, Philadelphia: New Society Publishers, 1982.

Moodie, T. Dunbar (with Ndatshe Vivienne and Sibuyi, British), 'Migrancy and Male Sexuality on the South African Gold Mines', *Journal of Southern African Studies*, vol. 14, no. 2, January, 1988.

Nicol, Abioseh, 'West Indians in West Africa', *Sierra Leone Studies: New Series*, no. 13, June 1960.

O'Brien, Patrick K., 'The Costs and Benefits of British Imperialism 1846–1914', *Past and Present*, no. 120, August 1988.

Page, Melvin E., 'The War of Thangata: Nyasaland and the East African Campaign, 1914–1918', *Journal of African History*, vol. 19, no. 1, 1978.

Park, J.H.W., 'Note on the Causes for Rejections of Volunteers for the Jamaica War Contingents', *The Jamaica Public Health Bulletin, 1917*, Jamaica: *Times* 1918.

Rathbone, Richard, 'World War 1 and Africa: Introduction', *Journal of African History*, vol. 19, no. 1, 1978.

Rich, Paul, 'Sydney Olivier, Jamaica and the Debate on British Colonial Policy in the West Indies', in Malcolm Cross and Gad Heuman (eds.), *Labour in the Caribbean*, London and Basingstoke: Macmillan, 1988.

Rohlehr, Gordon, 'Calypso Censorship: An Historical Overview', *ISER\UWI, Calypso Research Project: Seminar on the Calypso*, St Augustine, Trinidad, January 6–10, 1986.

Rutherford, Jonathan, 'Who's That Man?', in Chapman and Rutherford (ed.), *Male Order*, London: Lawrence and Wishart, 1988.

Samaroo, Brinsley, The Trinidad Working's Men Association and the Origins of Popular Protest in a Crown Colony', *Social and Economic Studies*, vol. 21, no. 2, June 1972.

Savage, D.C., and Munro, Forbes J., 'Carrier Recruitment in the British East Africa Protectorate, 1914–1918', *Journal of African History*, vol. 7, no. 2, 1966.

Scruton, R., 'Notes on the Sociology of War', *British Journal of Sociology*, vol. 38, no. 3, 1987.

Sharpe, C.A., 'Enlistment in the Canadian Expeditionary Force 1914–1918: A Regional Analysis', *Journal of Canadian Studies*, vol. 18, no. 4, Winter 1983–84.

Stanley, Peter, 'A Horn to put your Powder in: Interpreting Artefacts of British Soldiers in Colonial Australia', *Journal of Australian War Memorial*, 13 October 1988.

Thomas Roger, 'Military Recruitment in the Gold Coast during the First World War', *Cahiers D'Etudes Africaines*, vol. 57, no. 15, 1975.

Thompson, E.P., 'Eighteenth century English Society: Class struggle without class?', *Social History*, vol. 3, no. 2, 1978.

Travers, Tim, 'The Hidden Army: Structural Problems in the British Officer Corps, 1900–1918', *Journal of Contemporary History*, vol.17, no.3, July 1982.

Tylden, G., 'The West India Regiment 1795–1927 and from 1958', *Journal of the Society for Army Historical Research*, vol. 40, March 1962.

Vassell, Linnette, 'The Movement for the Vote for Women 1918–1919', *The Jamaican Historical Review*, vol. XVIII, 1993.

Walvin, James, 'Black Caricature: The Roots of Racialism', in Charles Husband (ed.), *"Race" in Britain: Continuity and Change*, London: Hutchinson, 1982.

Ward, Stephen R., 'Intelligence Surveillance of British Ex–Servicemen, 1918–1920', *The Historical Journal*, vol.16, no.1, 1973.

West, Guida and Blumberg, Rhoda Lois, 'Reconstructing Social Protest from a Feminist Perspective', in West and Blumberg (eds.), *Women and Social Protest*, New York: Oxford University Press, 1990.

Willan, B.P., 'The South African Native Labour Contingent, 1916–1918', *Journal of African History*, vol. 19, no. 1, 1978.

Williams, Keith, '"A Way Out of Our Troubles": The Politics of Empire Settlement 1900–1922', in Stephen Constantine (ed.), *Emigrants and Empire: British Settlement in the Dominions between the Wars*, Manchester and New York: Manchester University Press, 1990.

Winter, J.M., 'Some Aspects of the Demographic Consequences of the First World War in Britain', *Population Studies*, vol. 30, no. 3, 1976.

Winter, J.M., 'Britain's "Lost Generation" of the First World War', *Population Studies*, vol. 31, no. 3, 1977.

Winter, J.M., 'The Impact of the First World War on Civilian Health in Britain', *Economic History Review*, vol. 30, 1977.

Winter, J.M., 'Military Fitness and Civilian Health in Britain during the First World War', *Journal of Contemporary History*, vol. 15, no. 2, 1980.

Winter, J.M., 'Aspects of the Impact of the First World War on Infant Mortality in Britain', *Journal of European Economic History*, vol. 11, 1982.

Yarrow, Stella, 'The Impact of Hostility on Germans in Britain, 1914–1918', in Tony Kushner and Kenneth Lunn (eds.), *The Politics of Marginality: Race, the Radical Right and Minorities in Twentieth Century Britain*, London: Frank Cass, 1990.

Zeidler, Frank P., 'Hysteria in Wartime: Domestic Pressures on Ethnics and Aliens', in Winston A. Van Horne (ed.), *Ethnicity and War*, Milwaukee: University of Wisconsin, 1984.

Index

Index

Index

Index

Index

Index

(p) = photograph); (t) = table

CPSIA information can be obtained at www.ICGtesting.com
Printed in the USA
BVOW11s1606020914

365169BV00008B/344/P